SCARY WW2 HISTORY FACTS

CRAFTED BY SKRIUWER

Copyright © 2024 by Skriuwer.

All rights reserved. No part of this book may be used or reproduced in any form whatsoever without written permission except in the case of brief quotations in critical articles or reviews.

At **Skriuwer**, we're more than just a team—we're a global community of people who love books. In Frisian, "Skriuwer" means "writer," and that's at the heart of what we do: creating and sharing books with readers worldwide. Wherever you are in the world, **Skriuwer** is here to inspire learning.

Frisian is one of the oldest languages in Europe, closely related to English and Dutch, and is spoken by about **500,000 people** in the province of **Friesland** (Fryslân), located in the northern Netherlands. It's the second official language of the Netherlands, but like many minority languages, Frisian faces the challenge of survival in a modern, globalized world.

We're using the money we earn to promote the Frisian language.

For more information, contact : **kontakt@skriuwer.com** (www.skriuwer.com)

Disclaimer:
The images in this book are creative reinterpretations of historical scenes. While every effort was made to accurately capture the essence of the periods depicted, some illustrations may include artistic embellishments or approximations. They are intended to evoke the atmosphere and spirit of the times rather than serve as precise historical records.

TABLE OF CONTENTS

CHAPTER 1: SEEDS OF DARKNESS (1930S PRELUDE)

- *A Europe still scarred by World War I*
- *Economic devastation fueling radical ideologies*
- *Growing mistrust and resentment setting the stage for conflict*

CHAPTER 2: THE RISE OF TOTALITARIAN REGIMES

- *Hitler's ascent in Germany and Mussolini's Italy*
- *Stalin's iron rule in the Soviet Union*
- *Japan's imperial ambitions in East Asia*

CHAPTER 3: EARLY HORRORS ON THE EUROPEAN FRONT

- *Invasion of Poland sparking global war*
- *The "Phony War" and sudden Nazi offensives*
- *Norway, Denmark, Belgium, and the fall of France*

CHAPTER 4: THE EASTERN NIGHTMARE – OPERATION BARBAROSSA

- *German blitz into the Soviet Union*
- *Siege of Leningrad and atrocities in occupied territories*
- *POW starvation and partisan resistance*

CHAPTER 5: DARK DAYS OF THE HOLOCAUST BEGIN

- *Initial persecution of Jews, Roma, and other groups*
- *Einsatzgruppen mass shootings and ghettos*
- *Wannsee Conference planning the Final Solution*

CHAPTER 6: INSIDE THE GHETTOS AND CAMPS

- Everyday terror in overcrowded ghettos
- Forced labor, starvation, and disease
- Industrialized killing in extermination camps

CHAPTER 7: WEAPONS OF FEAR AND DESTRUCTION

- Advances in tanks, warplanes, and rocket technology
- Chemical and biological weapons research
- The terror of flamethrowers and incendiary bombs

CHAPTER 8: CIVILIAN NIGHTMARES – BOMBINGS AND TERROR

- The Blitz on Britain and massive Allied raids
- Axis reprisals on occupied populations
- Firestorms wiping out entire cities

CHAPTER 9: TWISTED SCIENCE AND HUMAN EXPERIMENTS

- Nazi euthanasia programs and camp medical abuse
- Unit 731 atrocities in Imperial Japan
- Ethics obliterated in the pursuit of "research"

CHAPTER 10: LIFE UNDER OCCUPATION – DAILY HORROR

- Curfews, rationing, and forced labor
- Puppet governments and collaborators
- Underground resistance and ruthless crackdowns

CHAPTER 11: THE PACIFIC FRONT'S GRIM REALITIES

- *Japan's lightning conquests across Asia*
- *Treatment of POWs and civilian populations*
- *Desperate resistance by Allied forces*

CHAPTER 12: SHOCK IN THE PACIFIC – PRISONERS AND EXPERIMENTS

- *Brutal conditions in Japanese POW camps*
- *Kamikaze attacks and the suicidal defense tactic*
- *Hidden horrors of medical "research" on captives*

CHAPTER 13: SECRET OPERATIONS AND PROPAGANDA

- *Espionage agencies and codebreaking triumphs*
- *Deception campaigns misdirecting enemy armies*
- *Psychological warfare shaping civilian and troop morale*

CHAPTER 14: STARVATION, SIEGE, AND SUFFERING

- *Blockades and the destruction of supply lines*
- *Leningrad's protracted siege and civilian tragedy*
- *Mass famines from Greece to China*

CHAPTER 15: CHILDREN OF WAR – LOST INNOCENCE

- *Evacuations, orphanhood, and child soldiers*
- *Youth indoctrination under Hitler Youth and similar groups*
- *Long-term trauma for a generation robbed of childhood*

CHAPTER 16: PSYCHOLOGICAL TACTICS AND FEAR

- *Totalitarian propaganda enforcing obedience*
- *Rumors, informants, and constant surveillance*
- *Terror bombings to shatter morale and ensure submission*

CHAPTER 17: THE TIDE TURNS – BRUTAL RETALIATIONS

- *Allied victories at Stalingrad, El Alamein, and Midway*
- *Scorched earth and partisan vengeance during Axis retreats*
- *Bloody retribution by liberated populations*

CHAPTER 18: THE FINAL THUNDER – ENDGAME HORRORS

- *Battle of the Bulge, the fall of Berlin, and VE Day*
- *Okinawa's desperate fight and the atomic bombings*
- *Japan's surrender amid cataclysmic devastation*

CHAPTER 19: AFTERMATH SHADOWS – TRIALS AND TORMENTS

- *War crimes proceedings in Nuremberg and Tokyo*
- *Displaced persons, famine, and rebuilding ruined cities*
- *Political realignments fueling the Cold War*

CHAPTER 20: LINGERING GHOSTS AND HAUNTING LESSONS

- *Impact on global politics, decolonization, and the UN*
- *Holocaust memory and the push for "Never again"*
- *Nuclear age fears and the imperative of historical vigilance*

CHAPTER ONE

Seeds of Darkness (1930s Prelude)

1. **Introduction: A Troubled Continent**
   In the early 1930s, Europe was like a bruised and battered fighter still struggling to stand after the punch of World War I. Villages, towns, and entire cities were torn up just a decade before, and the survivors were still trying to make sense of it all. Nations were broke; families had lost fathers, sons, and brothers. Many people were living in poverty or just barely holding on. There was a universal desire to avoid another conflict on the same scale as the Great War. But beneath this hopeful wish lay strong undercurrents of anger, fear, and revenge.

The sense of unease was not confined to just one country. All across Europe, people felt cheated by treaties, burdened by debts, and uncertain about what the future held. Meanwhile, in places like Germany, the combination of national shame and economic disaster created the perfect atmosphere for hateful ideas to take root. In Italy, the seeds of fascism had already sprouted, and in the Soviet Union, Joseph Stalin ruled with an iron fist—though most of Western Europe knew little of the horrors going on behind the closed curtain of communism.

Outside of Europe, other parts of the world were also in turmoil. In East Asia, Japan was beginning to flex its military muscles, slowly testing how far it could push toward its goal of an empire. Although few in Europe thought much about the actions of Japan at this early stage, those events would eventually become a critical piece of the global puzzle, leading to unimaginable destruction in the decade to come.

This chapter will shine a light on the state of the world at the start of the 1930s. We'll explore how the outcomes of World War I—especially the Treaty of Versailles—left devastating marks on countries' economies and psyches. We'll also see how these conditions became fertile ground for dangerous ideologies that promised quick fixes and strong leadership. With that in mind, we begin our journey into this era, where darkness slowly spread, unstoppable, until it plunged the world into the nightmare of the Second World War.

2. **The World War I Hangover**
   World War I ended in November 1918, leaving behind millions of graves and entire regions in ruins. When the war started in 1914, it was called "the war to end all wars," but that hopeful nickname would prove to be a tragic joke. By 1919, politicians from the victorious Allied nations—mainly Britain, France, and the United States—gathered in Paris to settle matters with the defeated Central Powers, which included Germany and the Austro-Hungarian Empire. Their aim was to find a lasting peace, but they were also eager to make Germany pay for the massive losses of life and resources.

The resulting Treaty of Versailles, signed on June 28, 1919, placed the main blame for the war squarely on Germany's shoulders. The treaty forced Germany to give up land, limit its military to a size that could barely police its own territory, and pay reparations that were astronomical. These reparations were meant to compensate the Allies for the damage caused during the war, but in practice, they crushed Germany's economy, leading to hyperinflation and joblessness.

For everyday Germans, the years following the war were humiliating. Their once-proud empire had collapsed, and many believed the country was sold out by its own politicians. While Germany's monarchy had ended, the new democratic government—known as the Weimar Republic—was off to a bad start. It had to deal with widespread bitterness among veterans and civilians alike. The economy was so bad that some people literally burned money for heat because banknotes were cheaper to burn than to use them to buy firewood. Stories of bread loaves costing wheelbarrows full of money fueled a sense of hopelessness and anger.

Despite the hardships, there was no immediate thirst for another war among most Europeans. The memory of the Great War was still raw. Families were left fatherless, and entire towns had lost nearly all their young men. Monuments to the fallen were built in every village, a constant reminder of the steep cost of modern warfare. Politically, though, the ground was shifting. People were searching for someone—or something—to blame for their misery, and charismatic demagogues were ready to step in, offering simple targets for their rage.

3. **The Great Depression's Grip**
    As if the post-war economic crisis wasn't enough, the global economy faced yet another blow in 1929 with the Wall Street Crash. The collapse of the American stock market sent shockwaves worldwide. American banks recalled loans they had made to European countries, leaving them in financial ruin. Companies went bankrupt, unemployment soared, and once again, people in many parts of the world found themselves unable to buy food or keep their homes.

In Germany, which was already reeling from the humiliations of Versailles, the Great Depression felt like the final straw. Millions lost their jobs, and the Weimar government looked more and more incompetent. Hyperinflation from the early 1920s returned in a different form, and a bitter sense of betrayal filled the air. It was during these tough times that extremist political parties found their voices and gained support.

Similar stories played out in other countries. Even the victors of World War I struggled. Britain and France had taken on massive debts to finance the war. Their economies were hurting, and their people were frustrated with their governments. In the Soviet Union, Stalin was implementing Five-Year Plans and forcing rapid industrialization, but at a terrible human cost. People in the West didn't fully grasp the scale of what was happening in the USSR, but rumors of forced labor camps and mass starvation began to trickle in.

Italy had already turned to fascism in the early 1920s under Benito Mussolini. He promised to restore the glory of the Roman Empire and to end economic chaos. While Mussolini's success was questionable, his strong-arm tactics, flashy uniforms, and patriotic speeches appealed to Italians tired of feeling weak. Their fear of communist revolution also pushed many to accept a fascist strongman as a necessary shield.

Against this backdrop of economic collapse and social unrest, the stage was set for even more frightening figures to appear. People were in despair, and when hope runs out, they often cling to whoever or whatever claims to offer a way out. In Germany, the man who would rise to power was Adolf Hitler, a name that soon became synonymous with terror and destruction on an unimaginable scale. But at the start of the 1930s, for many people, he was just a loud voice promising bread, jobs, and national pride.

4. **Early Echoes of Hate**
    Hate did not suddenly spring up in the 1930s. Anti-Semitism, racism, and xenophobia had existed in Europe for centuries. But the turmoil following World War I supercharged these hateful beliefs. Many ordinary citizens looked for scapegoats to explain their suffering. This often led them to blame minority groups, especially Jews, who were falsely accused of controlling banks and causing financial collapse.

Propaganda played a massive role in spreading these ideas. Newspapers, leaflets, and street orators began painting Jewish communities as parasitic outsiders. Conspiracy theories about global Jewish plots circulated, and lies were repeated so often that many people started believing them. This hatred wasn't restricted to Germany. Other countries had their own forms of racial and ethnic prejudices, which would later explode in different ways.

The Soviet Union, while officially against "bourgeois" oppression, also had its share of hidden hatreds. Stalin's regime targeted entire ethnic groups in mass deportations, though much of this was kept secret from the outside world. In Eastern Europe, many nations were grappling with large minority populations that didn't necessarily share the language or culture of the majority. Tensions simmered, stoked by propaganda that claimed these minorities were disloyal or inferior.

In America, a wave of isolationism swept the country in the early 1930s, as people wanted no part in another European war. Racism thrived there too, with groups like the Ku Klux Klan rising in influence. These attitudes contributed to a world climate of suspicion, xenophobia, and a belief that strong leadership was needed to sort things out. This belief in strong leaders often overshadowed moral concerns about how exactly these leaders planned to achieve their goals.

The seeds of World War II were planted in this poisoned soil. As we move through the decade, we see different groups—political parties, military circles, and extremist organizations—preparing for bigger moves. The atmosphere felt tense, as if everyone was waiting for a spark to set off a chain reaction. When the spark finally came, the subsequent inferno would consume much of the globe.

5. **Hitler's Early Path to Power**
   Adolf Hitler was born in Austria in 1889. He served in the German army during World War I and was shocked by Germany's defeat. Like many veterans, he returned to a society he barely recognized. In Munich, he got involved in the German Workers' Party (DAP), a small political group that aimed to unite Germans under a nationalist, anti-communist banner. Hitler discovered a knack for public speaking, mesmerizing audiences with passionate speeches filled with resentment and promises of revival.

The DAP changed its name to the National Socialist German Workers' Party—better known as the Nazi Party—and Hitler quickly rose to prominence within it. In 1923, he led an unsuccessful coup attempt called the Beer Hall Putsch, hoping to seize power in Bavaria and then march on Berlin. The plan failed, and Hitler was arrested. During his short prison sentence, he dictated the book *Mein Kampf* ("My Struggle"), outlining his extreme ideology. It combined intense German nationalism, anti-Semitism, anti-Bolshevism, and the idea of "Lebensraum," which meant Germany deserved more living space, especially in Eastern Europe.

Once released from prison, Hitler changed tactics. He realized that to gain power, he would need to work within the existing political system rather than try another coup. Over the next few years, he rebuilt the Nazi Party, creating a paramilitary wing called the SA (Sturmabteilung), which terrorized political opponents in the streets. Through carefully planned propaganda, mass rallies, and a promise to restore Germany's pride, the Nazi Party gained more and more popularity. By 1932, they were one of the largest parties in the Reichstag (the German parliament).

The Great Depression provided the perfect stage for Hitler. With unemployment skyrocketing and inflation eroding savings, many people were desperate. Hitler offered a simple message: Germany had been betrayed by traitors and humiliated by international vultures. He promised jobs, prosperity, and a purge of those he considered the "enemy within." To the disillusioned masses, this sounded like salvation. It didn't matter that much of it was based on lies and hate; Hitler's powerful speeches tapped into their anger, fear, and hopes.

6. **A Global Shift Toward Strongmen**
   Germany wasn't alone in turning to strong leadership. Across the continent, people were losing faith in democracy and liberal ideas that seemed incapable of fixing the economic mess. Italy had already set the trend by embracing Benito Mussolini, who established a fascist regime in the early 1920s. Mussolini's approach combined extreme nationalism, suppression of dissent, and promises of grandeur. He portrayed himself as the savior of Italy, reviving memories of the Roman Empire to stir patriotic pride.

In Eastern Europe, many newly formed states struggled to maintain order. Authoritarian leaders rose in places like Hungary, Romania, and Bulgaria, where the public was often told that only a firm hand could protect them from chaos. These regimes varied in severity, but they shared a common thread of suppressing political opposition and centralizing power. Some even saw Hitler as an inspiration.

Then there was the Soviet Union under Stalin. Though it was communist, it was just as totalitarian. Stalin tolerated no opposition, using secret police, forced labor camps, and purges to eliminate anyone he suspected of disloyalty. Millions died in famines or were executed during Stalin's rule. This brutal system pushed people in nearby countries to fear communism even more, which in turn made fascist or right-wing regimes seem like a "lesser evil" to some.

Altogether, democracy felt like it was on the retreat. The swirling storms of economic crisis, war trauma, and social change left people longing for stability. They looked for leaders who seemed confident and willing to crush any threats. Unfortunately, these strongmen also crushed human rights and freedoms, laying the groundwork for something far worse.

7. **Japan's Early Imperial Moves**

    While Europe was busy grappling with its economic woes and political upheaval, Japan was on a very different but parallel path. The nation had undergone rapid modernization since the late 19th century, transforming from a feudal society to a major industrial power. By the early 1930s, Japan felt it needed more natural resources to fuel its growing industries. Its eyes landed on territories in China, which was weak and divided by civil war.

In 1931, Japan orchestrated the Mukden Incident—an explosion on a section of railway near Mukden (now Shenyang) in Manchuria, which was controlled by Chinese forces. Japan blamed Chinese troops for the incident and used it as a pretext to invade Manchuria. The Japanese army swiftly took control, setting up a puppet state called Manchukuo. This aggressive move alarmed Western nations, but they were too wrapped up in their own problems to do anything substantial. The League of Nations, which was meant to mediate international conflicts, could only offer condemnation, which Japan ignored.

Manchuria's takeover was a key step in Japan's growing empire. It showed the world that Japan was ready to expand by force. It also showcased the weakness of the League of Nations, which would become more obvious in the coming years. Japanese propaganda painted these conquests as a noble mission to bring order and development to backward regions. In reality, the local population faced brutal occupation, with strict control enforced by the Kempeitai (Japanese military police) and the threat of sudden violence.

Within Japan, extreme nationalists and military officers were gaining more influence. They saw democracy as ineffective and Western nations as hypocritical. This mindset set Japan on a collision course with other powers in the Pacific. Though World War II is often considered primarily a European conflict until Pearl Harbor, these early Japanese moves in the 1930s were very much part of the story. They laid down the stepping stones for the Pacific Theater of the war, which would prove just as cruel and deadly as any fighting in Europe.

8. **The Eroding Peace**
   The 1930s started with uneasy peace, but day by day, event by event, that peace eroded. Germany's rearmament, Japan's invasion of Manchuria, Italy's ambitions in Africa—these were clear signals that the world was heading down a dangerous path. Diplomats made half-hearted attempts to patch things up, but they often operated out of fear and self-interest. Britain and France, for instance, were more concerned about their own empires and economic recovery than about maintaining a united front against aggression.

The League of Nations proved powerless. It had no army, and its resolutions were easily ignored. Countries that had joined the League hoped it would be a peaceful alternative to war, but the 1930s demonstrated that strong-willed aggressors could simply do as they pleased. Sanctions were either weak or never fully enforced. Some nations quietly hoped that by giving in to certain demands—like letting Germany reoccupy the Rhineland or turning a blind eye to Japan's activities in China—they could avoid a larger conflict. This policy of appeasement was most famously associated with British Prime Minister Neville Chamberlain, who sincerely believed he could negotiate with Hitler. But as we'll see, this approach only emboldened the dictators.

Inside Germany, Hitler tested international reactions step by step. He withdrew Germany from the League of Nations in 1933, started openly rebuilding the military in 1935, and reoccupied the Rhineland in 1936. Each time, the Allies complained but took no decisive action. These successes bolstered Hitler's standing at home. He looked like a hero, bravely standing up for German rights. The Nazi propaganda machine used every victory to fan the flames of nationalism.

9. **Street Violence and Paramilitaries**
   While leaders played their games of international diplomacy, real violence was happening on the streets in multiple countries. In Germany, the Nazi Party's paramilitary forces—the SA—roamed cities wearing brown uniforms, intimidating and beating political opponents. Socialists, communists, trade unionists, and even moderates felt their wrath. Local police often turned a blind eye, or in many cases, were sympathetic to the SA's cause.

By the mid-1930s, an even more fearsome group had emerged: the SS (Schutzstaffel). Initially formed as Hitler's personal bodyguard, the SS grew into a massive organization led by Heinrich Himmler. It was deeply ideological, promoting the concept of Aryan purity. Dressed in black uniforms, the SS cultivated an aura of terror and discipline. By 1934, during the "Night of the Long Knives," Hitler used the SS to purge the SA's leadership, solidifying his control over the party and the country.

The Soviet Union had its own version of terror in the form of the NKVD (People's Commissariat for Internal Affairs). Stalin's purges claimed the lives of untold numbers of party officials, military officers, and ordinary citizens who dared to question his policies. In Italy, Mussolini's Blackshirts enforced fascist rule with violence and intimidation. In Japan, extreme nationalists assassinated political rivals. Across the globe, the 1930s were marked by a rise in politically driven violence.

For the average person, this meant living with a growing sense of fear. Politics felt dangerous, and open debate often led to beatings or imprisonment. Many citizens chose silence, hoping to avoid trouble. Others became drawn into radical movements themselves, persuaded by fiery speeches and the promise of belonging to something bigger.

10. **A Growing Sense of Dread**
    As the 1930s wore on, it was as though storm clouds gathered over the entire world. In coffee shops and living rooms, people debated whether another large-scale war was coming. Newspapers carried headlines about Hitler's demands, Mussolini's invasions, and Japan's expansion in the Far East. Rumors flew about secret weapons, large-scale mobilizations, and alliances being made behind closed doors.

In Germany, the Nazi Party tightened its grip on every aspect of society. Children joined the Hitler Youth, where they were taught Nazi ideals from a young age. Posters declaring the superiority of the German "Master Race" appeared on walls, and anti-Jewish sentiment was normalized. The Nuremberg Laws of 1935 stripped Jews of their German citizenship and banned them from marrying or having relationships with "Aryans." The world saw these developments but mostly responded with shock rather than action.

At the same time, in Spain, a civil war broke out in 1936, pitting the Republican government against a nationalist rebellion led by General Francisco Franco. Germany and Italy supported Franco, using the conflict as a testing ground for new military tactics and equipment. The bombing of Guernica by the German Luftwaffe was a terrifying preview of what aerial warfare could do to civilian populations. The images of burning cities and fleeing refugees haunted Europe, but still, no one stopped the fascist tide.

By the close of the decade, it seemed obvious that some kind of major conflict was on the horizon. Those who had lived through World War I dreaded the thought of another. But the new generation of men who were in their twenties sometimes viewed war as an opportunity to prove themselves. The propaganda in Germany and Italy glorified the idea of battle, painting it as the highest form of service to the nation. This romanticized vision would soon clash with the brutal reality of modern total war.

11. **Conclusion: The Stage Is Set**
    The 1930s ended with a sense of inevitable doom. The seeds of darkness had fully taken root. Economies were still fragile, extremist ideologies were in power, and ordinary people felt powerless. The Treaty of Versailles had failed to prevent another war; the League of Nations was toothless; and powerful countries were led by men who saw violence as not just an option, but the solution to their problems.

In Germany, Hitler was no longer just a rabble-rouser but the Führer, a dictator with total control. In Italy, Mussolini's grip on power was solid. In Japan, militarists had the Emperor's blessing to expand. In the Soviet Union, Stalin was the unchallenged leader, ready to sign non-aggression pacts that would shock the world. And in Spain, Franco's victory signaled the resilience of fascism in Europe.

Yet, many people still clung to the hope that war might be avoided. Diplomats talked about meeting Hitler's demands, or at least keeping him satisfied enough not to spark a European-wide conflict. But Hitler and others had much bigger plans. The entire world was about to be plunged into a nightmare so deep that even the horror of World War I would seem mild in comparison.

CHAPTER TWO

The Rise of Totalitarian Regimes

1. **The Meaning of Totalitarianism**
   Before diving deeper into the specific dictatorships that emerged in the 1930s, let's understand what we mean by "totalitarianism." The word suggests a system where the state holds near-total control over the lives of its citizens. Individual freedoms are crushed. Political parties other than the one in power are banned, and dissent is met with brutal punishment. Propaganda becomes a tool for shaping minds, and secret police enforce the regime's will behind closed doors.

Totalitarian regimes thrive on fear. They create an atmosphere of paranoia, making people suspect their neighbors, friends, and even family members might be informants. Whether it's fascism under Hitler and Mussolini, or communism under Stalin, the blueprint is strikingly similar: a single leader worshiped almost like a god, a single ideology claiming to have all the answers, and a population too terrified or brainwashed to resist.

In this chapter, we'll look at how these regimes took hold in Germany, Italy, the Soviet Union, and to a lesser extent in other parts of Europe. We'll examine the methods they used to tighten their grip—methods that would lay the groundwork for some of the worst atrocities in human history. As we move forward, remember that these events didn't happen overnight. Each dictator climbed the ladder step by step, often using legal processes or exploiting crises to dismantle democratic institutions from within.

2. **Mussolini's Italy: The Fascist Template**
   Benito Mussolini was a restless figure who had once dabbled in socialism before World War I. But after the war, he realized that Italian society was ripe for a new kind of politics—one based on strong nationalism and anti-communism. Italy felt cheated by the Versailles peace settlement. The country had joined the Allies in World War I but didn't receive the territorial gains it had expected.
   Unemployment was high, and strikes plagued the economy. Mussolini saw an opportunity.

He formed the National Fascist Party in 1921, promoting an ideology that combined extreme nationalism, the glorification of violence, and hatred for communists and socialists. Mussolini's supporters, known as Blackshirts, used intimidation and violence against political opponents. In 1922, after a march on Rome, Mussolini was invited by the king to form a government. From there, he methodically dismantled the democratic system, banning other parties, censoring the press, and ruling by decree.

The Fascist regime glorified the state above everything else. Mussolini liked to be called "Il Duce" (The Leader), and he filled public spaces with symbols of Roman might—eagles, fascist bundles of rods, and statues echoing the glory of ancient emperors. People who disagreed with him could face imprisonment, exile, or worse. The regime also tried to control education, ensuring children were taught to revere Mussolini and fascism.

Though brutal, Mussolini's Italy served as a model for other dictators, including Hitler. Mussolini's earlier rise to power gave Hitler something to learn from. But while Mussolini could be vicious, he often lacked the single-minded fanaticism that would characterize Hitler's rule. Italy's brand of fascism was terrifying, but in many ways, it would be overshadowed by the full horror unleashed by Nazi Germany.

3. **Hitler's Germany: From Chancellor to Führer**
   When Adolf Hitler was appointed Chancellor of Germany on January 30, 1933, it was the culmination of a decade's worth of political maneuvering. President Paul von Hindenburg and other conservative elites believed they could control Hitler. They imagined he would be a useful tool to squash communism and restore order. They were wrong.

Almost immediately after becoming Chancellor, Hitler used the Reichstag Fire of February 1933 to claim that communists were plotting against the German state. He pushed through the Reichstag Fire Decree, which suspended civil liberties and allowed for mass arrests of communists and other political enemies. The Nazis then passed the Enabling Act in March 1933, giving Hitler the power to pass laws without parliamentary consent. It was, in effect, the death of German democracy.

Within months, all political parties aside from the Nazis were banned. Trade unions were dismantled, replaced by Nazi-controlled organizations. The press fell in line, either through intimidation or direct government takeover. The Gestapo (Secret State Police) was established to root out dissidents. Neighbors spied on neighbors, children reported parents, and a culture of fear consumed the population.

Hitler was also helped by an improving economy. As the regime pumped money into military projects and public works like the Autobahn, unemployment dropped. Many ordinary Germans began to believe Hitler was turning the country around. The harsh crackdowns on Jews, communists, and other "undesirables" were mostly ignored or accepted by a public eager for stability. By the time President Hindenburg died in 1934, Hitler combined the roles of Chancellor and President into one: "Führer and Reich Chancellor." From then on, no one could challenge his decisions.

4. **Nazi Propaganda and the Cult of Personality**
   No totalitarian regime can exist without propaganda. The Nazis understood this better than most. Joseph Goebbels, appointed Minister of Public Enlightenment and Propaganda in 1933, controlled every aspect of media—from newspapers and radio to films and public events. His goal was to shape German minds to accept Hitler's worldview without question.

Posters displaying heroic images of Hitler became ubiquitous. Films portrayed him as a man of destiny, chosen to rescue Germany from decay. Enormous rallies, like the Nuremberg rallies, featured rows of uniformed party members, dramatic lighting, and stirring music, all designed to create an emotional rush that bonded people to the Führer. School curriculums were altered to teach racial ideology. Teachers were instructed to emphasize German history as a tale of greatness interrupted by Jewish conspiracies and other "enemies."

Under this propaganda blitz, many Germans genuinely came to see Hitler as almost superhuman. Even those who were skeptical learned to keep quiet. Speaking ill of the Führer or questioning Nazi doctrines in public could lead to arrest, torture, or worse. The propaganda machine also extended beyond Germany's borders, with newsreels broadcasting carefully staged footage to show how peaceful and prosperous the Reich was becoming under Nazi rule.

Behind these polished images, though, were programs aimed at removing or destroying entire groups of people. Already, laws were in place to ostracize Jews from society. Political opponents and critics ended up in early concentration camps, which at this stage were built for "re-education" or forced labor. The darkest phases were yet to come, but the foundations were firmly laid.

5. **Stalin's Soviet Union: A Different Kind of Terror**
   While the world often draws a line between fascism and communism, Stalin's Soviet Union was just as totalitarian. By the 1930s, Stalin had consolidated power following Lenin's death in 1924. He introduced Five-Year Plans to industrialize the Soviet Union at breakneck speed, forcing peasants onto collective farms. The human cost was staggering. Famines swept across the land, most notably the Holodomor in Ukraine, where millions starved to death.

Stalin's regime relied on brutal methods to maintain control. The NKVD hunted down anyone labeled an "enemy of the people," a term so broad it could apply to almost anyone. Show trials took place, where old Bolsheviks and military leaders were accused of conspiracy and sabotage. Confessions were extracted through torture, leading to executions or life sentences in gulags, the Soviet labor camps. These purges destroyed the Red Army's leadership just as Europe was inching closer to war, but Stalin either didn't care or was too paranoid to stop.

Propaganda in the Soviet Union glorified Stalin as the "Father of Nations," a visionary leading the country to a workers' paradise. Gigantic portraits and statues of him were displayed in public squares. The Communist Party infiltrated every aspect of daily life. Children joined the Young Pioneers, learning Marxist-Leninist ideology from a young age. Citizens were encouraged to report "counter-revolutionary" behavior, and many turned on neighbors to protect themselves.

The difference between Stalin's terror and Hitler's or Mussolini's was in the ideology and the specific targets. Hitler focused on racial enemies—Jews, Roma, Slavs—while Stalin's enemies were often political or class-based—kulaks (wealthier peasants), Trotskyists, or anyone he deemed a threat. Yet the end result was still mass suffering, fear, and death on a vast scale. By the late 1930s, millions in the Soviet Union had perished or were rotting away in labor camps.

6. **Spain: A Dress Rehearsal for War**
   Spain hadn't fully industrialized and was racked by deep political divisions between conservatives, monarchists, liberals, and left-wing groups. In 1936, a group of right-wing army officers led by General Francisco Franco attempted a coup against the elected Republican government. The country split into Nationalist and Republican zones, and a brutal civil war began.

Fascist Italy and Nazi Germany saw a chance to test new weapons and tactics by supporting Franco's Nationalists. Mussolini sent troops and equipment, while Hitler sent aircraft and the infamous Condor Legion. On the Republican side, the Soviet Union provided limited support, and volunteers from around the world joined the International Brigades, believing they were fighting against the spread of fascism. Civilians bore the brunt of the war's savagery, with bombings like the one in Guernica shocking the international community.

The Spanish Civil War served as a laboratory for totalitarian warfare. German pilots practiced bombing techniques on Spanish towns, perfecting strategies they would later use on European cities. Propaganda soared on both sides, demonizing the enemy in stark black-and-white terms. Civilians caught in the middle suffered famine, disease, and terror. By 1939, Franco emerged victorious, establishing a dictatorship that would last until his death decades later. Spain's tragedy foreshadowed the horrors soon to engulf the rest of Europe.

7. **The Axis Forms**
   With the ideological lines drawn, certain alliances began to form. Italy and Germany found common ground in their shared fascist philosophies and expansionist goals. The two nations signed the Pact of Steel in 1939, promising mutual support in the event of war. Japan, though not strictly fascist, aligned with Germany and Italy through the Anti-Comintern Pact in 1936, aimed at

countering the Soviet Union's influence. Over time, these alliances would evolve into the Axis Powers.

The formation of the Axis was a huge development. It meant that Germany and Italy had a powerful partner in the East—Japan—whose imperial ambitions in Asia matched their own in Europe and Africa. This global partnership would stretch the resources of the eventual Allied forces thin, forcing them to fight on multiple fronts, thousands of miles apart.

Propaganda portrayed the Axis as a force of rejuvenation against the "decadent" democracies and the "evil" Bolsheviks. Hitler admired the samurai spirit of Japan, seeing it as a warrior culture akin to his vision of an Aryan empire. Mussolini, for his part, hoped to recreate the glory of Rome, even if it meant partnering with nations that had little cultural connection to Italy. Together, these leaders believed they could carve up the world among themselves.

8. **Appeasement: The Last Gasp of Avoiding War**
   In response to these developments, Britain and France flailed about with policies that ranged from timid protest to attempts at negotiation. Memories of the Great War were still fresh, and neither country was eager to jump into another conflict. Britain, in particular, believed it could maintain peace if it gave Hitler some of what he wanted. The hope was that a satisfied Hitler would stop making demands and that Europe could avoid war.

This policy reached its peak in 1938 when Hitler demanded the Sudetenland, a region of Czechoslovakia with a significant ethnic German population. In the Munich Agreement, Britain and France basically handed the region to Hitler, with British Prime Minister Neville Chamberlain proclaiming it "peace for our time." This move is widely seen as the high-water mark of appeasement.

While the Allies breathed a sigh of relief, Hitler viewed it as a sign of weakness. He became more convinced that Britain and France would not stop him if he continued to expand. Emboldened, he soon broke his promises, taking over the rest of Czechoslovakia. The lesson was clear: appeasement only fed the dictators' appetites. War seemed inevitable.

9. **Everyday Life Under Dictatorship**
   What was everyday life like for people in these totalitarian states? In Nazi Germany, many experienced a certain level of economic improvement—if they fit into the "Aryan" mold. Jobs were created through rearmament programs and public works. Leisure activities were organized by the "Strength Through Joy" program, offering subsidized vacations, theater tickets, and other forms of entertainment—always under watchful Party eyes.

For Jews, Roma, homosexuals, and others targeted by Nazi ideology, life became a living nightmare. They were forced out of jobs, barred from schools, and subjected to beatings or arrest. The Gestapo encouraged citizens to report any suspicious behavior. Children were indoctrinated in Hitler Youth or the League of German Girls, shaping their loyalty to the regime from an early age.

Similarly, in Stalin's Soviet Union, daily life was harsh. Residents faced long lines for basic goods, constant fear of denunciation, and an unrelenting stream of propaganda praising Stalin. Giant posters glorified industrial achievements, while behind the scenes, workers were expected to meet impossible production quotas. Failing to meet these quotas could lead to accusations of sabotage, potentially a death sentence.

In Mussolini's Italy, life was more regimented than in the pre-Fascist era. The regime tried to control cultural expression, and critics often vanished. Youth organizations taught obedience to Il Duce, while an ambitious public works program built roads and drained marshes. For those who could pay lip service to the regime and stay out of politics, life could remain relatively normal, at least compared to the extremes of Nazi Germany or Stalin's USSR.

10. **The Gathering Storm**
    By the late 1930s, the writing was on the wall. Hitler's Germany was rearmed and ready for action, Mussolini's Italy was hungry for colonial expansion (as seen in the invasion of Ethiopia in 1935), and Japan had already tested international limits by occupying Manchuria. The Soviet Union watched warily, worried about a possible two-front threat from Germany and Japan.

All the while, these dictatorships continued to solidify their holds on power. Opposition voices were silenced, propaganda drowned out reason, and scapegoats were targeted for every problem. Ordinary people, whether out of fear or genuine belief, often supported their leaders' ambitions, expecting that a glorious new era was just over the horizon.

Yet beneath the surface of these totalitarian states lay deep rot. Their success depended heavily on constant expansion and exploitation, whether of colonies, minority groups, or newly conquered territories. When resources began to run low, the only solution left was more conquest. This expansionist dynamic would soon tear Europe and the world apart.

As the decade rolled over into 1939, Hitler aimed his sights at Poland. Britain and France, finally realizing that appeasement had failed, promised to defend Polish sovereignty. The invasion of Poland in September would spark the official start of World War II. The dark seeds planted in the early 1930s were about to bear the most horrific fruit imaginable. In the next chapters, we will move from the build-up phase into the actual outbreak of war, examining the terrifying facts of how the conflict began to spiral into a global catastrophe.

CHAPTER THREE

Early Horrors on the European Front

1. **The Invasion of Poland (1939)**
   The spark that officially ignited World War II in Europe was the German invasion of Poland on September 1, 1939. For several months before that, tension had been building like storm clouds in the sky. Adolf Hitler made various demands over the city of Danzig (Gdańsk) and the Polish Corridor—a strip of land giving Poland access to the Baltic Sea—which many Germans saw as rightfully theirs. Britain and France had pledged to support Poland if it was attacked, but no one truly knew if they would follow through.

In the early hours of September 1, without a formal declaration of war, Hitler's forces crossed the Polish border from the west, north, and south. The Luftwaffe (German air force) launched devastating bombings on Polish cities and infrastructure. Meanwhile, the Wehrmacht (German army) used its infamous blitzkrieg tactics—lightning war involving fast-moving tanks supported by aircraft—to break through Polish defenses. Within days, Polish units were overwhelmed. Towns were devastated by aerial bombardments; columns of refugees clogged the roads, desperately trying to flee the fighting.

The bombing of Wieluń on that first day was especially brutal. German planes bombed the small town relentlessly. The aim was not just to cripple Polish forces—who were hardly present in Wieluń—but also to terrorize the civilian population. Buildings crumbled, and fires raged, with terrified families running for cover or dying beneath the wreckage. It was one of the first signs that World War II in Europe would not resemble the static trench warfare of World War I. This was a new, horrifying form of total war where civilians were direct targets.

Just over two weeks later, on September 17, the Soviet Union invaded Poland from the east under the terms of the secret Molotov-Ribbentrop Pact—a non-aggression treaty with Nazi Germany that contained a clause to divide Eastern Europe between them. The Polish army, already strained to the breaking point, found itself caught in a pincer. Polish forces fought bravely but were outgunned and outnumbered. By early October, Poland was completely occupied, carved up between the Nazis and Soviets.

2. **Unfolding Atrocities in Poland**
   With the occupation of Poland, the Nazi regime showed early signs of the brutality that would characterize the war. Special units known as Einsatzgruppen followed the advancing German army. Their job was to round up and eliminate anyone considered a threat—intellectuals, priests, community leaders, and Jews. While the full machinery of the Holocaust was not yet in motion, these squads

carried out mass shootings in forests, fields, and even town squares. Entire Polish villages were terrorized.

One chilling example was the Bydgoszcz "Bloody Sunday" in early September 1939. Rumors spread among German forces that Poles had attacked German residents. In retaliation, the Wehrmacht and SS shot hundreds of Polish civilians. Another example of early brutality was the treatment of Polish military officers and intelligentsia. The Nazis aimed to decapitate Polish society, removing anyone who might organize resistance. Universities were closed, professors were arrested or executed, and students had few options other than forced labor.

Nor was Soviet-occupied Poland spared. Many Polish officers and intellectuals ended up in NKVD prisons or were executed. The most infamous example was the Katyn Massacre in April and May 1940, where Soviet secret police systematically executed thousands of Polish military officers and elites. Though much of the Western world wouldn't learn the full truth of Katyn until later, this atrocity added another layer of darkness to the fate of Poland under foreign occupation.

3. **Britain and France Declare War: The 'Phony War'**
   Two days after Germany's invasion of Poland, Britain and France declared war on Germany, fulfilling their promise. Yet, they made no major offensive moves on the Western Front to relieve the pressure on Poland. Historians debate whether they should have launched an attack or if they were simply unprepared. Regardless, this period from autumn 1939 to spring 1940 became known as the "Phony War." Troops from both sides sat behind defensive lines, occasionally exchanging artillery fire, but no major battles erupted.

In Britain, citizens began preparing for the worst. Children were evacuated from major cities to the countryside to protect them from expected air raids. Gas masks were distributed. Blackout regulations were enforced at night to make it harder for enemy bombers to find targets. An uneasy calm settled across Western Europe, punctuated by occasional air-raid sirens that turned out to be false alarms. Meanwhile, the British Royal Navy moved to blockade Germany, and Germany's U-boats prowled the Atlantic in search of Allied shipping.

This strange lull allowed Hitler to consolidate his hold on Poland and shift forces westward for the next phase of his plan. While many soldiers on the Maginot Line—France's heavily fortified border—felt bored and restless, Germany quietly prepared for what would become a series of stunning invasions in the spring of 1940. The world would soon learn that Hitler had no intention of maintaining this fragile calm.

4. **The Invasion of Denmark and Norway**
   On April 9, 1940, German forces launched Operation Weserübung, the invasion of

Denmark and Norway. The move was swift and largely unexpected. Denmark, with a small army and a flat, open landscape, was overwhelmed within hours. The Danish government surrendered on the same day, hoping to spare its population from a disastrous battle. Although Denmark wasn't a major prize in terms of resources, its strategic location provided Germany with a direct route to Norway and control of the Baltic Sea approaches.

Norway posed a greater challenge due to its long coastline and fjords, which the German navy had to navigate under threat from British and Norwegian forces. Nevertheless, Germany succeeded in seizing key ports like Oslo, Bergen, and Narvik. Heavy fighting broke out in some regions; Norwegian and British troops attempted to hold positions, but they were outmaneuvered by German paratroopers and amphibious assaults. By June, Norway fell completely under German control.

The occupation of Norway was harsh. The Germans quickly installed a puppet government led by Vidkun Quisling—a name that would become synonymous with "traitor." Resistance movements formed, but the threat of brutal reprisals kept many Norwegians living in constant fear. Raids and arrests became common, and suspicion haunted small towns and large cities alike. The freezing winters and remote landscapes also made life difficult for both occupiers and locals. Germany saw Norway as an essential foothold for controlling the North Sea and protecting its iron ore shipments from Sweden, which were vital to the Nazi war machine.

5. **The Western Blitz: France and the Low Countries**
   While the world watched events in Scandinavia, the main blow came in May 1940. Germany unleashed a massive blitzkrieg on Belgium, the Netherlands, and Luxembourg—collectively known as the Low Countries—and then drove into France. This was a repeat of the Schlieffen Plan concept from World War I but executed with far more speed and precision. Panzer divisions under generals like Heinz Guderian and Erwin Rommel sliced through defenses, bypassing strongpoints, and leaving Allied forces scrambling.

The Netherlands capitulated in just five days after the devastating bombing of Rotterdam. The city's center was almost entirely destroyed by German aircraft, creating a firestorm that killed nearly a thousand civilians and left tens of thousands homeless. Faced with the threat of more bombings, Dutch forces laid down their arms. Civilians across the Low Countries were gripped by panic, fleeing with whatever belongings they could carry as German troops advanced.

Belgium held out slightly longer, but the result was the same. The Belgian fortress of Eben-Emael, thought to be impregnable, was taken by German glider-borne troops in a daring assault that stunned military observers worldwide. Belgian soldiers fought valiantly, but in the face of the German onslaught, they could not hold out for more than a few weeks. Once Belgium fell, the path into France lay wide open.

The German strategy involved driving through the Ardennes Forest—terrain that French and British commanders believed was too difficult for tanks to navigate. This miscalculation proved catastrophic. German Panzer divisions poured through the forest, bypassed the Maginot Line's fortifications, and encircled large groups of Allied troops. Terror spread through French cities as refugees clogged the roads, bombed and strafed by the Luftwaffe. By mid-June, Paris was within German reach, and the French government fled south.

6. **The Fall of France and the Armistice**
   On June 14, 1940, German forces entered Paris. The once-bustling capital was silent under occupation. Within days, the new French government led by Marshal Philippe Pétain sought an armistice, effectively surrendering the northern part of France to direct German control. The southern region became Vichy France, a nominally independent state but effectively under Nazi influence.

The speed of France's collapse stunned the world. Just months earlier, people remembered France as a major power—winner of the Great War. Now, the swastika flew over Paris. Hitler, exultant at this victory, forced the French delegation to sign the armistice in the same railway carriage used for the German surrender in 1918, a deliberate gesture of revenge.

Under occupation, life in France turned grim. The Gestapo and SS arrived, hunting for anyone who resisted. The puppet Vichy regime collaborated with Nazi policies, including the deportation of Jews to internment camps. French citizens faced rationing, curfews, and the constant threat of informers. The French Resistance did form, conducting sabotage and gathering intelligence, but any discovery by the Germans or the Vichy authorities could lead to torture, execution, or the destruction of entire villages.

7. **Dunkirk: A Glimmer of Hope**
   In the midst of the disaster in France, one event offered a small ray of hope for the Allies: the evacuation of Dunkirk. As the German Panzer divisions raced across northern France, they trapped nearly 400,000 British and French troops along the coast near the town of Dunkirk. Facing annihilation, the British launched Operation Dynamo, an emergency effort to rescue these stranded forces.

From May 26 to June 4, a motley fleet of warships, merchant vessels, fishing boats, and even pleasure yachts crossed the English Channel under constant Luftwaffe attacks. Over 330,000 soldiers were rescued and brought back to Britain. The images of British "little ships" braving bombs and strafing runs became legendary, a sign that even in the face of near defeat, there was resilience and courage.

Still, Dunkirk was more a retreat than a victory, leaving most of the heavy equipment behind. Yet for Britain, saving so many experienced troops meant the difference between having an army ready to fight another day versus losing almost all of its trained forces. Dunkirk became a symbol of unity, showing civilians and soldiers alike that they were in the war together, and that small miracles were still possible in a time of great darkness.

8. **The Battle of Britain: Terror in the Skies**

    After France fell, Hitler set his sights on Britain. Operation Sea Lion—Germany's plan for a cross-channel invasion—required air superiority. Thus began the Battle of Britain in July 1940. The Luftwaffe aimed to destroy the Royal Air Force (RAF) by bombing airfields, radar stations, and aircraft factories.

German aircraft like the Messerschmitt Bf 109 and the Junkers Ju 87 "Stuka" dive-bomber flew sortie after sortie over the English Channel. British pilots, often outnumbered, scrambled their Hurricanes and Spitfires to defend the homeland. Radar technology played a pivotal role, giving the RAF early warning of incoming raids. Despite heavy losses, the British pilots, famously labeled "The Few" by Prime Minister Winston Churchill, managed to keep the Luftwaffe at bay.

Frustrated with the RAF's stubborn resistance, Hitler changed tactics. He authorized the bombing of British cities in an effort to break civilian morale. This stage became known as "The Blitz." Night after night, London, Coventry, Liverpool, and other cities endured massive air raids. Homes were destroyed, families killed, and entire neighborhoods reduced to rubble. Blackouts turned cities into dark mazes, where people groped their way to shelters. Air-raid sirens wailed, and the distant hum of approaching bombers struck fear in every heart.

Yet, Britain did not collapse. While tens of thousands died and many more were made homeless, the bombings did not force a surrender. Instead, they steeled British resolve. Winston Churchill's speeches rallied the nation, reminding them they stood alone against Nazi tyranny. By late 1940, the Luftwaffe's losses had become unsustainable. Though the Blitz continued into 1941, Germany abandoned any serious plans to invade Britain. This was a critical turning point—Hitler's first major failure.

9. **The Balkan Campaign**

    Even as Germany bombed Britain, it turned its attention south to secure its flank before launching any massive campaigns in the East. Italy had entered the war in June 1940 on Germany's side, hoping to gain easy victories in North Africa and the Balkans. But the Italian military struggled, particularly in Greece. Mussolini's forces were repelled by the Greek army, embarrassing the fascist regime.

To rescue his ally, Hitler moved to invade Yugoslavia and Greece in April 1941. Yugoslavia fell quickly after being bombed relentlessly by the Luftwaffe, including the destruction of Belgrade. Then, German and Bulgarian troops pushed into Greece. British Commonwealth forces tried to help the Greeks, but they were outmatched. By the end of April, Greece was under Axis occupation. The island of Crete fell in May after a bold German airborne assault.

The occupation of the Balkans introduced a new wave of horrors. Resistance movements sprouted in Yugoslavia and Greece, but the reprisals by the Germans (and their local allies) were brutal. Entire villages were massacred if partisans were suspected of operating nearby. The harsh terrain and the complexity of ethnic divisions made the Balkan conflict especially vicious, with factions and rival groups carrying out their own campaigns of terror. This region would bleed for years under Axis rule, leaving behind a legacy of atrocities that still scars local memory.

10. **Civilian Terror in Occupied Europe**
    By mid-1941, Germany and its allies controlled a huge swath of Europe—from Norway's icy fjords in the north to the Mediterranean shores of Greece in the south. Civilians under occupation faced food shortages, forced labor, and the constant threat of arrests. The Gestapo and SS established networks of informers, and large numbers of Jewish people, political opponents, and others labeled "undesirable" were rounded up and transported to ghettos or camps. Though the full-scale genocide of the Holocaust would escalate in the coming months, the early signs of that machinery were already visible in places like Poland.

Daily life was dominated by fear. Curfews were strictly enforced. German patrols roamed city streets and rural roads, ready to punish even minor infractions with brutality. Resistance groups, while admired by many locals, often meant that entire communities could face collective punishment if a single partisan attacked an Axis soldier. Propaganda posters and radio broadcasts reminded everyone of the occupier's power, depicting Allied soldiers as monsters or criminals. Rumors of torture in prisons added to the climate of terror.

In France, the Vichy regime cooperated with Nazi authorities, introducing anti-Jewish laws and rounding up those deemed subversive. In the Netherlands, an efficient bureaucracy helped the Germans identify and isolate Jewish citizens. In Belgium, forced labor orders tore families apart. In Norway, local collaborators helped the Gestapo hunt down dissenters. None of these countries had experienced such a tight and violent grip since the Middle Ages, if ever. Human rights crumbled as the war machine devoured one nation after another.

11. **North Africa: Desert Warfare and Civilians**
    While much of the focus was on Europe itself, the war also raged in North Africa. Italy had colonies in Libya and sought to expand into British-controlled Egypt. The early Italian offensives went poorly, prompting Hitler to send in the Afrika Korps under General Erwin Rommel. Nicknamed the "Desert Fox," Rommel quickly proved adept at desert warfare. British and Commonwealth forces, led at different stages by generals like Archibald Wavell and later Bernard Montgomery, fought back and forth in a dynamic campaign.

Though less talked about than the European fronts, North Africa also saw its share of terror. Civilians in Libya and Egypt had to contend with shifting front lines, bombardments, and the threat of starvation as supply lines were cut. While the scale of atrocities was not as large as in Eastern Europe, local populations often lived in misery, watching foreign armies tussle over their homelands. Desert conditions—scorching heat, sandstorms, water shortages—added another layer of cruelty to the conflict.

Some Jewish communities in North Africa also faced persecution. Under Vichy French rule in Algeria, Morocco, and Tunisia, racial laws were introduced, and some Jews were interned in labor camps. Though these camps did not match the industrial-scale horrors of Auschwitz or Treblinka, they still represented a frightening extension of Nazi ideology into Africa. The seeds of darkness were indeed global, showing that no place was fully safe from the reach of total war.

12. **Cracks in the Axis Friendship**
    Despite its triumphs, the Axis alliance was not entirely harmonious. Mussolini's failures in Greece and North Africa frustrated Hitler, who had to divert German resources to bail out Italian forces. Japan was distant, mostly concerned with its

expansion in Asia. And in the background, the Soviet Union loomed—nominally allied with Germany through the Molotov-Ribbentrop Pact but deeply distrusted by Hitler. Stalin, for his part, eyed Germany warily, building up his army while purging his ranks of potential traitors, ironically weakening his officer corps.

The question on everyone's mind was: when would Hitler turn east? Germany's success in Western Europe left Britain isolated, but far from beaten. The uneasy non-aggression pact with the Soviet Union was set to expire at some point, at least in spirit, because Hitler had never really intended it to be permanent. His ideological hatred for Bolshevism and Slavs was well known. Meanwhile, Stalin believed he had more time to prepare, not fully grasping Hitler's willingness to risk a two-front war.

This tension between the Nazi regime and the Soviet Union, which had partly facilitated the start of the war in Poland, was about to explode. The next phase of the war, which we'll cover in Chapter Four, would be marked by a scale of violence and destruction Europe had scarcely imagined. The early horrors on the European Front were brutal enough, but the invasion of the Soviet Union—Operation Barbarossa—would introduce new depths of cruelty, setting the stage for the Holocaust to reach its most catastrophic phase.

13. **Refugees and Displacement**
    One underreported aspect of these early years is the massive displacement of people. Millions of civilians were uprooted as front lines shifted. Some fled aerial bombings, others were forced out by occupying powers. Children were separated from parents, entire families vanished in the chaos. Refugee columns stretched for miles along roads, vulnerable to air attacks and looting. Disease ran rampant in overcrowded camps, and local communities struggled to absorb the influx of homeless families.

The psychological toll was enormous. In practically every occupied or contested region, stories abounded of harrowing escapes, of livestock abandoned to starve, of beloved homes destroyed by bombs or confiscated by foreign soldiers. These tragedies might not always make the front page in war histories, but they formed the backdrop of countless personal nightmares. For many, the war was not about ideology or grand strategies; it was about surviving one more day with whatever food and shelter they could find.

14. **Underground Resistance**
    Despite the overwhelming power of the Nazi war machine, resistance movements gradually formed. From the Maquis in France to the Partisans in Yugoslavia, brave men and women risked everything to sabotage rail lines, smuggle weapons, gather intelligence, and shelter persecuted groups. In Belgium and the Netherlands, underground newspapers circulated, keeping hope alive. In Poland, the Home Army (Armia Krajowa) carried out clandestine operations, even

building secret schools to continue Polish education under the radar of the occupiers.

But resistance was dangerous. The Gestapo, SS, and local collaborators ruthlessly hunted down resistance cells. Torture was standard procedure for suspected partisans. Public executions or deportations were common reprisals. Entire communities could be wiped out in retaliation for a single act of sabotage. This brutality was meant to deter resistance, but in many cases, it only fueled deeper hatred for the occupiers.

15. **A Shifting Tide in the Air**
    While the early European campaigns heavily favored Germany, there were signs that the tide might eventually shift. The British victory in the Battle of Britain showed that Hitler's forces were not invincible in the air. American public opinion, once strongly isolationist, began to waver as news of Nazi aggression spread. President Franklin D. Roosevelt pushed for the Lend-Lease Act, providing Britain (and later the Soviet Union) with crucial military supplies.

Still, the immediate outlook in 1941 was grim for the Allies. Much of Europe lay under Nazi control, and Hitler was about to embark on his most ambitious offensive yet—an attack on the Soviet Union. Most German generals privately worried about fighting a war on two fronts, but Hitler's arrogance convinced him the Soviet Union would collapse quickly. As we'll see in the next chapter, Operation Barbarossa would open a new, horrific dimension of World War II, unveiling atrocities on a colossal scale.

CHAPTER FOUR

The Eastern Nightmare – Operation Barbarossa

1. **Prelude to the Invasion**
   Despite the non-aggression pact signed between Nazi Germany and the Soviet Union in 1939, both sides eyed each other with suspicion. Hitler detested communism and regarded Slavic people as inferior—destined to serve Germany's need for Lebensraum ("living space"). Stalin, for his part, believed Hitler might not strike so soon, especially while Britain was still unconquered. Both dictators were wrong in their assumptions. Hitler saw Britain's resilience as an annoying thorn but not an insurmountable threat. Convinced the Soviet Union could be toppled in a swift campaign, he set the date for invasion: June 22, 1941.

Codenamed Operation Barbarossa, this would be the largest land invasion in history. Over three million German soldiers, supported by thousands of tanks and aircraft, assembled along a massive front stretching from the Baltic Sea to the Black Sea. They were joined by Finnish forces in the north and Romanians in the south, as well as other Axis allies. The goal was to crush the Red Army, capture major cities like Leningrad, Moscow, and Kyiv, and seize the vast agricultural and industrial resources of the Soviet territories.

The Soviets were caught off guard. Stalin had received multiple warnings—from British intelligence, from spies like Richard Sorge in Tokyo, and even from German troop movements near the border—but he refused to believe Hitler would violate their pact so soon. As a result, on the eve of June 22, Soviet border units were under orders not to provoke the Germans. Planes sat parked in neat rows on airfields, waiting to be destroyed. Soldiers slept in their barracks, unaware that a maelstrom of fire was about to be unleashed.

2. **The Initial Onslaught**
   In the early morning hours of June 22, 1941, the German Wehrmacht, along with its allies, stormed across the Soviet frontier. The Luftwaffe struck Soviet airfields, destroying hundreds of planes on the ground before they could take off. Panzer divisions and motorized infantry units spearheaded the advance, smashing through Soviet border defenses. The Soviet Army, known as the Red Army, was ill-prepared. Communication lines were cut, panic spread, and entire divisions were encircled or annihilated within days.

Accounts from Soviet soldiers reveal the overwhelming shock of the invasion. Some describe waking up to the thunder of artillery and bombs, seeing their officers frantically trying to organize a defense, only to realize the enemy had already penetrated deep behind their lines. Others recall the confusion of retreat orders, counterattacks that made little sense, and supply lines that vanished. Civilians were equally stunned, with columns of refugees clogging roads in a desperate attempt to flee the relentless advance.

German forces in the north drove toward Leningrad, in the center toward Moscow, and in the south toward Ukraine. Success came quickly at first. The Red Army seemed to crumble. Soviet casualties soared into the hundreds of thousands within weeks. Thousands of tanks and artillery pieces were captured or destroyed. As entire Soviet armies were encircled, the Germans believed victory was near. But the Soviet Union's vastness and the grim determination of its people meant the fight was far from over.

3. **Brutality Against Civilians and POWs**

   From the outset, Operation Barbarossa was not just a military campaign. It was an ideological war that gave German forces "permission" to treat Soviet civilians and prisoners of war with unbridled cruelty. Hitler's instructions, known as the "Commissar Order," dictated that any Soviet political commissars captured should be executed immediately. Many German units took this as a license to kill or brutalize any Red Army soldier they considered to be "politicized."

The treatment of Soviet POWs was appalling. Instead of following the Geneva Conventions, German forces often left prisoners in open-air pens without food, water, or shelter. Thousands starved to death in these makeshift camps. Others were marched until they collapsed from exhaustion, then shot. The harshness of the Eastern Front was on a scale unseen in the earlier campaigns in Western Europe. It was fueled by Nazi racial ideology that labeled Slavs as subhuman.

Civilians fared no better. Einsatzgruppen, previously active in Poland, now rampaged across Soviet territory. Their mission expanded to include mass extermination of Jews, Roma, and anyone deemed a threat to Nazi rule. Entire villages were burned, with inhabitants shot or forced into mass graves. In some places, local collaborators joined in the killings, driven by anti-communist or anti-Jewish sentiments. The Eastern Front quickly became a land of horror, where normal rules of warfare disintegrated in the face of ideological fanaticism.

4. **Siege of Leningrad: Starvation as a Weapon**

   In the north, one of the most harrowing events of Operation Barbarossa was the Siege of Leningrad. By September 1941, German and Finnish forces encircled the city, cutting off all land routes. Hitler intended to starve Leningrad into submission, refusing any notion of surrender. Supplies could only enter through Lake Ladoga, often referred to as the "Road of Life" when it froze over in winter. But these efforts were not enough to feed the city's millions of residents.

As the siege dragged on, hunger became a daily torment. People ate pets, wallpaper paste, and sawdust in a desperate attempt to fill their stomachs. Thousands died each day from starvation, disease, and constant shelling. Bodies littered the streets. The winter of 1941-42 was brutally cold, exacerbating the suffering. Despite these horrors, Leningrad refused to capitulate. The siege lasted almost 900 days, making it one of the longest and deadliest in modern history. By some estimates, over a million civilians perished.

The psychological toll was immense. Survivors speak of haunting scenes—mothers cradling dead children, families tearing apart floorboards for firewood, and the eerie silence broken only by artillery blasts or the crash of bombs. People carried ration cards like lifelines, but rations were often a fraction of the minimal caloric need. The city turned into a cemetery, yet it never surrendered. This stubborn resistance bogged down Axis forces, diverting resources that might have gone toward other fronts.

5. **Einsatzgruppen and the Holocaust by Bullets**
   While the concentration camps are often the focal point of Holocaust discussions, the mass shootings carried out in the Soviet territories were equally horrific. Einsatzgruppen units, along with local auxiliary forces, carried out what is sometimes called the "Holocaust by Bullets." Rather than deporting Jews to camps, these mobile killing squads arrived in towns and villages, rounded up the Jewish population, and marched them to secluded sites—often forests or ravines—where they were shot.

Perhaps the most infamous massacre was at Babi Yar, a ravine near Kyiv. In late September 1941, over 30,000 Jews were ordered to gather. Believing they would be resettled, they arrived with belongings and small children in tow. Instead, they were stripped of clothing and valuables, lined up along the ravine's edge, and machine-gunned. Over two days, the ravine filled with bodies. Survivors recalled the relentless gunfire, the screams, and the earth itself seeming to move with the wounded trying to crawl free.

Such mass shootings were not isolated incidents. Thousands of similar executions took place throughout the occupied Soviet territories—smaller in scale but just as brutal. Local populations sometimes witnessed these killings firsthand, coerced into digging graves or burying bodies. Fear of similar fates kept many quiet. For the Nazis, this method of extermination was seen as a temporary solution until more "efficient" methods—like gas chambers—were scaled up. For those living through it, it was sheer terror.

6. **Battle of Kyiv and the Southern Front**
   In the south, German and Romanian armies advanced into Ukraine, a region prized for its fertile land and resources. The Battle of Kyiv, lasting from August to September 1941, became one of the largest encirclements in military history. Nearly 600,000 Soviet troops were captured or killed in the battle, a staggering loss. Hitler celebrated this as another step toward final victory. But it also delayed the push toward Moscow, costing the Germans critical weeks as winter approached.

Within occupied Ukraine, the Nazi regime imposed harsh rule. Cities like Kharkiv, Odesa, and Dnipro (then Dnipropetrovsk) faced shortages of food and medicine. Jewish communities were liquidated through shootings or forced into ghettos. The countryside was pillaged for grain and livestock to feed the German war effort. Resistance groups formed in the forests and marshlands, but any sign of partisanship invited brutal reprisals—entire villages could be razed.

For the Romanian troops, particularly around Odesa, the campaign also turned cruel. Massacres of Jewish citizens took place under Romanian occupation, sometimes rivaling the brutality of the SS. Meanwhile, the Red Army, battered but not broken, conducted strategic retreats and scorched-earth tactics to deny resources to the enemy. Villages were burned, factories dismantled, and fields ruined so the Germans would find nothing of value. For civilians, this meant devastation from both sides.

7. **Approach to Moscow: Operation Typhoon**
   By late September 1941, Hitler believed the Soviet Union was on the brink of collapse. He launched Operation Typhoon, the final drive to capture Moscow. German armies advanced rapidly, capturing prisoners and equipment in huge numbers. As they neared the Soviet capital, panic set in among local residents. Government offices began evacuating to Kuibyshev (now Samara). Some historians estimate that half of Moscow's population fled eastward.

However, the German offensive soon ran into two formidable foes: the Soviet will to defend the capital at all costs, and the brutal Russian winter. By October, heavy rains had turned roads into mud, trapping tanks and trucks. Then, temperatures plummeted, and snow began to fall. German troops lacked proper winter clothing, as Hitler had assumed the campaign would be over before winter. Meanwhile, fresh Soviet divisions arrived from Siberia, released by Soviet intelligence that deduced Japan would not invade from the east.

In December 1941, the Red Army launched a massive counteroffensive near Moscow. Exhausted and freezing, the Germans were pushed back. It was a crushing setback for Hitler, who had promised his generals they would stand victorious in Moscow's Red Square. Instead, they faced one of the coldest winters on record in a hostile land. The myth of German invincibility was shattered. While the Eastern Front would continue for years, this failed assault on Moscow marked a turning point where Nazi hopes of a quick victory died in the snow.

8. **Stalin's Terror Continues**
   Amid the chaos of the German invasion, Stalin's regime continued to show little mercy to its own people. Any sign of defeatism or collaboration could result in summary execution or deportation. Soldiers who surrendered or were captured were branded as traitors. If they managed to escape and return to Soviet lines, many faced interrogation and harsh punishment rather than a hero's welcome. Some families of POWs were arrested, accused of breeding traitors.

The NKVD also carried out hurried massacres of prisoners in regions about to fall to German forces. Prisoners—some political, some ordinary criminals—were executed en masse to prevent them from being freed by the Germans. Civilians living under Soviet control had limited news of the outside world. Propaganda insisted that the Red Army was fighting heroically and that any temporary setbacks were due to saboteurs or traitors. For the average Soviet citizen, especially in the path of retreat, life was a nightmare of uncertainty, fear, and displacement.

9. **Scorched Earth and Partisan Warfare**
   As Soviet forces withdrew from occupied territories, they adopted a scorched-earth strategy. Factories were dismantled and shipped east, crops burned, livestock slaughtered. Anything that could be of use to the German war machine was destroyed. This tactic was brutal on local populations, who were left with nothing but rubble. Yet, it also robbed the advancing Germans of supplies, forcing them to rely on long and vulnerable supply lines.

Partisan warfare became a significant factor behind German lines. Soviet partisans attacked convoys, blew up rail tracks, and assassinated collaborating officials. The response from the Germans was swift and merciless. For every partisan attack, entire villages might be punished. Civilians were hanged, shot, or deported to labor camps in Germany. Despite these reprisals, partisan activity grew, fueled by anger over Nazi atrocities.

Forests and swamps teemed with small bands of fighters who lived off the land or relied on secret supply drops from the Red Army. In places like Belarus, partisans effectively created "liberated zones" where German forces dared not venture without large escorts. These were dangerous times for everyone, as the line between partisan and civilian often blurred, giving the Germans an excuse for widespread terror.

10. **War of Annihilation**
    The conflict on the Eastern Front was truly a "war of annihilation," as Hitler had intended. Civilians were not just collateral damage; they were often deliberate targets. German propaganda painted the invasion as a crusade against "Jewish-Bolshevik" subhumans, fueling a sense of impunity in the troops. Plunder, rape, and murder became commonplace. At the same time, Soviet propaganda called for the total destruction of the invaders, portraying Germans as fascist devils who must be annihilated without mercy.

This clash of brutal ideologies left millions dead or homeless. Entire cities like Smolensk, Bryansk, and Rostov became battlegrounds repeatedly over the course of the war. Many towns were left in charred ruins, with only a fraction of their population surviving. Even animals suffered; livestock was wiped out, and forests burned, destroying habitats for local wildlife. The Eastern Front was total war in every sense—economically, militarily, and psychologically.

11. **The Toll on Soldiers**
    While the cruelty inflicted on civilians is often highlighted, the soldiers themselves endured hellish conditions. On the German side, morale plummeted as winter set in and the Soviets proved more resilient than expected. Frostbite claimed limbs, and supplies of winter gear were insufficient. Soldiers sometimes stripped clothing from Soviet dead, risking disease, just to stay warm. Dysentery and lice swept through the ranks, and the roads were choked with stalled vehicles.

Soviet soldiers faced even worse conditions. They were expected to fight a well-equipped invader, often with outdated rifles or limited ammunition. Political commissars kept a close watch, ready to punish any sign of retreat as cowardice. Despite this, many Soviet soldiers fought with fierce bravery, fueled by hatred of the invader and a desire to protect their homeland. Tank battles on the Eastern Front were massive and chaotic, with entire regiments wiped out in single engagements.

Prisoners of war, if captured, could expect no mercy from either side. Germans rarely adhered to international conventions, and the Soviets were often just as ruthless in retaliation. Camps for POWs were essentially death traps, riddled with disease and starvation. The few who managed to escape often found themselves wandering hostile territories, unsure if they would be shot by local militias or recaptured by enemy patrols.

12. **Changing Global Dynamics**
    Operation Barbarossa also changed the global political picture. Once Hitler invaded the Soviet Union, Britain found a new, albeit uneasy, ally in Stalin. Winston Churchill, who despised communism, declared support for the Soviet cause because the alternative—Nazi dominance—was far worse. British convoys began sending war supplies to Murmansk and Arkhangelsk via the treacherous Arctic route, enduring U-boat attacks and extreme weather to deliver tanks, planes, and other materiel.

The United States, still neutral at this point, became more sympathetic to the Allies. President Roosevelt extended Lend-Lease aid to the Soviet Union, providing crucial trucks, food, and ammunition. This assistance, while not decisive on its own, helped the Red Army recover from its initial losses.

Meanwhile, Japan kept an eye on events in the West, hesitant to open a second front against the Soviet Union. Tensions between the U.S. and Japan were rising over Japanese expansion in the Pacific, setting the stage for another dramatic turn in the global war. For the moment, the largest land war in history was raging in Eastern Europe, and the next big chapter would soon unfold when winter gave way to new offensives.

13. **The Road to Stalingrad**
    By the end of 1941, Operation Barbarossa had ground to a halt outside Moscow. However, Hitler was not dissuaded. In 1942, the German high command shifted focus south, aiming to seize the oil fields of the Caucasus. The push into Stalingrad became symbolic—both for Stalin, whose city bore his name, and for Hitler, who wanted to break Soviet resistance once and for all.

Though the Battle of Stalingrad is a story for another chapter, its seeds were planted during Barbarossa. The Red Army learned from earlier defeats and adopted new tactics. Stalin promoted capable generals like Georgy Zhukov. Soviet production ramped up, thanks in part to factories relocated east of the Urals, out of German bomber range. The bitterness of the early invasion, combined with propaganda focusing on Nazi atrocities, gave Soviet troops a sense of desperation and determination—they knew what would happen if they lost.

14. **The High Price of Barbarossa**
    In the grand sweep of World War II, Operation Barbarossa was a turning point that unleashed a level of suffering rarely seen in modern warfare. By the end of 1941, millions of Soviet soldiers had been killed, wounded, or captured. Countless civilians were trapped in occupied territories, subject to forced labor or extermination. German casualties, while lower in comparison, were still massive—hundreds of thousands of men lost in the first six months alone. The economic toll was also staggering. Germany had hoped to live off the land but found little nourishment in the devastated Soviet countryside. Vehicles broke down, ammunition ran low, and the unpredictability of Soviet counterattacks made supply lines precarious.

Yet, the Nazis pressed on, believing they could still force a Soviet collapse if they struck hard enough. This belief would lead them deeper into the Soviet Union's heartland, into brutal urban battles like Stalingrad and mountainous warfare in the Caucasus. As we will see in later chapters, the war in the East would become a grinding, merciless conflict that devoured whole armies and left behind a trail of atrocities unmatched in scale.

CHAPTER FIVE

Dark Days of the Holocaust Begin

1. **Prelude to Systematic Persecution**
   The Holocaust did not emerge out of nowhere. By the time the mass killings began in earnest, the Nazi regime had already spent years laying the groundwork of hatred and discrimination against Jewish people and other targeted groups. Even before the war, Jews in Germany were stripped of citizenship, forbidden to work in certain professions, and regularly humiliated in state-sponsored propaganda. Anti-Jewish violence was common in the streets, especially carried out by the SA (Stormtroopers) and later the SS.

In 1933, when Adolf Hitler rose to power, Germany's Jewish population was roughly 500,000—about 1% of the total population. Most German Jews considered themselves patriotic Germans and had served in World War I. They were integrated into society. But the Nazi Party insisted that Jews were an alien race responsible for Germany's problems, from the defeat in World War I to the economic crises of the 1920s.

After the Nuremberg Laws were enacted in 1935, Jewish people lost legal protections. They could not marry non-Jews or even have sexual relations with them. Jews were banned from public service jobs. Little by little, the world of German Jews shrank until many decided to leave. Yet emigration was difficult. Countries like the United States and Britain had strict immigration quotas. Many people were trapped. When war began in 1939, these discriminatory policies extended to all Jewish communities in occupied territories. The Nazi regime began to implement new, lethal methods, turning discrimination into systematic murder.

2. **Escalation of Violence in Occupied Poland**
   With the conquest of Poland in late 1939, the Nazis suddenly had control over a much larger Jewish population—around 3 million Polish Jews, plus many others considered "undesirable," such as Roma people, political dissidents, and those with disabilities. The Nazi leadership quickly realized that the earlier methods of forced emigration were no longer feasible. Instead, they began to force Jews into ghettos, separate neighborhoods or entire city districts sealed off from the outside world.

In 1940, the General Government (the Nazi administrative region of central Poland) issued orders to create large ghettos in cities like Warsaw, Łódź, and Kraków. These areas became overcrowded prisons. Jews from surrounding villages and towns were herded in, forced to abandon their homes and belongings. Families slept in cramped apartments or even on sidewalks. Food was scarce, medical care almost nonexistent, and disease spread rapidly. Typhus epidemics raged as sanitation collapsed.

Meanwhile, the SS and Gestapo carried out mass shootings and deportations whenever they saw fit. Early in the occupation, they also tested "killing vans," where victims were murdered by carbon monoxide. In some cases, local Polish police or other collaborators participated, either out of fear or bigotry of their own. The pace of violence grew. While the Nazis had not yet implemented the Final Solution's industrial-scale extermination policy, the seeds were planted. Terror and death had become everyday realities for Jewish communities throughout occupied Poland.

3. **The Madagascar Plan and Other 'Solutions'**
   In the early stages of the war, the Nazi leadership toyed with different ideas for how to rid Europe of Jews. One bizarre plan was to send them all to the island of Madagascar, off the coast of Africa. Known as the "Madagascar Plan," it was never more than a fantasy. Germany's naval situation made such mass deportations impossible. Another idea considered shipping Jews to the Siberian tundra, essentially abandoning them to a slow death. These proposals showed that from the start, the Nazis were bent on forcing Jews out of Europe—or destroying them if necessary.

By 1940 and 1941, as Nazi armies conquered more territories, these schemes gave way to more direct forms of violence. The invasion of the Soviet Union in June 1941, covered in Chapter Four, introduced new territories with massive Jewish populations. It also granted the SS a free hand to carry out mass shootings on a scale previously unseen. The so-called "Holocaust by Bullets" saw Einsatzgruppen (special killing units) follow the Wehrmacht, executing Jews, Roma, and Soviet political commissars. Mass graves dotted the countryside.

Though these shootings were deadly—claiming hundreds of thousands of lives—they were also considered inefficient by high-ranking Nazis. Organizing firing squads, digging huge pits, and finding remote sites was time-consuming. Soldiers suffered psychological stress from killing women and children at close range. Reports reached SS leaders like Heinrich Himmler that some men were showing signs of mental breakdown. This was one reason the Nazis began exploring more impersonal, industrialized methods of murder.

4. **From Persecution to Extermination**
   While most historians point to 1941 as the critical shift from persecution to extermination, the foundation was built long before. The Nazis used propaganda to dehumanize Jews, calling them "vermin" or "parasites." Schools taught children that Jews were biologically inferior. Neighbors grew accustomed to seeing Jews beaten or arrested without protest. Such conditioning allowed ordinary people to accept or at least ignore the growing violence.

Heinrich Himmler, head of the SS, and Reinhard Heydrich, chief of the Reich Main Security Office (RSHA), were key architects of this policy shift. Their aim was to make Europe judenfrei—"free of Jews." In late 1941, Hitler gave a series of verbal orders to intensify efforts to eliminate the Jewish presence in occupied territories. Construction began on purpose-built extermination camps, where the primary function was to kill as many people as possible, as quickly as possible.

In December 1941, the first extermination camp, Chełmno (also known as Kulmhof), became operational in German-occupied Poland. There, Jews were killed in mobile gas vans. Victims were locked in the cargo area while engine exhaust was pumped inside. At its peak, hundreds of people a day were murdered this way. This grim technology was soon expanded to larger killing centers like Bełżec, Sobibór, and Treblinka. The darkest days of the Holocaust were beginning.

5. **The Wannsee Conference**
    A key moment in the official orchestration of the Holocaust was the Wannsee Conference, held on January 20, 1942. A group of high-ranking Nazi officials, chaired by Reinhard Heydrich, met at a villa in the Berlin suburb of Wannsee. The topic was the "Final Solution of the Jewish Question." This meeting aimed to coordinate the bureaucratic machinery—officials from different agencies had to agree on how to classify, deport, and ultimately murder millions of Jews across Europe.

Remarkably, the meeting itself was brief and almost procedural. The minutes, known as the Wannsee Protocol, show that participants spoke in cold, bureaucratic language about methods for "evacuating" Jews to the East, where they would be worked to death or otherwise "dealt with." Although the exact phrases about mass killing were guarded, the implications were clear to all in attendance. The Nazis planned to kill every Jew in Europe, from France to the Soviet Union, from Norway to Greece.

The conference did not create the Final Solution; extermination was already underway. But Wannsee streamlined the process, ensuring that every branch of the German government worked in unison. It also confirmed that even highly educated individuals—lawyers, doctors, and civil servants—were complicit in genocide. They arranged schedules, calculated train capacities, and organized deportations with chilling efficiency.

6. **The Role of Propaganda and Secrecy**
    Even as the Holocaust expanded, Nazi authorities tried to keep many details hidden from the general German population. Certain euphemisms—like "special treatment" or "final solution"—were used in official documents to disguise the true nature of the operations. Propaganda continued to depict Jews as enemies of the state, criminals, or disease carriers. This constant dehumanization made it easier to accept rumors of harsh measures against them.

In occupied regions, the local populations often knew more. The sight of trains packed with Jews heading east became common. People saw men, women, and children crammed into cattle cars, locked inside without food or water. Sometimes the stench of death from nearby killing sites was impossible to hide. Yet terror kept many silent. Those who spoke out risked arrest or worse. Collaborators, motivated by fear or anti-Semitism, helped identify hidden Jews or seized Jewish property for themselves.

The SS also tried to erase evidence of mass murder. Graves were dug up, bodies burned, and documents destroyed. However, these efforts were imperfect. Allied intelligence gradually gathered information about these atrocities. Secret messages leaked from the camps or ghettos. The general German populace might not have known the full scale, but at least some had strong suspicions. As the war continued, the lines between ignorance, denial, and complicity blurred.

Extermination Methods: From Gas Vans to Gas Chambers
During the early phase of the Holocaust, the Nazis relied heavily on shootings and gas vans. But as the Wannsee decisions took effect, they shifted to larger extermination centers equipped with gas chambers. The reason was efficiency. Instead of moving the killing units to the victims, victims were brought to fixed killing sites, some disguised as transit camps or shower facilities.

- **Bełżec**: Opened in March 1942, using carbon monoxide gas generated by engines. Victims were forced into chambers that looked like shower rooms, then locked inside as the exhaust was pumped in.
- **Sobibór**: Began operations in May 1942, also using carbon monoxide. Over 200,000 people were murdered there before a prisoner revolt in October 1943 led the Nazis to close and dismantle the site.
- **Treblinka**: Perhaps the deadliest of these "Operation Reinhard" camps. Opened in July 1942, it had a similar system of deception—a fake train station, signs, and loudspeakers telling people they were being resettled. In reality, almost everyone who arrived was gassed within hours. Historians estimate that 700,000 to 900,000 people died there, mostly Jews from the Warsaw Ghetto and other parts of Poland.
- **Chełmno** (mentioned earlier): Operated gas vans primarily, but also used some primitive gas chambers.
- **Majdanek**: Part concentration camp, part extermination facility, near Lublin. It used Zyklon B gas (hydrogen cyanide) in its chambers.

The largest extermination camp complex, **Auschwitz-Birkenau** (often simply called Auschwitz), would become the central symbol of the Holocaust. Initially a concentration camp for Polish political prisoners, it expanded to include Birkenau (Auschwitz II) in 1941. There, multiple gas chambers and crematoria were built to kill and dispose of bodies on an industrial scale. Zyklon B pellets were dropped into sealed chambers, releasing lethal gas that killed hundreds at a time. We will explore life in these camps in detail in the next chapter.

8. **Impact on Other Targeted Groups**
    Although the Holocaust is primarily associated with the extermination of Europe's Jews, the Nazis also targeted other groups. The Roma and Sinti (often called "Gypsies") were persecuted, forced into camps, and subjected to medical experiments. An unknown number were killed—some estimates run as high as several hundred thousand. People with disabilities were singled out under the so-called **T4 Euthanasia Program**, which used gas chambers and lethal injections to murder those deemed "unfit" or "life unworthy of life." Homosexuals, political dissidents, and Jehovah's Witnesses were also imprisoned and killed in camps, though not always on the same scale.

Slavic populations, especially Poles and Russians, were marked for "decimation," meaning many were intended to be enslaved or starved to make room for German settlers. In territories like Ukraine, entire villages were burned down, and forced labor conscription took huge numbers of young men and women to work in German factories or on farms. The Nazi vision of racial hierarchy was broad and deadly, touching millions of lives across the continent.

9. **Resistance and Rescue Efforts**
    Despite the pervasive terror, there were acts of resistance. Jews in some ghettos formed underground movements. In the Warsaw Ghetto, the Jewish Combat Organization and other groups smuggled in weapons, printing illegal newspapers to keep morale high. In April 1943, as rumors spread about mass deportations to Treblinka, the Warsaw Ghetto Uprising began. Jewish fighters, poorly armed, held off German troops for nearly a month. Though the uprising was crushed and the ghetto razed, this act of defiance remains a powerful testament to courage in the face of certain doom.

Other resistance efforts took different forms. Some individuals rescued Jews by hiding them or forging documents. Diplomats like Swedish businessman Raoul Wallenberg in Budapest issued protective passports, saving thousands. In German-occupied Denmark, nearly the entire Jewish population escaped to neutral Sweden, thanks to a coordinated effort by Danish citizens. The numbers saved were small compared to those murdered, but every saved life was a moral victory against the Nazi machine.

10. **The Role of Collaboration**
    In discussing the Holocaust, it's crucial to recognize that not all atrocities were committed by Germans alone. In many occupied countries, local collaborators helped identify Jews, guarded ghettos, or participated in mass shootings. In Latvia, Lithuania, and Ukraine, nationalist or anti-communist factions sometimes

saw collaboration as a way to gain favor with the Germans. They believed it could lead to autonomy or independence from the Soviet Union. While some did it out of genuine hate for Jews, others acted out of fear for their own lives or simply seized the opportunity to profit by taking Jewish property.

Vichy France adopted anti-Jewish laws even stricter than those initially demanded by the Germans, rounding up and deporting thousands to the death camps. In countries like Romania, the Iron Guard regime carried out pogroms and massacres with little prompting. These collaborations complicate the narrative, showing that the Holocaust thrived not just on German evil, but also on the willingness (or apathy) of other societies to participate or look away.

11. **Knowledge of the Outside World**
    One of the haunting questions about the Holocaust is how much the outside world knew and why they did not act sooner. By 1942, reports of mass killings in Poland had reached the governments-in-exile in London. Jewish organizations in Switzerland received alarming accounts of gassings at Bełżec and Sobibór. Underground couriers smuggled out testimony of what was happening in the ghettos.

Allied governments debated the credibility of these reports; some considered them exaggerated. Others believed the best way to help was to defeat Nazi Germany militarily. Proposals to bomb the railway lines leading to Auschwitz or the gas chambers themselves were discussed but never executed. Some historians argue that the Allies could have done more, while others suggest limited resources and uncertainties made such actions impossible at the time. Regardless, for those being murdered, these debates were distant and irrelevant—they needed help that never arrived in time.

12. **Daily Terror in the Ghettos**
    The ghettos across Eastern Europe played a central role in the Holocaust's early stages. Many Jews spent months or years in these walled-off districts before deportation. Daily life meant scavenging for food, hiding from random beatings, and watching neighbors die of disease or starvation. Children often became crucial couriers, slipping through cracks in the walls to smuggle in bread or potatoes. If caught, they were usually shot on the spot.

In some ghettos, Jewish Councils (Judenräte) were forced to administer Nazi orders—drawing up lists for deportations or rationing out meager supplies. These councils faced impossible moral choices: if they refused, the Nazis would kill them and replace them. If they complied, they became complicit in their own community's destruction. This moral gray zone remains a painful subject among Holocaust survivors and historians alike.

13. **The 'Harvest Festival' and Killing Operations**
    By late 1943, the Nazis began winding down the ghettos and "Operation Reinhard" camps, having murdered a large portion of Polish Jewry. In November 1943, an operation called "Harvest Festival" (Erntefest) was launched to eliminate the remaining Jews in the Lublin district of occupied Poland. Over 40,000 were shot in mass executions at Majdanek, Poniatowa, and Trawniki camps. Machine-gun fire echoed day and night, and the ground was said to shake with the volume of bodies falling into the pits.

For survivors, the final liquidation of the ghettos and these mass shootings marked the end of any illusions about survival within Poland. Those who had avoided deportation to extermination camps or labor camps now faced near-certain death. Some escaped to the forests, joining partisan groups, living in makeshift shelters through harsh winters. Most, however, were caught. The sheer scale of these coordinated killing operations showed the depth of Nazi planning and the extent of their determination to destroy an entire population.

14. **Psychological Aspects of the Holocaust**
    The Holocaust was not just a physical genocide but also a psychological one. The Nazis aimed to strip Jews and other victims of their humanity—taking away names and replacing them with numbers, forcing them to wear identifying badges (like the yellow Star of David), and subjecting them to public humiliation. This process eroded hope and dignity, making it easier to manage large groups of terrified, demoralized people.

Meanwhile, the perpetrators often compartmentalized their actions. Guards at concentration camps might listen to classical music in the evening after a day of overseeing mass murder. SS officers sometimes rationalized their crimes as a "patriotic duty." Civilian bystanders in German towns near the camps may have convinced themselves that the rumors were exaggerated or that the prisoners were criminals who "deserved" their fate. This moral disengagement allowed the killing to continue with minimal resistance from within Nazi-occupied Europe.

15. **Survival Tactics**
    In the face of overwhelming terror, victims found ways to survive or resist psychologically. Some families hid in attics, basements, or farmhouses. Others acquired false papers to pass as Christian Poles or non-Jewish citizens. In the ghettos, underground schools and cultural events kept spirits alive, if only briefly. Secret diaries documented daily life and the atrocities witnessed. These acts of preserving culture and memory became small forms of defiance.

Young people sometimes formed clandestine groups that discussed post-war dreams: building a future free from hate, or even emigrating to British-controlled Palestine to start anew. While survival was a day-to-day challenge, the human spirit sometimes shone through in unexpected places. A simple gesture—like sharing a piece of bread—took on monumental meaning in a world designed to crush empathy.

16. **The Machinery of Death Shifts**
    By mid-1944, the Red Army was advancing into Eastern Europe. The Nazis began dismantling their extermination infrastructure to hide evidence of genocide. Death camps were blown up or abandoned, mass graves exhumed and burned. Prisoners were forced on death marches westward, as the SS wanted to keep them from being liberated. Even then, the killing did not stop. Many died on these marches from starvation, disease, or summary executions when they could no longer walk.

Auschwitz-Birkenau remained operational until January 1945, when the Soviets finally liberated the camp, discovering a few thousand survivors left behind. As the Allies pushed from both east and west, they encountered the ghastly remains of the Holocaust—piles of corpses, emaciated prisoners, and half-destroyed crematoria. The scale of what had happened took time to sink in, even for hardened soldiers who had seen combat on multiple fronts.

17. **The Human Cost**
    It is difficult to place an exact number on how many perished during the Holocaust. Most estimates suggest that around six million Jews were murdered. Over half of Europe's Jewish population was wiped out. The Roma and Sinti lost a significant portion of their communities, potentially several hundred thousand. Millions of Slavs, political prisoners, and others also died in camps, ghettos, or during forced labor. The Nazi attempt at genocide did not succeed in wiping out all Jews, but it shattered centuries-old communities across the continent.

Beyond the raw numbers are the individual stories: families torn apart, children left orphans, entire towns emptied of their Jewish populations. Centuries of cultural heritage—books, synagogues, traditions—went up in flames. For survivors, trauma persisted long after the war. Their testimonies provide a raw and haunting insight into how quickly a society can descend into barbarism under the sway of hateful ideologies.

18. **Allied Responses and Aftermath**
    When the Allied armies liberated the concentration camps in 1944 and 1945, they found living skeletons and warehouses stacked with stolen belongings—eyeglasses, shoes, gold teeth. Soldiers wept or vomited at the sight. Journalists and filmmakers documented the horrors, ensuring the world could not dismiss these crimes as propaganda. However, many Germans claimed ignorance or insisted they were only following orders.

Despite war crimes trials after the war—most famously at Nuremberg—many perpetrators escaped punishment. Some fled abroad, changed identities, or blended back into post-war life. Others received lenient sentences. The moral shock of the Holocaust, however, was so profound that it forced a worldwide reckoning with issues of racism, nationalism, and the fragility of civilization. Nations vowed that such atrocities should never be repeated, though history would show that genocide could—and did—happen again in different forms elsewhere.

19. **Why the Holocaust Matters in Understanding WWII**
    World War II is often portrayed as a struggle between Axis and Allied powers over territory and resources. While that is true, the Holocaust reveals a deeper horror: the war enabled a genocide that was planned and executed within the framework of a modern state's bureaucracy. Trains, schedules, budgets, and official stamps—these ordinary tools facilitated mass murder. This industrial and organized approach to killing made the Holocaust a unique event in world history.

Moreover, the Holocaust shows how propaganda, fear, and scapegoating can manipulate ordinary people into committing or tolerating extreme cruelty. It reminds us that war is not just about battles; it is also about what happens to vulnerable populations when ideologues take power. Understanding the Holocaust is essential to grasp the moral and human costs of World War II, beyond the usual statistics of tanks, planes, and naval fleets.

CHAPTER SIX

Inside the Ghettos and Camps

1. **Life Behind the Ghetto Walls**
   Before many Jews and other persecuted groups reached the camps, they endured life in overcrowded ghettos. Each ghetto functioned differently depending on location, but they shared common features: sealed borders, forced labor, starvation rations, and random acts of brutality. In Warsaw, the largest ghetto in German-occupied Europe, more than 400,000 Jews were crammed into an area of about 1.3 square miles. Families might share a single small room, often with no heating or plumbing.

Food in the Warsaw Ghetto was rationed at starvation levels—just a few hundred calories per person daily. Smuggling became a lifeline. Children, thin enough to slip through cracks in walls or under fences, sneaked out to buy or steal bread, risking beatings or death if caught. Disease spread quickly. Typhus epidemics claimed thousands of lives. Corpses sometimes lay in the streets, as funeral services were overwhelmed, and people were too weak or scared to help.

Ghetto police, often composed of Jewish volunteers or forced recruits under Nazi orders, patrolled the area to maintain "order." Their presence caused moral dilemmas: some tried to help community members in small ways, while others exploited their power, accepting bribes or collaborating in Nazi roundups. Survival entailed constant negotiation—bartering, bribing officials, or joining underground groups. Hope ebbed away as deportation trains rumbled out of ghetto stations, usually heading east to extermination camps.

2. **Forced Labor and Factories**
   In some ghettos, German or local authorities set up workshops or factories where Jews were forced to work for the war effort. In the Łódź Ghetto, for example, residents worked in textile production, making uniforms and other supplies. The ghetto's leader, Chaim Rumkowski, believed that productivity might protect them from deportation—if they were deemed "useful," perhaps the Nazis would spare them. But this was a false hope. While some individuals survived longer due to their labor value, most were eventually deported once they were no longer needed.

Working conditions were brutal. The workforce included children as young as eight or nine. Food rations did not match the physical demands of labor, leading to exhaustion and accidents. SS guards or local police often stood by with whips or guns to enforce quotas. Even basic safety measures, like protective gear or breaks, were virtually nonexistent. Many factories doubled as prisons, surrounded by barbed wire.

For some, forced labor offered a temporary reprieve from deportation. Work detail prisoners had slightly better rations or a chance to barter with guards. Still, disease and malnutrition took a heavy toll. If a person collapsed on the job, they risked a beating or a bullet. Even the luckier ones lived on borrowed time, uncertain if or when a transport to a death camp would arrive.

3. **Gestapo, SS, and the Reign of Fear**
   Inside ghettos, the Nazis wielded terror as their primary tool. Random "actions" were common: SS officers or Gestapo agents would storm in, dragging people out of their homes for deportation or execution. Sometimes they announced these actions in advance, leaving families in panic, trying desperately to hide or

bribe officials. At other times, the raids came without warning, at night, with no chance of escape.

The SS, led by Heinrich Himmler, and the Gestapo, under the broader control of the RSHA, coordinated these terror operations. Informants thrived in such an environment. Some ghetto residents, desperate to save themselves or their loved ones, betrayed neighbors. The Nazis cultivated an atmosphere where nobody could fully trust anyone else, fracturing the social bonds that might otherwise lead to unified resistance.

The psychological impact was enormous. Constant fear took a toll on mental health. Children grew up in a world where violence was the norm, witnessing beatings or shootings on a daily basis. Some lost the ability to cry or show emotion, becoming numb to horror. Parents struggled with guilt over not being able to protect their children. Spiritual leaders tried to maintain religious traditions, holding clandestine services or reading from Torah scrolls, even as the walls closed in around them.

4. **Transport to the Unknown**

    Eventually, most ghettos were either liquidated or drastically reduced in population as the Nazis ramped up the Final Solution. Deportation orders would arrive, instructing thousands of people to gather at a designated spot with their belongings. They were told they were being "resettled." Many hoped they might be taken to labor camps or farms. Others sensed something far worse awaited them.

The journey itself was harrowing. People were packed into cattle cars, often 50 to 100 per car, with little or no ventilation. Buckets served as toilets. No food or water was provided. The stench was overpowering, and the heat or cold (depending on the season) was unbearable. Some died en route. Pregnant women, the elderly, and children suffered especially. Those who tried to escape through small gaps faced armed guards stationed along the tracks.

After hours or days, the train would arrive at a place like Treblinka, Sobibór, or Auschwitz-Birkenau. Prisoners might see barbed wire, guard towers, and SS men with dogs. They had no idea that in many cases, they had just arrived at a death factory designed for systematic killing. The routine was always similar: men were separated from women and children. Luggage was confiscated. Documents or valuables were taken. Then, under the guise of showers or de-lousing procedures, victims were marched to the gas chambers.

5. **Arrival in Auschwitz-Birkenau**

    Auschwitz was a complex that included three main camps: Auschwitz I (the original concentration camp), Auschwitz II-Birkenau (the main extermination site), and Auschwitz III-Monowitz (a labor camp for the IG Farben chemical conglomerate). The train tracks led directly into Birkenau, where SS doctors, including the infamous Dr. Josef Mengele, conducted "selections." Those deemed fit for work were separated from those considered too weak or old. The latter were sent straight to the gas chambers.

For new arrivals chosen for labor, the first thing was a brutal welcome process. Heads were shaved. Prisoners had to strip, standing naked for hours in the cold while guards shouted and shoved them. They were issued striped uniforms or whatever rags were available. Their arms were tattooed with identification numbers, erasing their names and marking them as nothing more than camp property.

Barracks in Birkenau were wooden huts originally designed as horse stables. Hundreds crammed into each block, with three-tier bunk beds. Hygiene was impossible. Lice, rats, and disease were rampant. Prisoners received watery soup and a crust of bread each day. Starvation meant that many died within weeks. Others were pushed to back-breaking labor in construction, quarrying, or factory work for German companies. Guards often beat prisoners for no reason or set dogs on them. Murders could be arbitrary—anyone who displeased a guard risked a bullet or being reported to the SS.

6. **Gas Chambers and Crematoria**

    At the heart of Auschwitz-Birkenau were the gas chambers and crematoria complexes (II, III, IV, and V). These facilities were designed to kill thousands of people per day. Victims were herded into large underground chambers, told to undress, and sometimes given a piece of soap to maintain the illusion of a shower. Guards locked steel doors, and SS personnel poured Zyklon B pellets through vents in the ceiling. In minutes, the gas suffocated everyone inside.

Afterward, Sonderkommandos—special squads of Jewish prisoners forced to do this horrific work—removed bodies, shaved hair, and pulled out gold teeth before burning the corpses in huge crematoria ovens. The ashes were dumped in pits or rivers. Sonderkommando prisoners lived in slightly better conditions than other inmates but knew they were marked for death too. Periodically, the SS would liquidate these squads and form new ones to prevent any secrets from leaking. Some Sonderkommando members kept hidden diaries or took photographs, creating some of the few direct testimonies of the killing process.

7. **Dr. Mengele and Inhuman Experiments**

    Auschwitz also became notorious for medical experiments, particularly under Dr. Josef Mengele, known as the "Angel of Death." He was fascinated by twins and performed grotesque studies on them, injecting chemicals into their eyes, sewing them together, or trying to change their hair color. Other prisoners were used to test disease inoculations, chemical weapons, or hypothermia effects.

Such experiments resulted in countless agonizing deaths, disfigurements, and lifelong injuries. Victims often included children, lured by candy or kind words from Mengele, only to be subjected to excruciating procedures. The SS called these experiments "research," but they were nothing short of torture. While Mengele was the most infamous, many other Nazi doctors and scientists took part, pushing the boundaries of cruelty in the name of warped science.

8. **Survival Strategies in Auschwitz**
   Staying alive in a place designed for death required a mix of luck, resourcefulness, and connections. Some prisoners tried to get jobs in the camp kitchens or workshops, hoping for slightly better rations or a chance to steal scraps. Others learned to keep their heads down, avoid drawing attention, and form small support networks. Even a kind word or a shared piece of bread could mean the difference between hope and despair.

In secret, prisoners built a sense of community. They might trade stories, songs, or poems. Some found spiritual solace in covert religious gatherings. Political prisoners from various backgrounds—communists, social democrats, nationalists—sometimes united to share contraband food or to sabotage Nazi operations. A handful of escapes occurred, though they were incredibly risky. If an escape was discovered, the SS often inflicted collective punishment on entire barracks, sometimes executing dozens in retribution.

9. **Female Experiences in the Camps**
   Women faced additional horrors in the camp system. Many were subjected to sexual violence or coerced into prostitution in special "brothel barracks." Some were selected for forced sterilization experiments, which often caused severe infections or death. Pregnant women were usually sent directly to the gas chambers, as the SS deemed them unable to work. If a woman gave birth in camp, the baby was almost always killed, sometimes drowned in a bucket by an SS guard or kapo (a prisoner overseer).

Despite this terror, women also created support networks—sharing food, protecting children, and comforting each other during punishments or selections. Acts of kindness, however small, offered moments of humanity in a dehumanizing environment. Some women risked their lives to hide a newborn, though such attempts were rarely successful. The emotional toll of seeing children murdered before their eyes was immeasurable. Survivor testimonies often describe nightmares that continued long after liberation.

10. **Other Concentration and Extermination Camps**
    Auschwitz was the largest and most notorious, but it was part of a vast network of camps spread across Nazi-occupied Europe. **Majdanek** near Lublin functioned as both a labor camp and an extermination site, with gas chambers using Zyklon B and carbon monoxide. **Bergen-Belsen** in Germany became a place of mass

death from disease and starvation toward the end of the war. **Dachau**, the first Nazi concentration camp opened in 1933, primarily held political prisoners but expanded to include Jews and other groups. **Mauthausen** in Austria was known for its brutal quarry labor, where prisoners were worked to death hauling stones up the infamous "Stairs of Death."

In each camp, the fundamental purpose remained the same: to exploit prisoners for labor until they were no longer useful, then dispose of them. Daily life meant roll calls in the freezing dawn, forced marches, grueling labor, and constant threat of beatings or execution. Medical care was minimal. Even a minor illness could lead to selection for the gas chamber. Some camps had orchestras of prisoner-musicians forced to play while others marched to their deaths, adding an eerie soundtrack to the brutality.

11. **Resistance Inside the Camps**
    Despite the overwhelming odds, prisoner resistance did exist. In **Sobibór**, inmates staged a revolt in October 1943, killing several SS officers and guards. About 300 prisoners escaped, though many were recaptured or killed by pursuing patrols. In **Treblinka**, a similar uprising occurred in August 1943. Prisoners attacked guards, set buildings on fire, and fled into the woods. Only a small fraction survived, but these revolts disrupted the camps' function and demonstrated incredible bravery.

At Auschwitz, the Sonderkommando staged a revolt in October 1944, blowing up Crematorium IV with explosives smuggled by female prisoners who worked in a munitions factory. Although the revolt was crushed, it destroyed part of the extermination machinery and gave hope to other inmates that resistance was possible. These acts did not stop the mass murder, but they showed the human spirit's refusal to be entirely extinguished even in the face of systematic annihilation.

12. **Death Marches**
    As the Red Army advanced from the east in late 1944 and early 1945, the Nazis began evacuating camps in Poland. Prisoners were forced on marches westward, in freezing winter conditions, with little food or shelter. Anyone who lagged behind or collapsed was shot. These "death marches" caused the deaths of tens of thousands. Survivors recall seeing the roads littered with corpses, and hearing the constant gunshots as guards executed those who could not keep up.

Upon reaching camps in Germany or Austria, the prisoners were often thrown into already overcrowded facilities without adequate rations or sanitation, causing further deaths. Even at this late stage, the SS tried to maintain secrecy about the Holocaust. Some camps destroyed records, dismantled crematoria, and buried or burned evidence of mass murder. Yet the physical remnants and survivors would soon testify to the scale of the atrocities.

13. **Liberation and the Aftermath**
    Allied forces began liberating camps in early 1944 (in the east) and continued through 1945 (in the west). The Soviets reached Majdanek and later Auschwitz, discovering stockpiles of shoes, suitcases, and hair. British and Canadian troops entered Bergen-Belsen in April 1945, encountering thousands of unburied bodies and a mass of sick prisoners. American forces liberated Dachau and Buchenwald, capturing horrifying photographs and film footage that shocked the world.

Liberation did not mean an immediate return to normalcy for survivors. Many were gravely ill. Some were so traumatized they could barely communicate. Disease outbreaks persisted, and conditions in liberated camps were often dire until Allied medical teams restored order. Families had been torn apart, and countless survivors learned that spouses, children, or parents had perished. Displaced persons camps formed, as people had nowhere to go—especially those whose communities had been entirely wiped out.

14. **Testimonies and Trials**
    After the war, some survivors gave detailed testimonies to Allied war crimes investigators. These accounts formed the basis of evidence at trials like the Nuremberg Trials (1945-1946), where major Nazi leaders were prosecuted. Concentration camp guards, commandants, and doctors faced separate trials, although many escaped justice or received light sentences. The scale of the crimes was so vast that the legal system struggled to handle them all.

Testimonies revealed the day-to-day realities of camp life: the smell of burning bodies, the constant hunger, the terror of selections, and the sight of guards casually killing prisoners for amusement. Journalists and filmmakers documented these stories, showing the wider public that rumors of Nazi atrocities were indeed true, if not understated. Still, some civilians claimed ignorance or insisted they had no power to stop the genocide.

15. **The Psychological Scars**
    The emotional aftermath for survivors was profound. Many suffered from nightmares, anxiety, and survivor's guilt. Children who grew up in the camps missed crucial formative years. Reintegrating into society was hard. Antisemitism did not vanish overnight. In some places, returning Jews faced hostility or violence from neighbors who had taken over their homes and possessions. Others had to fight legal battles to reclaim stolen property.

Even decades later, survivors struggled with trauma. Relationships could be difficult because the experiences they endured were beyond normal comprehension. Yet some dedicated their lives to education and remembrance, insisting that the world should never forget. Their memoirs, interviews, and public speeches became a moral warning about the dangers of hatred, racism, and totalitarian ideologies.

16. **Medical and Scientific Exploitation**
    We must not forget the role of certain German companies and scientific institutions in exploiting camp labor. IG Farben, Siemens, Krupp, and others benefited from forced labor, paying the SS a small daily fee per prisoner. Prisoners labored in factories producing weapons, chemicals, or other goods vital to the Nazi war effort. Some companies used human subjects in unethical experiments, testing pharmaceuticals or extreme working conditions.

Many of these corporations continued to operate after the war. Some executives were tried for war crimes, but not all. The moral and ethical questions around corporate complicity in the Holocaust remain a dark chapter in industrial history. Documents and survivor testimonies revealed that profits often outweighed any concern for human life or dignity.

17. **Comparison to Other Genocides**
    Though the Holocaust stands as a unique event in many ways, it also shares similarities with other genocides—such as the Armenian genocide of 1915-1917, the Rwandan genocide of 1994, and others. Common threads include the role of propaganda, the dehumanization of a targeted group, and the complicity or silence of ordinary people. Studying these parallels helps us understand the Holocaust not as an isolated anomaly but as a horrific example of what can happen when hatred and power converge.

During World War II, the industrial scale of killing, coupled with modern bureaucracy, set the Holocaust apart. It was not a chaotic mass murder alone; it was carefully planned and executed using trains, gas chambers, and administrative networks. Reflecting on these mechanisms is essential to grasp how civilized societies can twist technology and organization toward pure evil.

18. **Acts of Kindness and Solidarity**
    Within the brutality of ghettos and camps, there were still sparks of humanity. Prisoners shared smuggled food, risked punishment to care for the sick, or helped hide children. Some non-Jewish Poles, Germans, and others put their lives on the line to shelter Jews. In the camp environment, any small kindness—like lending a spoon or giving away a tiny piece of bread—could be a monumental gesture of solidarity.

These acts underscore that even in the darkest conditions, people can choose compassion. They highlight the moral complexity: while many became perpetrators or collaborators, others refused to lose their sense of right and wrong. Their stories, though fewer, stand as a testament to human resilience and altruism under unimaginable pressure.

19. **Why Remember the Ghettos and Camps?**
    The ghettos and camps represent the culmination of Nazi ideology—a place where prejudice, propaganda, and policy combined to destroy millions. Learning about these places is crucial for understanding how an advanced nation could orchestrate such horror. It also underscores the importance of vigilance against dehumanizing language and policies in any society.

For survivors and their descendants, remembrance is personal—an homage to the murdered and a way to keep the memory alive so that it cannot be denied or trivialized. For the world at large, these stories serve as warnings. The potential for genocide exists whenever a group is defined as "less than human" and a government is willing to use violence unchecked. Understanding the details of daily life and death in the ghettos and camps is part of confronting that grim possibility head-on.

20. **Conclusion: A Window into the Abyss**
    The ghettos and camps were the epicenter of the Holocaust—places where bureaucracy and brutality merged to execute an unprecedented genocide. Victims lived in constant fear, juggling impossible moral choices and clinging to hope in a world engineered for despair. Their voices—through diaries, letters, testimonies—speak from the abyss, reminding us that every statistic was once a living, breathing person.

As the war shifted tides and Allied forces closed in, the Nazis tried to hide their crimes, but the evidence was too vast. Liberation revealed the skeletal survivors, the mountains of belongings, and the ashes of those who had no graves. Even decades later, the echoes of these atrocities linger, challenging us to remember and learn. The Holocaust remains a stark reminder of how thin the veneer of civilization can be.

CHAPTER SEVEN

Weapons of Fear and Destruction

1. **Introduction: A War of Rapid Technological Change**
    World War II was not only a clash of massive armies; it was also a gigantic laboratory of weapon development. In the span of just a few years, countries made huge strides in designing weapons that could destroy people, cities, and even entire regions more effectively than ever before. Nations poured vast amounts of money and labor into research labs and factories, hoping to gain a technological edge that would tilt the war in their favor.

What made this war so terrifying was the speed at which lethal technology advanced. Warplanes became faster and deadlier, tanks grew thicker armor and bigger guns, and submarines received better torpedoes. Old ideas such as poison gas reappeared in new forms, while entirely new concepts—like rockets and jet-powered planes—emerged. This chapter looks at some of the key weapons that generated fear on the battlefield and beyond. We'll see how some of these inventions changed the nature of combat, while others created lasting nightmares that still affect us today.

2. **The Tank Revolution**
    Tanks had first appeared in World War I, but they were slow, unreliable, and often broke down in mud-filled trenches. By World War II, every major power had developed improved tank designs. Germany's early success with "blitzkrieg" relied heavily on fast and coordinated tank divisions. Panzer models like the Panzer III and IV were initially strong, but as the war progressed, the Germans introduced even more menacing machines—the Panther, Tiger I, and later the Tiger II (King Tiger). These tanks had thick armor and powerful guns, making them extremely hard to destroy in open combat.
- **Tiger I**: A heavy tank with an 88mm gun, it could knock out enemy vehicles at long range. Allied soldiers trembled at the sound of a Tiger's rumbling engine. It was, however, expensive and complex to maintain.
- **Panther**: Considered one of the best German designs, combining firepower, armor, and speed. Despite mechanical issues, it struck fear into Allied crews, especially on the Eastern Front.

The Soviets responded with their own legends, notably the T-34. It was simpler to produce, had sloped armor that deflected shells, and performed well in all seasons. The T-34's wide tracks dealt with mud and snow far better than many German tanks. Later variants, such as the T-34/85, upped the firepower. Massive Soviet heavy tanks like the KV-1 and IS-2 also appeared, each carrying large-caliber guns capable of tearing holes in German steel.

The Western Allies had the American-made M4 Sherman, which was reliable, easy to mass-produce, but not as heavily armed or armored as the best German or Soviet tanks. British designs like the Matilda and Churchill saw improvements as the war continued, but they struggled early on against the German panzers in France and North Africa. Yet, the Allies' real advantage lay in production. Germany and the Soviet Union had powerful tank models, but the United States churned out massive numbers of Shermans, ensuring they could replace losses faster than the Germans. By the war's end, entire battlefields were littered with the burnt hulks of tanks, a testament to their critical role in the conflict.

3. **Air Power: Fighters, Bombers, and Fear**
    If tanks ruled the ground, warplanes dominated the skies. World War II saw enormous leaps in aircraft technology and tactics. Germany's **Luftwaffe** introduced the concept of close air support with planes like the Ju 87 Stuka dive-bomber, which terrorized both soldiers and civilians. The Stuka's siren—fitted intentionally—let out a horrifying scream as it dived, spreading panic before the bombs even dropped.

Fighter aircraft evolved rapidly too. Early German Bf 109s and British Spitfires, which fought during the Battle of Britain, represented advanced engineering for their time, but by 1944, new models with higher speeds and better armament entered the fray. The United States unleashed the P-51 Mustang, which excelled at escorting bombers deep into German territory thanks to its superior range and performance. On the Eastern Front, Soviet aircraft like the Il-2 Sturmovik provided critical ground-attack capabilities. Nicknamed the "flying tank," it supported Red Army advances and punished German ground troops.

Bombers proved crucial for strategic warfare. The British Royal Air Force (RAF) had the Avro Lancaster, and the US Army Air Forces deployed the B-17 Flying Fortress and B-24 Liberator. These heavy bombers could carry loads of bombs over long distances, targeting factories, rail hubs, and cities. Germany's defense rested on fighters like the Fw 190 and the Me 109, but as the Allied bombing campaign intensified, the Luftwaffe struggled to protect its own skies. Eventually, the Allies dominated the air, paving the way for destructive bombing raids that burned entire cities to the ground. We will explore the human consequences of these raids in Chapter Eight.

4. **The Naval War: Battleships, Carriers, and Submarines**
    On the seas, another arms race took place. Battleships—massive steel fortresses bristling with large-caliber guns—were once considered the pinnacle of naval power. By the late 1930s, Germany launched the Bismarck, a behemoth that captured the world's attention. Britain responded with its battleships like HMS King George V. Yet, the era of the battleship was starting to wane. The real game-changer was the aircraft carrier, demonstrated most dramatically in the

Pacific Theater. However, carriers also played some roles in the Atlantic and Mediterranean.

Germany's biggest threat to Allied shipping was not the battleship, but the **U-boat** (submarine). Operating in "wolf packs," U-boats terrorized convoys carrying food, troops, and equipment from North America to Britain. Early in the war, U-boats had tremendous success due to Allied unpreparedness and the use of Enigma-coded communications. Merchant ships were torpedoed in the dark of night, their crews lost to the cold Atlantic waters. British Prime Minister Winston Churchill later wrote that the U-boat threat was the only thing that ever really frightened him.

Eventually, Allied tactics improved. Technology like sonar (ASDIC), radar, and the cracking of the Enigma codes allowed escorts to hunt U-boats more effectively. Germany kept building new submarine models, including the advanced Type XXI "Elektroboot," but it came too late to change the war's outcome. By the end, the submarine campaign had claimed thousands of merchant ships and caused widespread fear, yet Germany failed to choke off Britain's supply lines completely.

5. **Rocket and Missile Technology**
   One of the most startling developments of World War II was the advent of rocket-powered weapons. German scientists, led by Wernher von Braun and others, developed the **V-1** flying bomb and the **V-2** ballistic missile, known collectively as "V-weapons." These represented a dramatic leap in warfare. The V-1 was essentially a small pilotless aircraft powered by a pulsejet engine. It flew in a straight line until it ran out of fuel, then crashed and detonated. The V-2 was far more advanced: the world's first long-range guided ballistic missile. It soared high into the atmosphere before plummeting down onto its target at supersonic speed—almost impossible to intercept.

These weapons, nicknamed "revenge weapons," were used by Germany primarily against Britain in an attempt to terrorize the civilian population into submission. The V-1's engine made a distinct buzzing sound, earning it the name "buzz bomb." When the buzzing stopped, the weapon fell silently toward its target. Londoners quickly learned to dread the moment the engine cut out. The V-2, on the other hand, arrived without warning. Civilians could be killed out of the blue, with no chance to seek shelter.

Thankfully for the Allies, these weapons appeared late in the war and in numbers too small to reverse Germany's fortunes. But they represented the dawn of a new era: warfare conducted by guided missiles, and eventually, rockets capable of intercontinental range. After the war, both the US and the Soviet Union scrambled to acquire German rocket scientists, technology, and documents, spurring the Cold War rocket race and, ultimately, the space race. But in the dark days of the 1940s, V-weapons were a source of terror that hinted at an even more frightening future.

6. **Chemical and Biological Weapons**
   World War I had introduced poison gas on a large scale, and the memory of gas attacks remained fresh in the minds of those who fought. During World War II, all sides possessed chemical weapons, including mustard gas, phosgene, and more advanced nerve agents like tabun and sarin (developed in Nazi Germany). Yet, for the most part, these weapons were not widely used on the battlefield. Fear of retaliation and the unpredictability of shifting front lines helped keep chemical warfare in check. Still, the threat loomed over the conflict.

In the East, Japan tested biological weapons on Chinese civilians and prisoners. The infamous Unit 731, led by Shiro Ishii, conducted horrifying experiments with plague, anthrax, and other pathogens, deploying them in Chinese villages. People were deliberately infected; some were dissected alive. These experiments were done in secret, but their results were meant to refine Japan's biological warfare capabilities. We will explore more on this in later chapters about the Pacific, but it's important to note here that World War II was a time when some nations toyed with unleashing diseases as a weapon of terror.

Germany, though it had advanced nerve agents, did not use them in battlefield conditions against the Allies. Historians have speculated about why. Some suggest Hitler, himself a victim of gas attacks in World War I, had a personal aversion. Others argue Germany feared Allied retaliation or that Hitler believed Germany's chemical war readiness wasn't superior enough for guaranteed success. Regardless of the reasons, the chemical and biological arsenal remained a terrifying "what if" scenario that could have made the conflict even more ghastly than it already was.

7. **Flamethrowers, Incendiaries, and Napalm**
   Few weapons inspire as much visceral fear as the flamethrower, which spews

ignited fuel to roast enemy positions or flush soldiers out of bunkers. Used by both Axis and Allied forces, flamethrowers were terrifyingly effective at close range. A single operator could spray a cone of fire into trenches, pillboxes, or caves, causing chaos among defenders. Yet, flamethrower operators were also prime targets. A single bullet piercing the fuel tank could create a horrific blowback, killing the operator and anyone nearby.

Incendiary bombs were another cause for alarm, especially for civilians. These bombs scattered flammable substances like magnesium, phosphorus, or later, napalm, igniting massive fires in urban areas. British and American air forces developed these bombs to maximize damage to cities, causing firestorms that turned neighborhoods into infernos. While the effect of these raids on wartime production is debated, the destruction to civilian life was undeniable.

Napalm—first developed in 1942 by a team in the United States—proved devastating in later stages of the war, though it became more infamous in subsequent conflicts. When dropped on cities or entrenched positions, napalm burned intensely and stuck to surfaces, including human skin, making it nearly impossible to extinguish. Such weapons blurred the line between soldiers and civilians, turning entire areas into hellish landscapes.

8. **Clandestine Ops and Spy Gadgets**
   Not all weapons were about brute force. Espionage agencies like Britain's Special Operations Executive (SOE), the American Office of Strategic Services (OSS), and Germany's Abwehr focused on sabotage and stealth. They developed silent pistols, explosive pens, and disguised devices that could kill or spy on enemies. Miniature cameras, cyanide capsules hidden in false teeth, and briefcase bombs were among the clandestine tools of the trade.

Resistance fighters in occupied countries used whatever they could get—homemade explosives, stolen military hardware, or submachine guns dropped by Allied planes. The famous Sten gun, produced cheaply in Britain, was a favorite among partisans. While these smaller-scale weapons might not match the industrial might of tanks and bombers, they instilled fear in occupying forces, who never knew where a hidden mine or ambush might be waiting.

9. **Kamikaze and Human Torpedoes**
   In the Pacific, Japanese desperation led to one of the war's most terrifying tactics: the **kamikaze** attacks. Pilots flew planes loaded with bombs directly into Allied ships, committing suicide in the process. These attacks were psychologically shocking; Allied sailors watching a plane dive straight at them knew the pilot had no intention of veering away. The Japanese Navy even experimented with human-guided torpedoes called "kaiten." A single occupant would steer the torpedo into an enemy vessel, sacrificing his life for the Emperor.

Though kamikaze attacks rarely sunk large warships outright, they inflicted serious damage and caused dread in Allied fleets. Sailors had nightmares about these sudden, unstoppable dives. For the Japanese pilots, this was framed as the highest form of sacrifice. The idea of a "living bomb" changed the calculus of naval engagements. Even advanced radar or anti-aircraft defenses struggled to stop a plane that refused to return. The psychological impact was as potent as the physical destruction.

10. **Jet Aircraft and the Dawn of a New Age**
    Late in the war, Germany introduced the world's first operational jet-powered fighter, the **Messerschmitt Me 262**. Capable of speeds up to 540 mph, it could outrun most Allied piston-engine fighters. In the hands of skilled pilots, the Me 262 was devastating against Allied bombers. However, it arrived too late and in too few numbers to stop the Allied air offensive. Fuel shortages, lack of trained pilots, and Hitler's meddling—he wanted the jets to be used as bombers rather than fighters—prevented them from altering Germany's fate.

Britain and the United States also had jet prototypes in the works, such as the Gloster Meteor. While these saw limited service, they foreshadowed the post-war era, where jet planes would become standard. The appearance of jets introduced a new dimension: air combat beyond the propeller's limitation, with speeds that tested pilots' physical limits. They also hinted at future wars where supersonic flight, ballistic missiles, and nuclear payloads would dominate—a chilling prospect when we consider how quickly technology was evolving.

11. **Weapons of the Eastern Front: Artillery and Rocket Launchers**
    On the massive Eastern Front, where distances and the scale of battles were enormous, heavy artillery and rocket launchers played a crucial role. The Soviets fielded the **Katyusha** rocket launcher, a simple yet effective system that could fire a salvo of rockets in rapid succession. Nicknamed "Stalin's Organ" by German troops, the Katyusha's howling launch terrified enemies, and the impact of dozens of rockets slamming down within seconds caused massive damage.

The Red Army also relied on massive artillery pieces, sometimes pulling them by tractors across muddy or frozen terrain. German forces were not behind in artillery, deploying formidable cannons, including railway guns like the **Schwerer Gustav**, which fired shells weighing several tons. While impressive, these giant guns often had limited practical value—difficult to transport and slow to operate. Still, their psychological impact was huge. Hearing the thunder of such artillery in the distance reminded both soldiers and civilians that nowhere was truly safe on the Eastern Front.

12. **Amphibious and Special Assault Vehicles**
    World War II saw the largest amphibious invasions in history, such as the D-Day landings in Normandy on June 6, 1944. These operations demanded specialized

landing craft like the Higgins boat (LCVP) to carry infantry from transport ships to shore under fire. The Allies also developed amphibious tanks—like the "DD tank," a Sherman modified with a collapsible canvas screen to float and propel itself onto beaches.

While many of these inventions struggled to perform in rough seas, they still represented a leap forward in combined arms tactics. Armies had to coordinate air, sea, and land forces to push through defended coastlines. The sight of thousands of landing craft approaching the shore was awe-inspiring and terrifying. For the defenders, the knowledge that advanced vehicles could climb right onto the beaches and deliver tanks or troops directly into the fight added a new dimension to coastal defense.

13. **Handheld Weapons: The Soldier's Tools of Survival**
    In the massive scope of World War II, it's easy to focus on tanks, planes, and bombs. But individual firearms still shaped the war at a personal level. The average infantryman relied on bolt-action rifles like the British Lee–Enfield, the German Karabiner 98k, or the Soviet Mosin–Nagant. Semi-automatic rifles—like the American M1 Garand—offered a higher rate of fire, giving the US infantryman a notable edge in firepower.

Submachine guns (SMGs) such as the German MP 40, the Soviet PPSh-41, and the American Thompson were deadly in close-quarters combat. Lightweight and firing pistol-caliber rounds, SMGs were favored by commandos, paratroopers, and tank crews. Germany introduced the **StG 44**, often considered the first modern assault rifle. It fired a medium-power cartridge with a select-fire mechanism (semi-auto or full-auto), providing a balance of range and controllability. The StG 44's design would influence post-war assault rifles like the AK-47.

Grenades and portable anti-tank weapons also evolved. The American "bazooka" and the German "Panzerschreck" gave infantry a fighting chance against tanks at close range, although using them required nerves of steel. These handheld weapons underscored that even with high-tech machines dominating the battlefield, the individual soldier's experience remained raw, personal, and terrifying.

14. **Psychological Warfare**
    Not all weapons were physical. Propaganda broadcasts, leaflets dropped from planes, and loudspeaker trucks tried to demoralize enemy troops or convince civilians to surrender. Germany's **Lord Haw-Haw** and Japan's **Tokyo Rose** broadcast messages in English to sow doubt among Allied ranks. Meanwhile, the Allies dropped leaflets over German lines, claiming the war was lost and encouraging desertion. Some leaflets included detailed instructions on how to surrender, hoping to reduce the enemy's will to fight.

These tactics sometimes involved subtle manipulation—false promises of good treatment or highlighting the horrors that awaited if troops continued resisting. While the direct impact of propaganda is debated, it certainly played a role in shaping public opinion and soldier morale. In many cases, such messages fueled fear and uncertainty, which, by itself, could be as effective as bullets in weakening resistance.

15. **Resource Wars and Fuel Crises**

    A weapon is only as useful as its supply of ammunition and fuel. World War II saw repeated crises over raw materials like oil, rubber, and steel. The German war machine famously struggled with fuel shortages as Allied bombers targeted synthetic oil plants. The Japanese empire went to war partly to secure oil and rubber in Southeast Asia, knowing its industrial sector could not survive on domestic supplies alone.

This desperate scramble for resources influenced strategies and the development of alternative technologies. For instance, Germany produced synthetic fuel from coal and built more electric-powered submarines. Japan tried to stretch out existing supplies by converting civilian ships and vehicles into less efficient war machines. By late in the war, many German tanks and trucks simply ran out of diesel or gasoline, stranded on the battlefield. These shortages made advanced weapons worthless unless supplied with the fuel and parts they needed.

16. **Inflicting Terror or Finding Victory?**

    One could ask: did these fearsome weapons actually decide the war, or was it the mass of simpler, more reliable equipment combined with raw manpower and industrial might? Historians often argue that while advanced weapons like the Tiger tank or the V-2 rocket were technologically impressive, they did not by themselves guarantee victory. Germany's "wonder weapons" used precious resources and arrived too late. Meanwhile, the Allies focused on mass production of serviceable designs like the Sherman tank or the B-24 bomber.

Nevertheless, the psychological dimension of these weapons was massive. Civilians in London lived in constant dread of V-2 rockets; Soviet troops loathed encountering the dreaded Tiger; Allied convoys feared the silent approach of a U-boat. Terror became a force of its own. Leaders hoped that by deploying terrifying technology, they could break the opponent's will. This strategy sometimes backfired, uniting people in anger rather than prompting surrender.

17. **The Atomic Bomb: The Dawn of Ultimate Fear**

    No discussion of World War II weapons is complete without mentioning the atomic bomb—unleashed by the United States in August 1945 against Hiroshima and Nagasaki. While these events took place late in the conflict and primarily affected the Pacific Theater, the development of the atomic bomb (the

Manhattan Project) cast a looming shadow over every aspect of warfare. The bomb's power dwarfed even the fiercest conventional weapons. A single plane could now annihilate an entire city in one blast.

Although the bombs effectively ended the war with Japan, they introduced the world to the concept of nuclear annihilation—a fear that would dominate the post-war era. Scientists like J. Robert Oppenheimer who worked on the Manhattan Project later expressed deep moral qualms. The atomic bomb was the ultimate triumph of scientific progress twisted for warfare. In a single flash, it revealed humanity's potential for self-destruction on an unimaginable scale.

18. **Collateral Damage and Morality**

    The relentless pursuit of more destructive weapons triggered ethical questions that persist to this day. Civilians often suffered the most—caught in bombed cities, trapped by artillery barrages, or subjected to forced labor in factories producing more engines of death. The moral line between combatants and non-combatants blurred. Did the ends justify the means? Many Allied leaders believed massive bombing campaigns would shorten the war, saving lives in the long run. German commanders reasoned that terror weapons like the V-1 and V-2 might demoralize Britain into seeking peace. In practice, each new invention raised the stakes for ordinary people, turning them into unwilling targets of advanced killing tools.

Lessons Learned—or Not Learned
World War II's weapons revolution showed the world that science and industry could produce terrifying results when shaped by total war. In the conflict's aftermath, these lessons did not simply vanish. Rather, they evolved. Nations raced to develop nuclear

weapons, ballistic missiles, and chemical/biological arsenals even more potent than those of the 1940s. Warfare changed forever, and many of the technologies first glimpsed in WWII formed the basis for future militaries worldwide.

This leads to a sobering thought: if the horrors unleashed by conventional and early nuclear arms in WWII caused such devastation, what would happen in a new global conflict with far more advanced technology? Historians, ethicists, and ordinary citizens grapple with this question. The memory of entire cities incinerated and millions killed stands as a grim reminder of what can happen when destructive potential is allowed free rein.

Conclusion: The War's Inescapable Arsenal
From heavy tanks rolling through the mud on the Eastern Front to rockets raining down on London, the weapons of World War II embodied the darkest side of human ingenuity. Nations fought with everything from rifles and hand grenades to ballistic missiles and near-invisible submarines. Civilians became targets, factories churned out arms day and night, and scientists pushed the boundaries of what was possible—often with devastating results.

These weapons did not exist in a vacuum. They were fueled by ideology, desperation, and a global struggle for dominance. In the next chapter, we will look more closely at how these weapons were turned against civilian populations. Bombing campaigns, terror tactics, and occupation policies would bring fear and suffering to millions who never set foot on a battlefield. If Chapter Seven shows us the arsenal of WWII, Chapter Eight exposes how that arsenal translated into everyday nightmares for ordinary people across the planet.

CHAPTER EIGHT

Civilian Nightmares – Bombings and Terror

1. **Introduction: The Home Front Under Siege**
   For most of history, wars were fought primarily on battlefields, with civilians often caught in the crossfire but not always as direct targets. World War II changed that dynamic forever. From the very beginning, entire cities became strategic objectives—bombed or occupied to break the enemy's will and disrupt production. Civilians could no longer hide behind distance or neutrality. Air raids, artillery shelling, and outright terror campaigns brought the front line into people's living rooms.

This chapter explores the suffering of civilians under bombardment, occupation, and mass terror. We'll see how entire neighborhoods vanished overnight and how families were torn apart by bombs that rained down without mercy. We'll also look at how occupying armies used fear to control populations, resulting in harsh punishments, forced labor, and daily intimidation. If war on the battlefield is horrifying, then war visited upon the unarmed is a different depth of nightmare entirely.

2. **The Blitz on Britain**
   One of the first major bombing campaigns against civilians in World War II was **the Blitz** on Britain. After the fall of France in 1940, Hitler hoped to force Britain to surrender by pounding its cities from the air. Beginning in September 1940, the Luftwaffe targeted London almost every night for nearly two months. Later, the raids expanded to other cities like Coventry, Birmingham, and Liverpool.

Night after night, citizens sought refuge in bomb shelters, including the London Underground stations. Families huddled together in cramped conditions, listening to the distant drone of approaching German bombers. When the bombs fell, the earth shook, buildings collapsed, and fires raged across city blocks. Anti-aircraft guns lit up the sky, but they weren't enough to prevent widespread damage. The Blitz killed around 40,000 British civilians and destroyed or damaged over a million homes.

Despite the terror, British morale didn't collapse. Winston Churchill's government used propaganda to praise the resilience of everyday people—"Keep Calm and Carry On." However, that stoic image often glossed over the real despair and trauma. Families emerged from shelters to find their homes reduced to rubble and loved ones buried beneath the wreckage. Recovery crews worked day and night to pull survivors out, with many rescue efforts turning into body recovery. Still, the Blitz served as a preview of far worse devastation to come in other parts of the world.

3. **Operation Gomorrah: The Firebombing of Hamburg**
   In the summer of 1943, the Allies launched **Operation Gomorrah**, a massive bombing campaign against the German city of Hamburg. For eight days, British and American bombers dropped thousands of tons of explosives, including incendiary bombs designed to ignite firestorms. A firestorm occurs when fires merge into a single inferno, creating hurricane-like winds that feed the flames with oxygen. Temperatures can reach over 1,000 degrees Celsius, making survival nearly impossible.

Hamburg experienced one of the deadliest firestorms of the war. Streets melted, and people were incinerated. Some suffocated when the flames consumed all the oxygen in underground shelters. Tens of thousands died in a single week. The haunting stories from survivors include seeing tornadoes of fire, with houses exploding in heat so intense that metal objects fused. A once-proud city was reduced to scorched ruins, with only blackened shells of buildings standing amid piles of ash.

Many German civilians, previously shielded from the realities of the war, now understood the full weight of Allied air power. The campaign aimed to cripple German industry and morale. While it did destroy essential war factories, it also killed large numbers of ordinary people, including refugees who had fled bombed-out areas elsewhere. Scenes of charred bodies in the streets hammered home the new face of total war: entire populations turned into targets.

4. **Dresden: Controversy and Destruction**
   By 1945, the Allies had air superiority and could strike nearly any German city at will. One of the most infamous and controversial raids occurred on Dresden in February 1945. Often called the "Florence on the Elbe," Dresden had been relatively untouched by bombing compared to other major German cities. It was

a cultural center with beautiful architecture. However, it also had factories producing war goods and rail links that were crucial for German troop movements.

Between February 13 and 15, British and American bombers dropped massive loads of high-explosive and incendiary munitions, igniting another firestorm. The resulting inferno raged, consuming historic churches, museums, and residential areas. Thousands of people died, with exact figures debated—but estimates range from 25,000 to over 30,000. The city became a surreal landscape of flames and smoke that some survivors described as "apocalyptic."

Controversy surrounded the raid because many questioned whether Dresden was a legitimate military target, given that Germany was already near collapse. Critics accused the Allies of engaging in terror bombing aimed solely at killing civilians. Defenders of the operation argued that Dresden played an essential role in German logistics. Regardless of one's viewpoint, the devastation was undeniable, and Dresden became a symbol of total war's merciless extremes.

5. **The Siege of Leningrad: Starvation as a Weapon**
   While bombing campaigns ravaged Western Europe, the East saw its own form of civilian horror—**sieges**. We touched on the Siege of Leningrad in Chapter Four, but it's worth revisiting its impact on civilians. German and Finnish forces encircled the Soviet city, cutting off all land routes. Hitler's plan was to starve Leningrad into submission, forbidding the acceptance of any surrender.

For nearly 900 days, Leningrad's residents lived on meager rations, sometimes as low as a few hundred calories per day. Winters were brutal. Temperatures dipped well below freezing, yet people lacked heat or adequate clothing. Corpses froze in the streets; some families resorted to cannibalism in their desperation. Libraries burned books as fuel; citizens tore apart wooden houses for firewood. By the time the siege ended, over a million Leningraders had died, making this one of the deadliest sieges in history.

The deliberate targeting of civilians through starvation highlighted another terrifying tactic of World War II: controlling food supplies to break the enemy's resistance. Stalin's government also enforced harsh discipline; desertion or theft of rations could lead to execution. So, while German shells rained down on the city, Soviet authorities clamped down internally. Civilians found themselves trapped in a vice of external and internal terror, barely able to survive the onslaught.

6. **Japanese Occupation in Asia**
   Civilians in Asia were not spared. Japanese forces, driven by imperial ambition, occupied vast swaths of China, Southeast Asia, and the Pacific islands. Occupation often meant systematic cruelty, forced labor, and fear. In places like

Nanking (Nanjing), the Japanese Army perpetrated an infamous massacre in December 1937—known as the Rape of Nanking—slaughtering hundreds of thousands of Chinese civilians and prisoners of war. Mass rapes, looting, and execution contests became the gruesome reality. Though this occurred before the official start of WWII in Europe, it set the tone for Japanese occupations elsewhere.

Throughout the war, Japanese military police, the Kempeitai, suppressed local populations with brutal methods. Resistance fighters or suspected opponents were tortured, decapitated, or used as slave labor. Comfort women—forced sex slaves, many from Korea or China—were another horrifying aspect of Japanese occupation. Entire villages lived in constant dread of random reprisals or punishments. Famines broke out in areas where Japanese authorities requisitioned rice and other food supplies for their troops.

Allied prisoners of war fared no better under Japanese rule, forced to build railways (like the Burma Railway) and roads under inhuman conditions. Civilians also had to endure Allied bombing raids, particularly later in the war when the US targeted cities like Tokyo with incendiary bombs. So even those living under Japanese occupation encountered terror from both the occupying forces and the skies above.

7. **Crimes Against Humanity in Eastern Europe**
   German occupation in Eastern Europe was similarly brutal. We've seen the Holocaust's systematic murder of Jews and other groups, but beyond that, ordinary Slavic populations—Poles, Ukrainians, Belarusians—faced forced labor, reprisals, and daily oppression. The occupation policies in Poland, for example, led to the deaths of millions of non-Jewish Poles from starvation, overwork, or outright murder. The **Warsaw Uprising** in 1944 saw Polish resistance fighters attempt to liberate the city from German control. In retaliation, the Germans razed entire districts, killing tens of thousands of civilians.

Further east, in Ukraine and Belarus, partisan activity was met with scorched-earth reprisals. If a German patrol was ambushed near a village, the Nazis would often burn that village to the ground, executing residents. This savage pattern repeated itself across countless hamlets. Soviet forces, when they reconquered these areas, sometimes inflicted their own terror, accusing locals of collaboration or punishing entire communities for perceived disloyalty.

8. **Italy Under Bombs and Armistice**
   Italy, initially an Axis power, faced Allied bombings after the United States and Britain began offensives in the Mediterranean. Cities like Naples, Rome, and Milan suffered air raids. When the Allies landed in Sicily in July 1943, the war became a stark reality for Italian civilians. The collapse of Mussolini's regime led

to confusion. German troops rushed in to occupy parts of Italy, bringing the same harsh tactics they employed elsewhere.

Northern Italy turned into a battleground between German occupiers, Italian fascist loyalists, and partisans. Civilians caught in the middle endured raids, public executions, and random violence. The countryside was dotted with small villages that each had stories of mass shootings or burnings at the hands of retreating German soldiers. Allied bombings continued in urban centers, aiming at factories and rail networks but often hitting residential neighborhoods.

By the war's end, Italy was left with shattered infrastructure and a society deeply divided between former fascists, partisans, and those who simply tried to survive. The memories of occupation atrocities and bombed-out cities would haunt Italians for decades.

9. **Bombing the Pacific Cities: From Tokyo to Hiroshima**
   While chapters ahead will dive more into the Pacific conflict, we cannot ignore the terror inflicted on Japanese civilians by Allied bombing campaigns later in the war. The **firebombing of Tokyo** on March 9–10, 1945, remains one of the most destructive air raids in history. B-29 bombers dropped incendiary bombs that sparked a massive firestorm. Wooden houses burst into flames, and entire districts were consumed in hours. Casualty estimates vary, but at least 80,000 to 100,000 people died that single night—numbers comparable to or exceeding many European raids.

Other Japanese cities, including Kobe, Osaka, and Nagoya, faced similar fates as the US shifted to incendiary bombing tactics. Civil defense measures in Japan were weak; firefighting services and shelters were inadequate. Civilians learned to dread the midnight wail of sirens, knowing they might have only minutes to flee. These nightmares culminated in the atomic bombings of Hiroshima and Nagasaki in August 1945, which unleashed a new level of destruction and horror. But even before the nuclear attacks, Japan's civilians bore the brunt of intense bombing that leveled large portions of their cities.

10. **Resistance vs. Retaliation**
    Civilian terror was not merely a byproduct of strategy; sometimes it was deliberate retaliation for resistance activities. In occupied France, the **Oradour-sur-Glane** massacre in June 1944 saw an SS unit kill 642 villagers, including women and children, as revenge for partisan attacks. In Greece, entire villages were wiped out for harboring resistance fighters. Similar stories come from Yugoslavia, where resistance movements fought fiercely, and German or Italian forces responded with mass executions.

These brutal reprisals aimed to scare locals into submission, hoping they would stop helping partisans. Instead, the cycle of violence often fueled more hatred. People who lost loved ones joined underground movements out of vengeance. Villagers who watched their neighbors executed were unlikely to cooperate with the occupiers. While terror tactics could suppress open revolt in the short term, they fanned the flames of rage in the long run.

11. **Refugees and Displacement**
    All this destruction forced millions of civilians to flee. People crowded onto roads with whatever belongings they could carry, hoping to find safety in less threatened areas. Columns of refugees were not safe from bombs, artillery, or strafing planes. Many starved or fell ill along the way. Others found themselves trapped between warring armies, forced to move repeatedly as front lines shifted.

Across Europe, the Middle East, and Asia, refugee crises became a hallmark of WWII. Towns that escaped direct bombing struggled to house and feed huge numbers of displaced persons. Diseases like cholera, typhus, and dysentery spread rapidly in overcrowded camps or makeshift shelters. Government agencies and charities tried to help, but resources were strained. Often, the best they could do was provide a few blankets and rations, leaving refugees to cope with cold winters and scarce medical care.

12. **Children of War**
    Children faced some of the worst realities of the war, robbed of normal school routines and thrown into worlds of chaos. In Britain, many children were evacuated from cities to the countryside (the so-called "evacuees"), often separated from parents for months or years. They lived with strangers, coping

with homesickness and fear. On the continent, children weren't so fortunate if bombs fell on their towns. Some ended up orphans, wandering through ruins, surviving on scraps.

In occupied areas, children witnessed executions, humiliations, and the deportation of friends or neighbors. Some tried to fight back as part of underground resistance groups—smuggling messages or sabotaging occupiers in small ways. Others were forced into labor or used as child soldiers in desperate last stands, such as in Nazi Germany's final defense or Japanese-held territories. The psychological trauma for these young people was immense, shaping an entire generation with deep scars.

13. **Daily Life Under Occupation**
    Beyond bombings, simply living under an occupying army was a nightmare for many. Curfews, ration cards, and the ever-present threat of arrest meant constant tension. Soldiers billeted in civilian homes could confiscate property at will. Some families tried to cooperate to survive, while others risked everything by supporting local resistance groups. Women lived with the added fear of sexual violence from occupying troops. Black markets flourished, with goods like coffee, sugar, and cigarettes trading at astronomical prices.

Propaganda posters demanded loyalty. Radios blared official broadcasts. Schools were forced to teach the occupier's language or ideology. Even small acts of disobedience—like listening to banned radio stations—could land one in a concentration camp or prison. Spies and informants lurked around every corner, making trust a luxury. People learned to keep their heads down and avoid drawing attention, a survival tactic that ate away at their dignity and sense of community.

14. **Bomb Shelters and Survival Tactics**
    As air raids became more common, civilians dug shelters in backyards or under buildings. Governments built public bomb shelters, though these were often cramped and insufficient. In London, many people took shelter in subway stations; in Berlin, the city's subways also served as improvised refuges during Allied bombing. Some tried to reinforce basements with steel beams or sandbags, but direct hits from larger bombs meant even well-built shelters could collapse.

Survival sometimes depended on luck. Neighbors might group together, sharing supplies and comforting each other in darkness as bombs whistled overhead. After the raid, they emerged into smoldering streets, praying their homes still stood. Over time, a grim routine developed: sirens, frantic rush to shelters, waiting for the all-clear, then stepping outside to see which part of the city had been flattened. This cycle repeated nightly in many European and Asian cities.

15. **Psychological Warfare on Civilians**
    Bombing was not just about destroying factories or infrastructure; it was meant to break morale. Leaders like Britain's Arthur "Bomber" Harris believed that by hitting German cities hard enough, civilians would force their government to surrender. Similarly, Japanese militarists believed attacks on Chinese cities would crush Chinese resistance. But it rarely worked as planned. Many populations reacted to bombings with anger rather than submission. Instead of rebelling against their leaders, people often united in defiance.

However, the psychological toll was immense. Civilians lived in perpetual anxiety. Air-raid sirens triggered panic attacks. Children wet the bed or refused to sleep alone. Some adults turned to black humor, while others sank into depression. The daily fear drained people's spirits. Even if entire societies did not collapse, individuals crumbled under the unrelenting stress of possibly dying at any moment.

16. **The Long Arm of Atrocities: POWs and Forced Labor**
    Millions of civilians and prisoners of war were forcibly moved to labor camps. The Nazis deported workers from occupied countries into Germany to replace men who had gone to fight. The conditions for these foreign workers were often appalling—long hours, little food, and abusive treatment. The same was true in the Soviet Union's forced labor system under Stalin, though on a different ideological basis. Japan also used forced labor in its conquered territories, as mentioned earlier, building railways and fortifications at massive human cost.

For civilians, forced labor disrupted family structures and decimated local economies. Many never returned home, dying of disease or overwork. Those who did come back were often traumatized, struggling to fit into communities that had changed drastically in their absence. Children grew up without parents; farms went untended; entire towns lost their young men and women to factories across distant lands.

17. **Healthcare Crises and Disease**
    Amid bombings and occupation, healthcare systems buckled. Hospitals that weren't destroyed outright were overwhelmed with casualties. Medical supplies ran low, and doctors or nurses were drafted into military service. Diseases like tuberculosis and typhus spread in bomb shelters, ghettos, or refugee camps, where crowding and poor hygiene were rampant. Civilians sometimes had to rely on folk remedies or black-market drugs. Malnutrition weakened immune systems, creating a vicious cycle of illness.

In the last years of the war, Germany and Japan both faced collapsing infrastructures. Electricity, water, and sanitation systems broke down under bombing. Civilians scrounged for water from broken pipes or wells. Sewage spilled into streets, contaminating what little food was available. In such conditions, even minor cuts could become lethal infections. Suffering extended well beyond direct combat casualties, showing that war's impact stretched into every corner of civilian life.

18. **Propaganda and False Hope**
    During these nightmare conditions, propaganda poured in from all sides. Nazi radio promised "miracle weapons" that would turn the tide. Allied broadcasts claimed the war's end was near. In occupied regions, rumors circulated daily: "The Allies have landed in the west," or "The Red Army is just miles away." People clung to these bits of hope, even when reality was bleak. For some, these stories kept them going, fueling a will to survive another day.

Others felt betrayed as the war dragged on. Each new rumor that liberation was imminent only to see it postponed chipped away at morale. Occupation governments forced newspapers to publish inflated stories of victories, but many civilians saw the truth in the form of retreating armies or bombed-out rail yards. Disillusionment and exhaustion took hold, creating a psychological climate of mistrust and despair.

19. **The Resilience and the Cost**
    Despite the horror, many civilians displayed remarkable resilience. Communities organized soup kitchens, volunteered in fire brigades to battle the flames, or formed secret schools in occupied areas to keep children educated. Women often became linchpins of survival, juggling black-market trading, child-rearing, and manual labor while men were off fighting or imprisoned. Local churches or community halls turned into makeshift hospitals or shelters.

Yet, the cost of this resilience was staggering. Millions of civilians died, and entire cities were obliterated. Generations grew up traumatized, haunted by images of burning houses and loved ones lost. When the war finally ended, survivors emerged into landscapes of rubble and grief. Many found their homes gone, their families scattered, their future uncertain. While soldiers might return from the front, civilians had no clear line between war and peace; the war had come to them, and the scars would last a lifetime.

CHAPTER NINE

Twisted Science and Human Experiments

Introduction: Science in Service of Horror
World War II witnessed not only the development of advanced weapons but also the misuse of science in ways that defied moral comprehension. On both the Axis and Allied sides, governments enlisted doctors, chemists, biologists, and engineers for wartime research. Much of this research was directed toward weapons, but in some extreme cases, it involved direct experimentation on human beings.

While the Holocaust is often remembered for gas chambers and mass shootings, it also included medical experiments that inflicted agony on prisoners. In the Far East, Imperial Japan conducted appalling biological warfare tests on Chinese civilians and Allied prisoners. Even some Allied programs to understand human limits in war danced on the edge of what was ethical. This chapter explores these grim aspects of the war—where lab coats and stethoscopes became tools of torture, and where the thirst for scientific advancement or ideological "proof" led to inhumane acts.

Nazi Euthanasia and the T4 Program
Before the gas chambers of Auschwitz or Treblinka were set up, the Nazis had already begun a program to eliminate those deemed "unfit" or "life unworthy of life." Officially, this was called "Aktion T4," named after the address Tiergartenstrasse 4 in Berlin, the headquarters of the operation. Launched in 1939, the T4 program targeted mentally ill and disabled Germans—children and adults. Hitler had signed a secret authorization allowing doctors to kill disabled patients in various institutions.

- **Methods Used**:
    - Lethal injections of morphine or other drugs.
    - Starvation.
    - Gradual introduction of gas chambers in some clinics, foreshadowing the techniques later used in death camps.

Doctors falsified records to hide the true cause of death from relatives, claiming pneumonia or other illnesses. Families were often told that their loved ones had died from "natural causes." It's estimated that over 70,000 people were murdered under T4 before public protests within Germany forced the program to become more clandestine. Nonetheless, the infrastructure and experience gained during T4 directly influenced the creation of large-scale extermination facilities for Jews, Roma, and others. T4 thus formed a brutal blueprint for genocide, showing how medical professionals could be twisted into mass murderers in white coats.

Medical Experiments in Concentration Camps
Within Nazi concentration camps like Auschwitz, Dachau, Ravensbrück, and Buchenwald, certain SS physicians carried out "research" under the guise of benefiting German soldiers or proving racial theories. The most notorious among them was **Dr. Josef Mengele**, stationed at Auschwitz.

- **Experiments on Twins**: Mengele had a special fascination with identical and fraternal twins, believing that understanding how their bodies worked might unlock secrets of heredity. He performed gruesome procedures—injecting dyes into their eyes, cutting limbs, attempting to conjoin twins, or infecting one twin with a disease to see how the other reacted.
- **Sterilization and Reproductive Experiments**: Some doctors tested chemical injections or radiation to see if they could achieve mass sterilization of "undesirable" groups, particularly Jewish and Roma women. These procedures caused intense pain, infections, and permanent damage.
- **Hypothermia and High-Altitude Trials**: At Dachau, inmates were immersed in ice-cold water or exposed to high-altitude conditions in low-pressure chambers. The aim was to learn how long German pilots could survive if shot down over cold seas or high altitudes. Prisoners died horrible deaths, often suffocating or freezing while doctors recorded data.

Survivors, if they existed, were left with disfiguring injuries or lifelong trauma. Many victims were killed afterward so that autopsies could be performed. The SS recorded findings carefully, showing a shocking level of detachment. Scientists who participated claimed they were serving the Reich or advancing medicine, but in reality, the experiments served as a front for torture grounded in racist and eugenic ideologies.

Heinrich Himmler's Obsession with "Racial Science"

Reichsführer-SS Heinrich Himmler played a key role in encouraging these experiments. Deeply influenced by pseudoscientific theories of Aryan superiority, he funded research at institutions like the **Ahnenerbe**, a Nazi think tank dedicated to uncovering ancient Germanic heritage and proving Aryan racial myths.

- **Anthropological Studies**: SS researchers measured skull sizes, nose lengths, and eye color among camp inmates, trying to categorize them as "racially inferior."
- **Disease Testing**: Himmler approved experiments on typhus, tuberculosis, malaria, and other ailments, seeing them as opportunities to develop vaccines or cures to protect German soldiers—without any ethical constraints.
- **Personal Visits**: He visited concentration camps, pressuring doctors to push boundaries. He wanted practical results quickly, making him a driving force behind many lethal experiments.

While these studies often produced questionable data—due to uncontrolled conditions, malnourished test subjects, and incompetent methods—the Nazis were so steeped in their ideology that the brutality continued. Himmler's personal interest in such "research" gave camp doctors free rein to commit atrocities in the name of science.

Unit 731 and Japan's Biological Warfare

On the other side of the world, Imperial Japan conducted its own horrifying experiments under **Unit 731**, based in Harbin, Manchuria. Led by Lieutenant General **Shirō Ishii**, this secret research group focused on biological and chemical weapons. Thousands of prisoners—Chinese civilians, POWs from various Allied nations, and others—became unwilling guinea pigs.

- **Disease Experiments**: Plague, anthrax, cholera, and typhus were deliberately introduced to living subjects. Researchers dissected victims while they were still alive (often without anesthesia) to observe the disease's progression in real-time.
- **Frostbite and Dehydration**: Prisoners were locked in freezers or exposed to sub-zero temperatures until their limbs froze. Ishii's team then attempted various thawing methods, sometimes using scorching water, to see what worked best to "treat" frostbite in Japanese soldiers.
- **Weapons Testing**: Unit 731 tested grenades, flamethrowers, and bombs on bound prisoners to gauge effective blast radii. They even dropped plague-infested fleas from aircraft over Chinese towns, sparking outbreaks.

This program was shrouded in secrecy. Ordinary Japanese soldiers and citizens knew little about it. Documents were destroyed near the war's end, but enough evidence survived to confirm the scale of atrocities. American authorities, after Japan's surrender, reportedly offered immunity to many Unit 731 doctors in exchange for their research data—information that remained classified for decades. This shocking deal meant that several perpetrators escaped prosecution, a fact that still stirs controversy among historians and survivors' descendants.

Lesser-Known Experiments and Allied Ethical Quagmires
Although the Axis powers committed the most notorious experiments, the Allies were not entirely free from questionable practices. Some examples include:

- **Mustard Gas Tests on Soldiers (US and UK)**: In the early years of the war, both the US and Britain secretly tested mustard gas on their own service members to study its effects and develop better protective gear. Soldiers often did not fully understand the risks and suffered burns, lung damage, or chronic illness.
- **Malaria Studies in the United States**: The US Office of Scientific Research and Development conducted controlled malaria infection studies on prisoners in state penitentiaries, offering shortened sentences for participation. Though not as brutal as Nazi or Japanese experiments, these prisoners were not always aware of the potential long-term consequences.
- **Soviet NKVD "Interrogation Sciences"**: While not strictly "medical," the Soviet secret police performed forced psychiatric treatments or drug-induced interrogations on political prisoners, believing such methods could force confessions. Little data survived, but testimonies suggest detainees endured agonizing procedures in KGB or NKVD facilities.

While these Allied efforts were not as systematically homicidal or ideologically driven as Nazi or Japanese programs, they highlight that wartime desperation blurred ethical lines even in democratic societies.

Pseudoscience and Racial Theory
Many experiments stemmed from racist or eugenic beliefs. Nazis clung to the idea that Germans belonged to a "Master Race," while other ethnic groups were biologically inferior. Japanese imperial propaganda placed the Yamato race above others, justifying cruelty toward Chinese, Koreans, and Western POWs. Scientists who should have been guided by objective inquiry instead searched for "proof" that validated these prejudices.

Ironically, the data collected was often useless. Malnourished prisoners, chaotic camp conditions, and sadistic methods meant results were scientifically flawed. Methods lacked control groups or proper experimental protocols. Nevertheless, these "findings" were cited as evidence supporting racist ideologies. When the war ended, legitimate researchers condemned much of this work as pseudoscience. Yet the damage had been done; thousands had suffered or died under the pretense of scientific progress.

Victims' Voices: Survivor Accounts
Survivors of these experiments, though few, have provided haunting testimonies. A Jewish twin who endured Mengele's injections at Auschwitz might describe daily terror

of waiting for the next summons, the excruciating pain of procedures with no anesthesia, and the sorrow of seeing siblings die on cold operating tables. Chinese villagers who survived plague bombings by Unit 731 recount entire families perishing in feverish agony. Allied POWs forced to endure chemical tests or exposure to pathogens speak of betrayal by their captors, who saw them as expendable.

These personal stories illuminate the raw human suffering behind the clinical notes. Where official Nazi or Japanese documents speak of "subjects," survivors remember real people with names, families, and aspirations—reduced to lab animals. Their accounts reveal how easily humans can inflict torment on others when ideology or perceived national necessity overrides moral restraint.

Post-War Trials and Controversies
After the war, the International Military Tribunal at Nuremberg prosecuted some of the leading Nazi doctors in the **"Doctors' Trial"** of 1946–47. Prominent figures like Karl Brandt and others were convicted for war crimes and crimes against humanity. The trials exposed the brutality of their experiments, leading to the establishment of the **Nuremberg Code**, a set of ethical guidelines for human experimentation that emphasized voluntary consent and a prohibition on unnecessary suffering.

However, the aftermath for Unit 731 was far more controversial. Many of its members escaped prosecution because US intelligence agencies wanted their biological warfare data for Cold War research. Shiro Ishii and several colleagues lived out their lives free from prison. In subsequent decades, some survivors and families of victims tried to sue the Japanese government, but official acknowledgment and compensation were limited. Japan's education system often glossed over or minimized these crimes, creating tension between Japan and other Asian nations even to this day.

In the Soviet Union, public discussion of NKVD abuses was suppressed. Some Allied nations, like the United States and Britain, kept quiet about their own questionable research programs. While the Nazi doctors' prosecution became a high-profile affair, not all perpetrators of wartime medical crimes faced justice. This incomplete accountability left deep wounds and raised ethical dilemmas about how societies handle dark aspects of their past in pursuit of scientific or strategic advantage.

Legacy: The Nuremberg Code and Medical Ethics
The brutality of wartime experiments spurred a global reckoning with medical ethics. The **Nuremberg Code (1947)** spelled out principles like informed consent, the right to withdraw from an experiment, and the necessity of minimizing harm. This code influenced later ethical guidelines, including the **Declaration of Helsinki (1964)** by the World Medical Association, setting standards for research on human subjects.

Yet, controversies still arise today—whether in military research, pharmaceutical trials in developing countries, or psychological experiments that push ethical boundaries. World War II's legacy reminds us that science, stripped of morality, can become a tool of unimaginable cruelty. The code established a benchmark, but as history has shown, guidelines are only as strong as the willingness of researchers and governments to follow them.

Scientific Gains vs. Moral Costs
A grim question arises: did these experiments produce any medical benefits? Some defenders have claimed that data on hypothermia or infectious diseases helped shape modern treatments. However, the mainstream medical community largely rejects using findings from Nazi or Unit 731 studies, arguing that the methods were scientifically flawed and morally tainted. Even if certain bits of information could be gleaned, relying on them risks legitimizing the atrocities.

Hence, mainstream consensus is that the moral cost far outweighed any possible scientific gain. A legitimate path to knowledge must respect human dignity, something that was systematically violated in these "labs" of the Third Reich or Imperial Japan. Many argue it's better to discard unethical data rather than validate it, to ensure that such horrors never become an acceptable price for progress.

Parallel Horrors: Non-Consensual Sterilizations in Occupied Lands
Aside from the concentration camps, Nazi occupiers imposed forced sterilization programs in some Eastern territories. Women deemed racially "unacceptable" or carrying hereditary diseases were targeted. Teenage girls might be tricked into going to clinics for "check-ups," only to discover afterward that they'd been rendered infertile. Similar patterns occurred in certain Japanese-occupied regions, though on a smaller scale.

These policies aimed to erase future generations of the "inferior" or subjugated populations. Survivors often only learned they were sterilized when they tried to start families years later. The mental and emotional trauma of realizing one cannot have children—due to a procedure forced upon them during occupation—echoed long after the war's end. Historians consider these acts a form of slow genocide, undermining a people's ability to reproduce and preserve their cultural identity.

Experiments on POWs in Germany and Japan
Beyond the well-known medical horrors, both Germany and Japan used Allied POWs in lethal research or forced them into extreme conditions. In Germany, some British and Soviet prisoners were exposed to mustard gas or forcibly infected with diseases. In Japan, POWs from Australia, Britain, the Netherlands, and the US sometimes ended up in Unit 731 or related programs.

Those who survived seldom received recognition or compensation. Military and political leaders post-war often downplayed these incidents to maintain diplomatic relations. POW testimonies reveal the sense of helplessness—captured soldiers already faced harsh conditions, but being singled out for "scientific" torture added another layer of despair. Some turned to religion or camaraderie to endure, but many died unnamed in labs or bunkers, their bodies incinerated to hide evidence.

Civilian Conscription for Experiments
It wasn't just prisoners of war or concentration camp inmates who suffered. In occupied countries, local populations could be coerced into "medical checks" that led to experiment-like testing. In Eastern Europe, the SS sometimes marched villagers into makeshift field labs, measuring reaction to pathogens or toxins. In China, entire towns were used for Unit 731's field tests—bombing them with plague-infested fleas or anthrax-laced powders.

Survivors describe mass infections, quarantines enforced at gunpoint, and seeing black-uniformed soldiers taking notes while people died agonizing deaths. The term "maruta," meaning "logs," was used by Unit 731 personnel to refer to human test subjects, indicating how little they valued these lives. This dehumanizing language made it psychologically easier for perpetrators to carry out atrocities.

SS and Gestapo Collaboration
Many camp medical experiments required cooperation between the SS and the Gestapo. The Gestapo rounded up prisoners, while the SS guarded facilities and provided infrastructure. Some detainees were specifically selected for experiments based on age, gender, or condition. If a prisoner resisted, the Gestapo had full authority to torture or execute. This synergy between police and "scientific" staff amplified the terror.

In some camps, kapos (prisoners granted limited authority) were coerced into assisting. They might be ordered to restrain fellow inmates or help with disposal of bodies. Refusal meant punishment or death. This structure spread moral culpability across various ranks, obscuring individual responsibility. After the war, many lower-level participants claimed they were just following orders, complicating efforts to assign blame precisely.

Chemical Weapons Testing in Concentration Camps
Though large-scale chemical warfare didn't erupt in WWII (thankfully), the Germans tested lethal gases like **phosgene** and **tabun** on camp inmates. The idea was to see how quickly these agents killed and what protective measures could be devised for German troops. Victims were locked in chambers or open-air pits while gas canisters were detonated. Observers recorded symptoms: choking, convulsions, vomiting blood.

This had direct connections to the potential deployment of chemical agents on the battlefield if Hitler chose to use them. The fact that such testing occurred demonstrates how close the world came to a chemical nightmare. Had Hitler decided to break the taboo, these experiments might have paved the way for mass chemical attacks on Allied soldiers or civilians.

Impact on Post-War Science

Paradoxically, the war catalyzed significant medical breakthroughs in legitimate fields—penicillin mass production, blood transfusion techniques, improved surgical methods. But the dark underbelly of unethical experiments overshadowed these positive advances. After 1945, Western scientists aimed to distance themselves from anything resembling Nazi or Japanese methods. The push for formal ethical codes grew, culminating in the Nuremberg Code and later guidelines.

At the same time, some data from German aviation or Japanese frostbite experiments was quietly circulated among Allied researchers. The question of whether to use or discard knowledge gained through torture remains ethically fraught. Overall, the war shaped the medical and scientific community's stance on human experimentation: any benefits from unethical methods are outweighed by moral condemnation, shaping research standards for generations.

Public Revelation and Denial

Civilians in Germany and Japan often claimed ignorance of these experiments, focusing instead on their own hardships under bombing or occupation. When evidence came to light—through trials, testimonies, or discovered documents—some refused to believe their countrymen could commit such deeds. Revisionists argued that the scale or severity was exaggerated by Allied propaganda.

Survivors seeking recognition or compensation struggled against this denial. Families of victims who had disappeared in labs had to prove it in courts that often lacked documentation. Over time, as more eyewitness accounts and archival material surfaced, public understanding grew. In Germany, discussions of medical war crimes became part of the broader reckoning with the Nazi past. In Japan, the process was slower and more contentious, especially regarding Unit 731, due to political sensitivities and the Cold War dynamic with the United States.

Human Dignity Under Threat

The central horror of these experiments lies in their systematic denial of human dignity. Whether in the name of racial theory, scientific curiosity, or military necessity, people were tortured and killed like lab animals. This total disregard for basic humanity set a precedent for how monstrous a modern state can become when it wields absolute power and abandons moral restraint.

The experiments also highlight how complicity can spread. Physicians, lab assistants, guards, bureaucrats issuing funds—all played a role in sustaining these programs. Some feared for their own lives if they resisted; others believed wholeheartedly in the ideology. Understanding these dynamics is crucial for recognizing potential warning signs in future societies.

CHAPTER TEN

Life Under Occupation – Daily Horror

1. **Introduction: An Unwanted New Order**
   When we think about an occupying army, we often imagine soldiers marching through city squares, flags replaced, and government offices taken over. But beneath that outward display of control lay countless acts of violence, exploitation, and terror. For people in occupied regions—Poland, France, Norway, Greece, and many other places—the war was not just a distant conflict. It moved into their homes, took over their streets, and shaped every waking moment.

This chapter explores the grim reality of daily life under Axis occupation. We'll see how Nazi Germany, Fascist Italy, and Imperial Japan governed conquered territories through fear and force. We'll examine the puppet regimes they set up, the forced labor they demanded, and the subtle (and not so subtle) ways ordinary people tried to survive or resist. Daily horror meant more than just bombs or battles; it meant living with oppressive rules, ration cards, curfews, and the knowledge that a careless word could lead to arrest—or worse.

2. **Immediate Changes: Curfews, Flags, and Propaganda**
   Once an invading force took control, the first step was to impose new authority. Streets were patrolled by foreign soldiers, local officials were replaced or coerced into cooperation, and propaganda posters appeared overnight. In cities like **Warsaw**, German signs replaced Polish ones, and the swastika flew atop government buildings. In **Paris**, Nazi banners draped iconic monuments. The occupiers made sure everyone understood who was in charge.

Curfews were a common tactic. Civilians had to be off the streets by a certain hour, or they risked arrest. Radios were confiscated or re-tuned to broadcast the occupiers' messages. Censorship became a daily headache. Newspapers were forced to print stories praising the new regime or condemning the old leaders. Some people found themselves listening to forbidden radio broadcasts from London or Moscow in secret, risking severe punishment if caught.

3. **Puppet Governments and Collaborators**
   Often, the occupier set up a **puppet government** made of locals who were willing (or pretended) to cooperate. In **France**, this took the form of the **Vichy regime** under Marshal Pétain after the German armistice. In Norway, Vidkun Quisling led a collaborationist government so notorious that his name became a synonym for "traitor." These regimes tried to strike a balance between appeasing the occupiers and maintaining some sense of national identity. They often ended up implementing the occupier's policies—such as deportation of Jews, forced labor, and suppression of resistance.

For many citizens, collaborating was a survival strategy. Some believed they could soften the harshest measures or protect their families by working with the occupiers. Others, driven by ideological sympathy or personal ambition, embraced the new regime wholeheartedly. Collaboration carried a steep social price: neighbors viewed collaborators as sellouts, and after liberation, they often faced public humiliation, arrests, or summary executions.

4. **Rationing and Starvation**
   Food became a central issue. Occupying armies seized resources, feeding their soldiers first and shipping surplus back to the homeland. Local populations were left with whatever remained. Ration cards were introduced, restricting civilians to minimal amounts of flour, sugar, meat, and other staples. In some places, like **Greece** under Italian and German occupation, famine loomed large, with thousands dying from malnutrition.

Long lines formed outside bakeries and shops, with people arriving hours before they opened. Black markets thrived, but prices were exorbitant. A loaf of bread could cost a month's wages. Some families resorted to barter, trading valuables for potatoes or beans. In the countryside, farmers had to turn over quotas of grain and livestock to occupation authorities, leaving only scraps for themselves. Starving peasants and city dwellers alike faced the daily dilemma of feeding their children or preserving seeds for the next planting season.

5. **Forced Labor and Deportations**
   The occupiers often needed labor for factories, farms, and construction projects. They rounded up men and women, shipping them off to work camps in Germany, Italy, or Japan—or forced them to build roads and railways in the local territory.

In Eastern Europe, this was especially brutal. The Nazi "Generalplan Ost" envisioned using Slavic people as slave labor before eventually clearing them out for German settlers.
- **Recruitment Drives**: Sometimes disguised as "voluntary work," but refusal meant prison or worse.
- **Labor Transports**: Crowded train cars carried workers west to German factories. Families were torn apart.
- **Work Conditions**: Long hours, scarce food, harsh discipline. Sabotage attempts were punished severely.

Deportations overlapped with racial policies: Jewish communities were deported to ghettos or camps, while non-Jewish Poles or other Slavs might be sent to forced labor camps. In Asia, the Japanese used conscripted Korean and Chinese labor for mines, railroads, and industrial complexes. Survival rates were low, with disease and exhaustion claiming many lives.

6. **Daily Violence: Beatings, Arrests, and Executions**
   Occupation soldiers and police wielded almost unchecked power. A perceived insult, a curfew violation, or even looking "suspicious" could trigger a beating or an arrest. In rural areas, small garrisons punished entire villages for partisan attacks. The methods included:
- **Hostage Taking**: Authorities randomly selected locals as hostages, warning that if partisans struck again, the hostages would die.
- **Public Executions**: To instill fear, suspected resistance members were hanged or shot in the town square. Sometimes, the occupiers forced crowds to watch.
- **Sweep Operations**: Soldiers combed through neighborhoods, arresting people on flimsy suspicions. Families might never see a relative again, without explanation.

This atmosphere of constant threat permeated daily life. People learned to keep their heads down, avoid eye contact with soldiers, and conceal any sign of patriotism or dissent. Children grew up thinking that uniformed men carried fear in their wake, a far cry from the protective figure of a neighborhood policeman in peacetime.

7. **Religious and Cultural Suppression**
   Occupation authorities often sought to erase local identity. Churches or synagogues were destroyed or converted into storage facilities. Public gatherings—like festivals or national celebrations—were banned. Schools were forced to teach the occupier's language or ideology. Teachers who resisted were fired or arrested.

In some places, religious leaders tried to protect their congregations. Priests hid valuables or even people in church basements. Rabbis organized secret worship in attics, risking deportation if discovered. Cultural societies went underground, preserving books, art, and music that the occupiers deemed subversive. This clandestine effort to keep a culture alive served as a form of silent resistance, even if it carried great risk.

8. **Women Under Occupation: Exploitation and Abuse**
   Women faced unique hardships. Many became the primary providers for their families while husbands, brothers, or fathers were off fighting, imprisoned, or in forced labor. They had to negotiate with occupation officials for rations, risk traveling to black markets, and protect their children from danger. Sexual violence was widespread. Soldiers considered local women "spoils of war," leading to rapes, forced prostitution, and the establishment of "comfort stations" by the Japanese military.

In some cases, women collaborated in minor ways—sleeping with an occupying soldier for extra food or better treatment. Others formed or joined resistance groups, acting as couriers or spies because they were less likely to be suspected. But the stigma remained, especially after liberation, when those who had relationships with enemy soldiers were sometimes publicly humiliated (their heads shaved, paraded through streets, etc.). The moral gray zones of survival under occupation left deep scars.

9. **Children: Growing Up in Fear**
   For children, occupation meant a stolen childhood. Schools were disrupted or co-opted to teach propaganda. Playgrounds might be commandeered for military use. Many kids had to work on farms or in small family businesses just to put food on the table. In some urban centers, gangs of orphaned children roamed the streets, scavenging for scraps.

The psychological toll was immense. Children normalized violence, seeing shootings or bombings as part of daily life. A child in Warsaw might hide in cellars during SS raids; a child in Nanjing might witness Japanese soldiers executing neighbors. Some children participated in small acts of resistance—delivering messages, hiding ammunition, or acting as lookouts. Their innocence eroded quickly, replaced by a cynicism and wariness rarely found in peacetime youth.

10. **Resistance: Sabotage, Underground Newspapers, and Partisan Warfare**
    Not everyone under occupation bowed to the new regime. **Resistance movements** sprang up in nearly every occupied land. Their tactics varied:
- **Sabotage**: Blowing up bridges, cutting telephone lines, derailing trains.
- **Propaganda**: Printing clandestine newspapers to counter occupier propaganda. In France, papers like *Combat* or *Libération* were circulated secretly, boosting morale and spreading news of Allied advances.
- **Guerrilla Warfare**: Partisan units in Yugoslavia, the Soviet Union, and elsewhere waged hit-and-run attacks. They ambushed patrols, rescued downed Allied pilots, and destroyed supply depots.

- **Intelligence Gathering**: Spies or informants passed crucial information about troop movements to Allied forces. Local knowledge of terrain proved invaluable.

Resistance was dangerous. If the occupiers discovered a cell, everyone involved risked torture or death. Reprisals often fell on innocent civilians. Yet these movements kept alive the hope of eventual liberation and showed that submission to tyranny was not universal.

11. **Allied Support and Controversies**
    Allied nations sometimes aided resistance groups with weapons drops, radio equipment, or secret agents. The British Special Operations Executive (SOE) and the American Office of Strategic Services (OSS) coordinated with local partisans. These efforts helped sabotage enemy logistics, tying down large numbers of occupation troops.

However, controversies arose when local uprisings were encouraged but not adequately supported. One example is the **Warsaw Uprising** of 1944. The Polish resistance expected Soviet assistance but found the Red Army halted on the Vistula River, allowing Germans to crush the uprising. The city was left in ruins, and tens of thousands of civilians perished. Allegations that Stalin deliberately let the uprising fail to weaken anti-communist Poles highlight the murky alliances and political games overshadowing ground-level realities.

12. **Economic Exploitation and Resource Extraction**
    Occupying powers drained conquered regions of resources to fuel their war machines. In **France**, Germany seized agricultural output, coal, and manufactured goods. In **Manchuria**, Japan took iron, timber, and agricultural

products. Factories were retooled to produce arms for the occupier. Local workers received minimal wages or were coerced into forced labor.

This left local economies in shambles. Small businesses closed, farmland was overused, and inflation soared. People who once led comfortable lives found themselves selling heirlooms or family treasures to survive. The black market became a parallel economy, where anything from bread to gasoline could be bought at insane prices if you had gold, jewelry, or connections. Survival overshadowed all else, pushing moral boundaries to the limit.

13. **Propaganda Ministries and Indoctrination**
    To solidify control, occupiers established propaganda offices. In Nazi-occupied territories, Joseph Goebbels's Ministry of Public Enlightenment and Propaganda extended its reach. Radio stations broadcast German achievements, while local newspapers repeated Nazi slogans. Posters depicted Allied soldiers as monsters or criminals. In Japanese-occupied regions, propaganda hammered home the idea of the "Greater East Asia Co-Prosperity Sphere," claiming they were liberating Asians from Western colonialism.

Citizens were bombarded with these messages. Some believed them out of fear or ignorance; others feigned compliance. Underground jokes circulated, mocking outlandish claims of victory as the war turned against the Axis. But voicing open skepticism was risky, as informers lurked everywhere.

14. **Healthcare Under Occupation**
    Medical facilities became scarce. Occupying armies often commandeered hospitals, reserving them for their soldiers. Civilians had limited access unless they had connections or bribed medical staff. Doctors who resisted working with occupiers might lose their licenses—or vanish. In rural areas, basic medicines were nonexistent. People returned to folk remedies or smuggled supplies from other regions.

Epidemics spread swiftly when clean water and sanitation broke down. Typhus, dysentery, tuberculosis, and other diseases thrived in overcrowded housing or prisons. Occupation authorities rarely prioritized civilian health, focusing instead on their own troops. This neglect turned minor illnesses into lethal threats, especially for children and the elderly.

15. **Cultural Repression: Burning Books and Erasing Identities**
    Occupiers often aimed to erase the cultural backbone of conquered peoples. The Nazis, for instance, destroyed Polish libraries, museums, and churches. Jewish, Slavic, and other minority cultures were systematically dismantled. Japanese

occupiers forced Koreans to adopt Japanese names, banned the Korean language in schools, and requisitioned cultural artifacts.

Such actions stripped communities of their heritage. Libraries that survived might hide precious books in secret rooms. Artists and intellectuals went underground or fled. Illegal gatherings kept traditional music and dances alive. This quiet resistance proved pivotal for restoring national identity after liberation.

16. **Harsh Winters and Housing Crises**
    In regions with cold climates—like the Soviet Union or parts of Northern Europe—winter magnified suffering. Occupiers confiscated fuel, leaving civilians with minimal heating. Homes destroyed by shelling forced families to shelter in barns, cellars, or makeshift huts. Frozen roads complicated the delivery of any relief. Starvation escalated when crops froze.

Urban housing shortages plagued cities like Warsaw, Berlin, or Leningrad. Overcrowded apartments housed multiple families, tension flaring over scarce resources. Disease spread easily. For many, daily life became a struggle against cold and hunger, overshadowing any political concerns.

17. **Small Acts of Kindness and Solidarity**
    Despite the terror, stories of kindness punctuated the gloom. Neighbors shared rations or hidden supplies with those who had nothing. Some local officials quietly bent rules to protect families from deportation. Priests or monks offered shelter in monasteries. Farmers left sacks of potatoes at night for hungry townsfolk. Such gestures, though small, meant survival and reminded people that humanity still existed.

Women often led these solidarity efforts, organizing communal cooking or childcare. They formed supportive networks to help with laundry, sewing, or burying the dead. While these acts did not end the occupation, they preserved a sense of dignity and community against the brutal machinery of war.

18. **The Psychological Weight of Occupation**

    Beyond physical suffering, the mental strain was immense. People lived in constant fear of betrayal by collaborators or secret informants. Trusting someone could mean life or death. Paranoia grew, and friendships fractured under suspicion. Sleep was often difficult—any knock on the door after dark could herald an SS raid or a Kempeitai search.

Children absorbed this fear, becoming hyper-alert to adult conversations or changes in routine. Some developed deep anxiety disorders that lasted well after the war. The daily pressure of survival overshadowed hopes, dreams, or future plans. For many, life narrowed to the next meal or the next safe hiding place.

19. **End of Occupation: Liberation and Its Aftermath**

    As the war turned against the Axis, liberation came at different times to different places. The Allies landed in Normandy in June 1944, freeing parts of France that had been under Nazi rule for four years. The Soviet Red Army pushed the Germans out of Eastern Europe, though this often replaced one form of oppression with another, especially in places like the Baltic states. Japan's capitulation in August 1945 freed large parts of Asia.

Liberation brought euphoria but also chaos. Collaborators were punished, sometimes violently. Resistance heroes emerged from hiding. Families tried to reunite, though many discovered loved ones were dead or missing. Cities lay in ruins, economies were wrecked, and bitter memories lingered. Some who had cooperated with the occupiers argued they did so to save lives. Others faced public humiliation or vigilante justice. The scars of occupation did not vanish with the new flags waving over city halls.

20. **Conclusion: The Quiet Hell of Occupation**

    Daily life under occupation was a relentless blend of fear, deprivation, and enforced submission. From forced labor and ration lines to raids and public executions, each day brought new tests of endurance. Yet, in this crucible of suffering, acts of resistance and humanity also shone through—showing that even under the boot of tyranny, people found ways to preserve dignity, culture, and hope.

CHAPTER ELEVEN

The Pacific Front's Grim Realities

1. **Introduction: Japan's Path to War**
    While Germany's blitzkrieg swept across Europe, another storm was brewing in East Asia. Japan had been modernizing and expanding since the late 19th century, defeating Russia in 1905 and annexing Korea in 1910. By the 1930s, Japan aimed to become the dominant power in Asia, seizing resources to fuel its growing empire. The Depression years only intensified Japan's ambition, as military hardliners gained influence and pointed to nearby territories—particularly China, Southeast Asia, and the Pacific islands—as sources of raw materials.

Conflict began in earnest with the invasion of Manchuria in 1931, then escalated into a full-scale war against China in 1937. The world watched, but Western nations were preoccupied with their own crises. Tensions with the United States rose sharply after the occupation of French Indochina. Washington imposed embargoes on steel and oil exports to Japan. Feeling cornered and in need of resources, Tokyo launched a surprise attack on Pearl Harbor in December 1941, dragging the US into the war. Thus, the Pacific Theater exploded, spanning from the jungles of Burma to the coral atolls of the Central Pacific. This chapter covers the early phases of Japan's rampage and the terror faced by civilians under the rising sun.

2. **Pearl Harbor and the Spread of War**
    In a matter of hours on December 7, 1941, Japan's carrier-based planes devastated the US Pacific Fleet at Pearl Harbor, Hawaii. Battleships like the USS Arizona were sunk or heavily damaged. Over 2,400 Americans died in the attack, and many planes were destroyed on the ground. Although the strike was meant to cripple American naval power, it also ignited fury and a thirst for revenge in the United States. President Franklin D. Roosevelt declared December 7 as "a date which will live in infamy," and war was declared.

Simultaneously, Japanese forces attacked American bases in the Philippines, Guam, and Wake Island. They also struck British colonial holdings such as Hong Kong and Malaya, aiming to secure resource-rich areas quickly, while the Allies reeled. Within weeks, Japanese troops entered Manila, took Hong Kong, and pushed British forces back in Malaya. The fall of Singapore in February 1942 shocked the world; a supposedly impregnable British fortress surrendered to a smaller Japanese force after chaotic battles and disastrous leadership decisions. Tens of thousands of Allied troops became prisoners, setting the stage for a brutal captivity.

3. **Conquest of the Dutch East Indies and Other Territories**
   Japan's hunger for oil and rubber led it to invade the Dutch East Indies (modern Indonesia). The region's oil fields were vital for Japan's war machine. Allied defenses were a patchwork of American, British, Dutch, and Australian forces (ABDA Command) lacking cohesive leadership. Japanese air superiority, combined with swift naval strikes, overwhelmed ABDA units. By March 1942, the Dutch East Indies had fallen. The Japanese took control of vital oilfields in places like Balikpapan and Palembang.

In Burma (Myanmar), Japanese columns advanced from Thailand, driving Allied defenders back. British colonials and Indian troops retreated in disarray, often cutting roads behind them to slow the enemy. Civilians caught in the middle found themselves trekking through disease-ridden jungles. The newly formed Burma Railway would soon become a site of horror for POWs forced to build it, famously known as the "Death Railway."

4. **Occupation Policies: The "Greater East Asia Co-Prosperity Sphere"**
   Japan justified its conquests with the idea of liberating Asia from Western colonialism, calling it the "Greater East Asia Co-Prosperity Sphere." In practice, this often meant replacing one harsh colonial rule with another. Though some local populations initially welcomed the Japanese—hoping for relief from Western oppression—they quickly discovered that Tokyo's promises of brotherhood were hollow. Local economies were reorganized to feed Japan's war effort; natural resources were shipped out, local industries taken over.

The Japanese military police, the **Kempeitai**, enforced strict obedience. They used informants, torture, and public executions to suppress dissent. Political leaders or intellectuals who resisted were thrown into prison. Stories circulated of entire villages razed for harboring guerrillas or refusing to hand over rice quotas. Local men were conscripted into labor battalions, building roads, airfields, and fortifications under brutal conditions. Women lived under the constant fear of sexual violence or forced prostitution in military-run "comfort stations."

5. **The Fall of the Philippines and the Bataan Death March**
   One of the early symbols of Japanese cruelty occurred in the Philippines. American and Filipino forces, led by General Douglas MacArthur, tried to hold back the Japanese invasion but were pinned down on the Bataan Peninsula. Starvation and disease ravaged the defenders. By April 1942, they surrendered. What followed became infamous as the **Bataan Death March**.

Over 70,000 weakened, starving prisoners were forced to walk about 65 miles in the tropical heat with almost no water or food. Japanese guards beat, bayoneted, or shot stragglers. Some accounts describe prisoners collapsing from thirst, only to be executed on the spot. Others talk of men who tried to drink from roadside puddles, risking bullets.

At night, the prisoners were crammed into filthy pens without supplies. By the time the march ended, thousands had died. Survivors then faced internment in prison camps under equally harsh conditions.

6. **Life in Occupied Southeast Asia**
   For civilians across Southeast Asia—Malaya, Singapore, the Dutch East Indies, and Burma—occupation life was an unending ordeal. Japan demanded local collaboration: officials who had once served British, Dutch, or American colonial administrations were told to continue their jobs but under Japanese directives. A language policy was imposed in many areas, forcing people to learn Japanese for official business. Schools were reorganized to teach Japanese history and culture.

Food shortages soon loomed. Large portions of the rice harvest or rubber and tin output were appropriated for Japan's use. Black markets flourished, but prices were astronomical. Meanwhile, forced labor squads scoured the countryside for able-bodied men. In some regions, entire families were uprooted and relocated closer to roads or rail lines, allowing the occupier to tighten control. The Kempeitai's reign of terror ensured that any sign of rebellion or hidden Allied sympathies was ruthlessly crushed.

7. **Propaganda and Indoctrination**
   The Japanese occupiers bombarded local populations with propaganda. Newspapers praised the Imperial Army's victories and depicted Western powers as evil colonizers. Radio broadcasts insisted that Asia must unite under Japan's benevolent leadership. Posters showed smiling locals saluting the Emperor, claiming they were finally free from Western exploitation.

Yet reality clashed with rhetoric. While some nationalists were initially swayed, the everyday brutality wore down any goodwill. Executions for minor infractions were common. Civilians were forced to bow in the direction of Tokyo. Racial arrogance pervaded the ranks of Japanese officers, who considered themselves superior not only to Westerners but also to the Asians they claimed to be liberating. Resentment simmered, fueling underground resistance movements despite the threat of lethal reprisals.

8. **Guerrilla Warfare in the Jungles**
   Just as European resistance groups formed in Nazi-occupied territories, guerrilla forces arose in Southeast Asia. In the Philippines, local fighters and remaining American soldiers launched ambushes from mountainous hideouts. Chinese communities in Malaya supported Communist guerrillas who fought the Japanese. Burmese nationalists, initially allied with Japan to oust the British, grew disillusioned and turned to sabotage or intelligence-gathering for the Allies.

Jungle warfare was brutal. Supplies were scarce, diseases like malaria ravaged fighters, and local villagers faced harsh reprisals if they were caught aiding partisans. The

Japanese responded with scorched-earth tactics, burning villages suspected of harboring rebels and executing anyone found with weapons. Some accounts describe entire communities slaughtered after a single rifle was discovered hidden nearby. Fear became the occupiers' favored method of control.

9. **Atrocities in China: Beyond Nanjing**

   Japan had been waging war in China since 1937. The atrocities in Nanjing (1937–1938) were only the start. Over the next several years, Japanese forces implemented a "Three Alls" policy in some regions—"Kill All, Burn All, Loot All"—to break Chinese resistance. Villages suspected of harboring Communist or Nationalist guerillas were systematically destroyed. Men were executed, women raped, and homes torched. Crops were burned to starve the population.

Biological and chemical warfare experiments, as discussed in Chapter Nine, were carried out by Unit 731 and related units, leading to plague outbreaks and horrifying medical torture. Civilians lived in terror of "mopping-up" operations in which entire areas were cleared of suspected guerrillas. People seeking safety in major cities found them heavily policed, with routine searches and forced labor conscriptions. Millions of Chinese died from famine, disease, forced labor, and direct violence during Japan's occupation—an overlooked tragedy compared to the more commonly cited events in Europe.

10. **Comfort Women: Sexual Slavery**

    One of the most disturbing elements of Japan's wartime occupation was the forced prostitution system known as "comfort women." Tens of thousands (some estimates suggest hundreds of thousands) of women, primarily from Korea and China but also from the Philippines, Indonesia, and other territories, were coerced or tricked into serving in military brothels. Some were promised factory or nursing jobs, only to be trapped in "comfort stations" near the front lines.

The conditions were harrowing. Women faced daily rape by multiple soldiers, physical abuse, and venereal diseases. Attempts at escape or resistance often led to beatings or execution. Basic healthcare was minimal. Many women died in these stations or took their own lives to escape the nightmare. After the war, survivors faced social stigma and rarely found justice. The Japanese government largely evaded responsibility for decades, sparking ongoing controversy and calls for redress that persist to the present.

11. **The Turning Tide: Midway and Guadalcanal**

    Initially, Japan seemed unstoppable. But the tide began to turn in mid-1942. In the **Battle of Midway** (June 4–7, 1942), US carrier planes ambushed and sank four Japanese aircraft carriers, crippling Japan's naval air power. This decisive victory put Japan on the defensive in the Central Pacific. Next, the Allies launched a grueling counteroffensive in the Solomon Islands, starting with **Guadalcanal**

(August 1942–February 1943). These battles were fought in steaming jungles, with disease, hunger, and exhaustion as constant companions.

Japanese troops, fiercely devoted to the Emperor, rarely surrendered. Their motto "death before dishonor" meant they often fought to the last man. Allied soldiers discovered that capturing an island was never complete until they rooted out every hidden bunker or cave. Meanwhile, the Japanese lacked sufficient supply lines, forcing them to scavenge local resources. Civilians caught in these battle zones endured bombardments, crossfire, and the terror of unpredictable occupant behavior. Even Allied liberators, though welcomed, brought their own brand of destruction to once-quiet villages.

12. **Island Hopping and Brutal Combat**
    By 1943–1944, the Allies adopted an "island hopping" strategy—bypassing heavily fortified Japanese strongholds and capturing strategically valuable islands. Key battles erupted in the Gilbert, Marshall, Mariana, and Palau Islands. The fighting was savage. On **Tarawa** in November 1943, US Marines suffered massive casualties in just 76 hours, encountering ferocious resistance and well-dug defenses. Civilians, if present, found little mercy in such infernos.

In the **Marianas** (Saipan, Tinian, Guam), entire local populations—often Japanese colonists or indigenous Chamorro—were caught between the advancing Americans and the entrenched Imperial Army. Japanese propaganda claimed that American soldiers would torture and kill civilians, prompting mass suicides on Saipan's cliffs, including parents jumping with their children. The psychological warfare took a horrifying toll. Even when Allied policy aimed to save civilian lives, the swirl of fanaticism, rumors, and combat chaos led to tragedies.

13. **Kamikaze Strikes**
    As the Allies drew closer to Japan, the Japanese military resorted to increasingly desperate measures. The **kamikaze** tactic—suicide attacks by pilots crashing bomb-laden planes into Allied ships—began in late 1944. This new approach was terrifying for Allied sailors. The speed and determination of kamikazes caused significant damage, especially off the coast of the Philippines and later at Okinawa. Although not a direct occupation tactic, it reflected Japan's absolute refusal to surrender and foreshadowed the horror that might be unleashed if Allied forces had to invade the Japanese home islands.

Civilians on these contested islands suffered the brunt of the violence. Japanese garrisons forced them to build defenses or supply them with food. When Allied bombardments commenced, entire towns were flattened. Evacuation was often impossible. Some residents tried hiding in caves or jungles, only to face starvation or get caught in firefights. The front line shifted unpredictably, making everyday survival a gamble.

14. **Retreat and Scorched Earth**
    As the Japanese retreated across Southeast Asia, they burned crops, destroyed infrastructure, and executed prisoners or forced laborers. The idea was to leave nothing of value for advancing Allied forces. In the Philippines, Japanese troops under General Yamashita adopted a brutal scorched-earth policy in Manila, turning a once-thriving city into a battlefield. Tens of thousands of civilians died in the crossfire, while Japanese marines committed rampant atrocities, including rapes and murders in hospitals and churches.

The same pattern appeared in Burma, Malaysia, and elsewhere. Roads were cratered, bridges blown up, and local populations forcibly moved or killed. Disease swept through these devastated regions, with cholera, dysentery, and malaria flourishing in the wreckage. Even as Allied armies "liberated" territories, they found traumatized survivors, burned villages, and an infrastructure on the brink of collapse.

15. **POWs in the Pacific**
    Unlike the more "regulated" (though still harsh) treatment of POWs by Germany in the West, Japanese camps were notoriously brutal. The Imperial Japanese Army operated under the Bushido code, which viewed surrender as dishonorable. Hence, captured enemies were deemed beneath contempt. Thousands of POWs died constructing railways (most famously the Burma-Thailand Death Railway), roads, and airfields. Beatings, starvation, and disease were standard. Guards withheld medical supplies, often leaving men to suffer tropical ulcers that rotted down to the bone.

The death rate among Allied POWs in the Pacific was dramatically higher than in Europe—some estimates suggest 25–30% compared to under 5% in German camps for

Western POWs. Civilians interned in places like Santo Tomas in Manila or Changi in Singapore faced similarly grim conditions, with minimal food rations and overcrowding. Some guards relished cruelty, forcing prisoners to stand in the sun for hours, feeding them infested rice, or punishing them at whim. Allied soldiers liberated from these camps often emerged skeletal and psychologically scarred.

16. **Resistance within Japan's Expanding Empire**
    Just as Nazi rule provoked underground resistance in Europe, Japan's empire saw covert opposition. Chinese guerrillas behind enemy lines waged relentless sabotage. Filipino resistance fighters guided US forces and attacked Japanese garrisons. Malayan Communists harassed supply lines. Burmese independence groups turned on their former Japanese allies when the promise of liberation turned to oppression. Even in the Dutch East Indies, local nationalists realized Japan would not simply hand over independence, so they shifted to subversion.

All these efforts risked horrific reprisals. Civilians suspected of aiding partisans were tortured or executed. But the flame of rebellion continued to burn, fueled by cultural pride, rage at occupation atrocities, and hope that the Allies might one day return. When Allied operations finally moved into these regions, local knowledge proved invaluable—helping the Allies navigate jungles, gather intelligence, and coordinate surprise attacks.

17. **Civilian Experience in Japan's Home Islands**
    While Japan's conquering armies brutalized foreign populations, its own civilians eventually faced crippling shortages and incessant Allied air raids. By 1944–1945, US bombers ranged freely over Japanese skies, dropping incendiaries on cities largely built of wood and paper. The March 1945 firebombing of Tokyo killed an estimated 80,000 to 100,000 in one night, and subsequent raids destroyed large portions of Osaka, Kobe, Nagoya, and other urban centers.

Students and housewives joined the Volunteer Fighting Corps, training with bamboo spears or basic weapons. Propaganda told them to fight to the death if the Americans invaded. Meanwhile, the blockade of Japanese shipping caused rampant shortages of food and fuel. Malnutrition spiked, disease spread, and entire families starved. Thus, even as Japan inflicted horrors on conquered peoples, its own citizenry endured terrifying bombings and near-famine as the war neared its climax.

18. **Manila Massacre and the End Near**
    One of the final, brutal chapters in the Pacific was the **Battle of Manila** (February–March 1945). Determined to defend the Philippine capital, isolated Japanese units went on a savage rampage. They burned neighborhoods, executed hospital staff, and massacred civilians in schools, convents, and private homes. Tens of thousands died in the crossfire or as deliberate targets of Japanese fury.

American artillery destroyed much of the city trying to root out entrenched defenders. By the battle's end, Manila lay in ruins, with civilian casualties estimated at 100,000 or more. It was among the most brutal urban battles in the Pacific.

As Allied forces closed in on Japan's perimeter, the stage was set for even bloodier confrontations on Iwo Jima and Okinawa. Both sides knew that a fight on the Japanese home islands would eclipse all previous horrors. Allied leaders dreaded the casualties an invasion would cost, while Tokyo's militarists vowed to fight until the last Japanese citizen. This confrontation would ultimately be cut short by the atomic bombs dropped on Hiroshima and Nagasaki in August 1945, but the cost in civilian and military lives by that point was already staggering.

19. **Legacy of the Pacific Front's Brutality**
    The Pacific war was characterized by racism and a sense of cultural superiority on both sides. The Japanese saw Westerners as decadent imperialists; many Americans and Europeans viewed the Japanese as treacherous barbarians, especially after atrocities like Bataan. The brutal nature of island combat, with limited scope for surrender, fed mutual hatred. Civilians in Southeast Asia and China endured years of oppression, forced labor, and famine, culminating in millions of deaths.

Even after the war, Japan's reluctance to fully acknowledge its war crimes—especially regarding comfort women and Unit 731—fueled tension with neighboring nations. The memory of horrific battles, mass civilian deaths, and POW cruelty lingered. Veterans struggled with trauma, and entire regions lay in ruins. Though overshadowed in Western memory by events like D-Day or the Holocaust, the Pacific Theater's violence, scale, and suffering rivaled anything in Europe.

20. **Conclusion: Under the Shadow of the Rising Sun**
    Japan's lightning conquests in 1941–1942 changed the fate of Asia forever. Civilians in China, the Philippines, Malaya, Burma, and countless other territories were plunged into a dark new order. Forced labor, mass executions, and famine became everyday realities. Meanwhile, the Allies—initially caught off guard—gradually regrouped, launching bloody counteroffensives that turned every Pacific island into a lethal battleground. The war in Asia showed how easily the line between soldier and civilian could vanish under an imperialist ideology claiming racial destiny and total obedience to the Emperor.

CHAPTER TWELVE

Shock in the Pacific – Prisoners and Experiments

Introduction: A Different Kind of Hell
For many Western soldiers, capture by the Germans in North Africa or Europe meant grim detention but at least some adherence—albeit imperfect—to the Geneva Convention. In contrast, falling into Japanese hands frequently spelled a sentence far worse than mere imprisonment. Japan's cultural ethos, rooted in the Bushido code, viewed surrender as a deep shame. Consequently, Allied POWs were often treated as subhuman. Rather than just holding them, the Imperial Japanese Army saw them as forced labor resources or subjects for barbaric "experiments."

This chapter focuses on the experiences of POWs and civilian internees in the Pacific Theater. We touch on forced marches, railroad construction, medical horrors, and the psychological torment inflicted daily. While Unit 731's atrocities against Chinese civilians have been discussed, here we expand on the suffering endured by Allied prisoners who became unwitting test subjects. We also examine the small acts of courage and solidarity that emerged in these camp environments—a sliver of light amidst the darkness.

Conditions in Pacific POW Camps
Compared to their counterparts in Europe, Allied prisoners in the Pacific faced drastically worse conditions. Camps were scattered across Southeast Asia, China, Japan's home islands, and even remote Pacific atolls. Many facilities were makeshift, converting old warehouses, stables, or barbed-wire enclosures. Guard towers overlooked cramped barracks with leaky roofs, dirt floors, and inadequate bedding. Food rations were

minimal, often just a bowl of rice or thin soup per day, sometimes accompanied by rancid fish or vegetables.

- **Diseases**: Dysentery, beriberi, malaria, cholera, and tropical ulcers were rampant. Medical supplies were rare, and camp doctors (if available) could do little without proper medicine.
- **Punishments**: Japanese guards or Korean overseers (often conscripted into the Japanese Army) beat prisoners for minor infractions like talking back, failing to bow correctly, or being too slow at work.
- **Work Details**: POWs woke at dawn, marched to labor sites, and worked until dusk with few breaks. Back at camp, they might receive a meager meal before collapsing from exhaustion.

Forced Labor: The Death Railway

The Burma-Thailand Railway (often called the **Death Railway**) exemplifies the cruelty of forced labor under the Japanese. Built to supply Japanese forces advancing into Burma, it stretched over 250 miles through dense jungles, mountainous terrain, and malaria-infested swamps. The project was supposed to last years, but Japan insisted it be completed in a matter of months to boost the war effort.

- **Construction Hell**: Prisoners toiled day and night, hacking through rock with picks and shovels. Mudslides, floods, and swarms of insects were constant. Minimal tools meant men had to rely on brute strength.
- **The Hellfire Pass**: One of the harshest sections, where POWs carved through solid rock in blistering heat. Guards whipped or beat stragglers. At night, the flickering torchlights on the walls gave it a hellish glow, inspiring the macabre nickname.
- **Disease and Death**: Malaria, dysentery, and cholera swept the camps, exacerbated by malnutrition and exhaustion. Corpses piled up; burial details worked continuously. Some POWs were literally worked to death.

By the time the railway was completed in late 1943, tens of thousands of Allied POWs and even more local laborers (romusha) had perished. Survivors carried physical and psychological scars that haunted them for the rest of their lives.

Life Under the Kempeitai

While all Japanese soldiers could inflict terror, the **Kempeitai** (military police) had a special reputation for sadism. They ran specialized interrogation and punishment centers in occupied territories and within POW camp systems. Prisoners suspected of sabotage, escape attempts, or espionage were transferred to Kempeitai-run facilities for "questioning." Torture methods ranged from waterboarding to electric shocks, beatings with bamboo canes, and forced kneeling on sharp objects for hours.

Civilians who tried to smuggle food to POWs or relay messages also risked arrest by the Kempeitai. Reprisals extended to families—wives, children, or parents might be seized to coerce confessions. The mere sight of the Kempeitai uniform filled prisoners and locals alike with dread. Even some ordinary Japanese soldiers feared them, knowing that any sign of disloyalty or "insufficient patriotism" could land them in the same torture chambers.

Human Guinea Pigs: Medical Experiments on Allied POWs
Though Unit 731 mainly targeted Chinese civilians, there are documented cases of Allied POWs used for medical experiments in various Japanese-run facilities. These ranged from forced infection with diseases like cholera or dysentery to blood transfusion tests in which POWs were drained of blood to see how much they could lose before dying. Some survivors recall being given injections without explanation, followed by fever, vomiting, or strange rashes.

In certain camps, Japanese doctors tested newly developed drugs or treatments for battlefield wounds—deliberately inflicting injuries, then observing how different medicines worked. Some accounts describe POWs strapped to tables as chemicals were applied to open wounds, or toxins were introduced into their systems. Those who survived rarely recovered fully, suffering lifelong complications. Official records of these experiments were often destroyed at war's end, but enough eyewitness accounts and partial documents confirm their existence.

Civilian Internees: Captivity and Hardship
Alongside military POWs, thousands of Western civilians living in Southeast Asia or the Pacific—such as missionaries, colonial administrators, businesspeople, and their families—were also interned. Camps like **Changi** in Singapore and **Santo Tomas** in Manila housed entire families under Japanese guard. Although these internment camps were less labor-intensive, conditions still involved overcrowding, hunger, and disease.

Women gave birth with little medical help. Children grew up behind barbed wire, learning to fear the daily roll calls and watch their parents starve. Some internees had the relative luxury of forming committees to distribute limited supplies, but the Japanese camp commandant held absolute power. Punishments or executions for suspected infractions were not uncommon. After the liberation of these camps, Allied troops discovered malnourished prisoners struggling with diseases caused by months or years of poor sanitation and diet.

Escapes and Secret Radio
A small percentage of POWs attempted escapes. Stories abound of men forging passes, sneaking out under the cover of night, or using stolen uniforms. Most attempts ended in capture and brutal punishment, including beheadings. In some lucky cases, escapees found local resistance groups, which helped them evade recapture or guided them to Allied lines.

Secret radios were another lifeline for POWs. Constructed from smuggled parts, these clandestine devices picked up news of Allied successes. Hearing about victories at Midway, Guadalcanal, or in Europe offered prisoners hope. They might then discretely spread the good news through camp rumor. However, discovery of a radio often led to mass beatings, extended punishment, or the execution of those involved.

Religious Faith and Coping Mechanisms
Facing daily horror, many prisoners leaned on faith or camaraderie. Impromptu church services in hidden corners of the camp offered solace. Christian POWs recited Bible passages, even if they had to memorize them due to confiscated Bibles. Others turned to meditation or mental exercises to stave off despair. Companionship among fellow prisoners was crucial: sharing scraps of food, nursing each other through illness, or providing emotional support after a beating.

Small acts of defiance—like saluting in the Allied style, secretly making national flags, or carving regimental badges—helped men remember their identity. Sketchbooks or diaries, often hidden from guards, captured the daily grind and the occasional moment of relief. Any sense of normalcy was precious, whether it was organizing a makeshift theater performance or exchanging jokes to lighten the gloom.

The Thai-Burma Railway Beyond POWs: Asian Laborers
While Allied attention focuses on Western POWs, the majority of forced laborers on projects like the Thai-Burma Railway were Asian. Javanese, Malayan, Burmese, Thai, and other romusha were rounded up by the Japanese or tricked with false promises of paid work. They labored under even worse conditions than Allied prisoners, often with no oversight or international attention. Mortality rates soared, with some estimates suggesting hundreds of thousands perished.

Romusha lived in filthy jungle camps, lacking even the minimal rations sometimes granted to POWs. Language barriers made it difficult for them to communicate their suffering, and after the war, their stories were overshadowed by the Western POW narrative. Yet, for these Asian workers, the railway was a genocidal experience, many left uncounted and unmourned, forgotten in unmarked graves along the tracks.

Executions and War Crime Trials

As the war raged on, the Japanese high command sometimes issued kill orders for POWs if liberation seemed imminent. This spurred incidents like the **Palawan Massacre** in the Philippines (December 1944), where retreating Japanese troops herded Allied prisoners into air-raid shelters and set them on fire, machine-gunning those who fled. Similar orders threatened all POW camps, though not all were carried out.

After Japan's surrender in August 1945, the Allied occupation forces investigated countless war crimes. Military tribunals were held, most famously the **Tokyo Trials**, sentencing high-ranking Japanese officials. Some POW camp commandants and guards faced separate trials. But many, especially those involved in Unit 731 or lesser-known atrocities, escaped prosecution, sometimes shielded by the US in exchange for research data. For the survivors who testified, these trials were a chance to voice the torments they had endured, yet justice often felt incomplete.

Kamioka Mines, Omuta, and Forced Labor in Japan

Not all POWs remained in Southeast Asia; some were shipped to Japan itself. They found themselves working in coal mines, steel mills, or manufacturing plants. The Kamioka mines in central Japan, for instance, employed hundreds of captured Allied troops under brutal supervision. Men worked underground in dangerous conditions, inhaling toxic dust. Accidents were frequent, medical care nonexistent. Guards punished any sign of sluggishness or mistakes.

The mines were a vital part of Japan's war economy, producing metals needed for weapons. Many companies—like Mitsubishi or Nippon Steel—profited from forced labor. POWs recalled hauling heavy loads for hours on end, with watery soup as their only sustenance. When US bombing raids targeted industrial areas, these captive laborers found themselves stuck in factories with no bomb shelters. Survival depended on luck.

Cannibalism Cases

One of the darkest revelations of the Pacific war was incidents of cannibalism by certain Japanese units, especially in New Guinea and other remote jungle areas. Starvation, harsh conditions, and a breakdown of discipline led some soldiers to kill and eat Allied prisoners or local civilians. Testimonies describe horrifying scenes where straggling soldiers captured lone POWs, murdered them, and consumed the flesh. While not widespread, such cases highlight the absolute collapse of moral restraint under extreme pressure.

Survivors who witnessed or escaped these atrocities carried deep psychological scars. Even seasoned officers in the Imperial Army sometimes turned a blind eye, prioritizing survival at all costs. Post-war trials for these crimes were complicated; evidence often relied on few witnesses, many of whom were also traumatized or deceased.

Civilian Comfort Women from Allied Territories
Though "comfort women" are commonly associated with Korea or China, Allied territories like the Philippines, Dutch East Indies, and Malaysia also provided victims. Some Dutch women were seized from internment camps, forced into military brothels. This revelation emerged during post-war investigations, leading to testimonies that shocked European audiences who assumed such brutality only targeted Asian women. The women were subjected to repeated sexual assaults and frequent beatings if they resisted.

After liberation, many survivors felt too ashamed to speak publicly, fearing stigma from their own communities. Some families disowned them, blaming them for "dishonoring" themselves, ignoring the violent coercion involved. Those who did testify found the Japanese war crime tribunals only partially responsive, as occupying powers often prioritized other strategic matters over these crimes.

Hidden Heroes: POW Doctors and Volunteer Nurses
Amid the horror, POW doctors and volunteer nurses emerged as unsung heroes. Scraping together meager supplies, they attempted surgeries or treated tropical diseases with improvised remedies. Antibiotics like penicillin were nearly unobtainable, so medics resorted to folk treatments—boiled herbs, maggots to clean wounds, or fashioned homemade splints from bamboo. Their resourcefulness saved countless lives.

Stories of compassion abound: camp doctors risking punishment to hide extra medicine for gravely ill prisoners, nurses sneaking in stolen food. Such acts bolstered morale. Even as men died around them, the presence of a dedicated medical figure offered a sense of hope. Camp logs, where they existed, reveal heartbreaking decisions—choosing which patient to treat first when supplies were limited.

Resistance and Sabotage Behind the Wire
Some POWs engaged in covert resistance. Underfed but determined, they tampered with machines in factories, producing flawed parts or slowing assembly lines. In docks or mines, they "accidentally" broke tools or allowed equipment to be damaged. Guards often failed to detect this sabotage or simply ascribed it to ignorance. The risk was enormous: if caught, torture or execution followed.

Additionally, intelligence networks sometimes operated within camps. POWs might memorize Japanese troop movements seen en route to labor sites, passing the info to secret Allies outside. A few bold individuals planned major breakouts, but success rates were minimal. Even sharing morale-boosting rumors or forging officer signatures on official documents to secure lesser tasks represented small acts of defiance, reminding prisoners that they were still soldiers of their respective nations.

The Long Wait for Liberation
For prisoners taken in 1942, captivity lasted over three years. News trickled in, sometimes months out of date, about Allied offensives in the Central Pacific, Italy's surrender, D-Day in Europe, and more. POWs clung to hope each time they heard about a major Allied victory, picturing liberation on the horizon. But the Japanese high command refused to yield. In some final months, certain guards became harsher, sensing defeat yet lashing out in frustration.

By mid-1945, Allied bombers appeared in Japanese skies more frequently. Some POWs in Japan witnessed the firebombing of nearby cities. The spectacle of massive air raids ironically lifted spirits—evidence that the Allies were winning. However, it also heightened fear that their captors might kill them en masse if an invasion loomed. The dropping of atomic bombs on Hiroshima and Nagasaki in August 1945 eventually forced Japan's surrender. It was not until the official ceasefire on August 15 that POWs truly believed they might survive.

Liberation: The Aftermath for POWs
When Allied forces finally liberated camps, they found emaciated prisoners near death. Some men weighed half their pre-war mass, bones protruding under skin riddled with sores. Dysentery and malaria raged. Rescue operations hurried in with food and medical supplies, but refeeding had to be done carefully—shocked digestive systems could not handle sudden large meals. Emotional scenes ensued: men weeping at the sight of Allied flags, hugging rescuers, or staring blankly in disbelief.

Reunion with families took months. Many POWs were sent to hospitals for prolonged rehabilitation. Some never recovered from physical ailments. Others carried invisible psychological wounds—nightmares, severe anxiety, or guilt for surviving when so many died. Some found their homes irrevocably changed; loved ones had moved on, died, or no longer understood the horrors they had endured.

War Crimes Documentation and Trials
In the wake of Japan's surrender, Allied war crimes teams interviewed liberated prisoners, collecting testimonies of abuse, forced labor, and experiments. This evidence fueled trials in Tokyo and other locations, including the International Military Tribunal for the Far East (IMTFE). High-profile figures like Prime Minister Hideki Tojo were convicted, while camp commandants and certain Kempeitai officers faced separate proceedings.

Yet, the complicated politics of the early Cold War shaped the scope of these trials. American occupation authorities, interested in Japan's rapid reconstruction as a buffer against communism, sometimes limited or overshadowed the process. Victims of sexual slavery and medical experiments found themselves marginalized. Many lower-level perpetrators slipped through cracks or received lenient sentences, overshadowed by the big-name trials of generals and politicians.

Forgotten Theaters: The Legacy of POWs in Asia
In the West, the European theater often overshadowed the Pacific. POWs returning from Japanese camps felt that their stories were less publicized, overshadowed by the concentration camps in Germany or the final battles in Europe. They struggled to articulate the scale of horror they had endured, especially the punishing forced labor that resembled slavery. Some described feeling overshadowed by the Allied celebrations over V-E Day (Victory in Europe), even though the Pacific war dragged on.

Memory of these atrocities lingered in Southeast Asia too, but local populations had their own tragedies—occupation, famine, or forced labor—that overshadowed the plight of Allied POWs. Over time, veterans' memoirs, documentaries, and historical research brought more attention to the brutalities in the Pacific. Yet, the sense remains that this corner of WWII history never received the same universal recognition as events in Europe. For survivors, recognition came late, sometimes well after their prime years had passed.

CHAPTER THIRTEEN

Secret Operations and Propaganda

Introduction: War in the Shadows
While gunfire and bombs dominated the headlines, a parallel struggle took place behind the scenes during World War II—a clandestine world of spies, saboteurs, codebreakers, and propagandists. These invisible armies did not fight on open battlefields. Instead, they gathered intelligence, disrupted enemy lines, and manipulated public opinion. In many ways, these secret operations and propaganda campaigns were as critical to the war's outcome as tank battles or aerial bombardments.

This chapter delves into the hidden side of World War II. We'll explore how espionage agencies sprang up in response to the Axis threat, how codebreakers pried open enemy communications, and how propaganda shaped entire populations' perceptions. We will also see how these covert efforts sometimes blurred moral lines—spreading disinformation, manipulating the media, and even plotting assassinations. In the end, the secret war proved pivotal, though its successes and failures remained unknown to the public for years, sometimes decades, after the war ended.

Early Espionage: SIS, Abwehr, and Others
At the war's outset, the major powers already had intelligence services, but these organizations were often small and underfunded. For Britain, the **Secret Intelligence Service** (SIS, also known as MI6) traced its roots to World War I, but it had to rapidly expand its network to counter Nazi Germany. Germany's own military intelligence, the **Abwehr**, took orders from the Wehrmacht high command, though its effectiveness varied. The Soviet Union's **NKVD** (later to become the KGB) kept tight control over espionage and internal security, employing a network of informants across Europe.

- **German Abwehr**: Led initially by Admiral Wilhelm Canaris, the Abwehr was tasked with gathering intelligence about enemy forces. Yet, internal factionalism and Nazi ideological meddling hindered its efficiency. Some Abwehr officers grew disillusioned with Hitler, secretly working to undermine him.
- **British SIS and Security Services**: MI6 focused on gathering foreign intel, while MI5 handled domestic counterintelligence. They recruited agents in occupied Europe, set up spy rings, and tried to intercept German communications.
- **Soviet NKVD**: Known for ruthless efficiency. Stalin's paranoia, however, led to purges of top intelligence officers, weakening the organization just before Nazi Germany invaded. Nonetheless, Soviet spies still managed to penetrate Nazi circles and even placed moles in Western governments.

Breaking the Codes: Ultra and Enigma

One of the biggest triumphs of the Allied secret war was the cracking of German **Enigma** and Japanese **Purple** codes. The most famous effort was **Ultra**, centered at Britain's Bletchley Park. Here, mathematicians like Alan Turing led teams that constructed early computing machines (the "Bombe" devices) to decipher Enigma-encrypted messages.

- **Enigma's Complexity**: This rotor-based encryption machine allowed countless permutations, changing daily. The Germans believed Enigma to be unbreakable.
- **Polish Pioneers**: Even before the war, Polish cryptanalysts had made significant progress on Enigma. When Poland was invaded, they shared their findings with Britain and France, laying a foundation for Ultra.
- **Impact on the War**: By reading German U-boat communications in the Atlantic, the Allies rerouted convoys to avoid wolf packs, reducing shipping losses. In North Africa, Ultra intelligence helped Field Marshal Montgomery counter Rommel's moves. On the Eastern Front, the Soviets received some intelligence from Ultra via British channels, though Stalin's distrust sometimes limited its use.

Meanwhile, American cryptanalysts at **Station HYPO** in Hawaii and other facilities deciphered Japanese codes, including the "JN-25" series. Breaking these ciphers led to major victories like **Midway**, where foreknowledge of Japanese plans allowed the US Navy to ambush and sink four enemy carriers. Both the Axis powers underestimated Allied codebreaking success, a blunder that gave the Allies a massive intelligence advantage.

The Special Operations Executive (SOE)

One of Britain's boldest initiatives was the creation of the **Special Operations Executive (SOE)** in July 1940, described by Winston Churchill as an organization set to "set Europe ablaze." The SOE recruited men and women—sometimes from refugee communities or diaspora groups—trained them in sabotage, guerrilla warfare, and covert communications. They were then parachuted into occupied territories to assist local resistance movements.

- **Training**: Agents learned how to handle explosives, forge documents, use hidden radios, and evade capture.
- **Missions**: SOE teams in France worked with the Maquis to blow up rail lines, sabotage factories, and coordinate with the Allied D-Day invasion. In Yugoslavia, they aided Tito's partisans with weapon drops. In Burma, the SOE supported indigenous guerrillas.
- **Risks**: If caught, agents faced torture and execution. Female operatives like Violette Szabo or Nancy Wake became legendary for their bravery, though many died in Gestapo custody.

In parallel, the US formed the **Office of Strategic Services (OSS)**—a precursor to the CIA. Under Major General William "Wild Bill" Donovan, the OSS mounted similar operations in Europe and Asia, forging links with resistance fighters and conducting sabotage missions behind enemy lines.

German and Japanese Covert Operations

The Axis powers also deployed spies and saboteurs, though with mixed results. German intelligence networks infiltrated some Allied countries, but Britain's MI5 was adept at capturing or "turning" German agents. Known as the "Double-Cross System," MI5 used captured spies to feed disinformation back to Berlin. As a result, many German operations in Britain were effectively controlled by British intelligence—a humiliating failure for the Abwehr.

- **Operation Pastorius (1942)**: A German attempt to land saboteurs on the US East Coast. They came ashore in submarines with explosives to target industrial sites. However, one saboteur defected, leading to the group's swift capture by the FBI.
- **Japan's Intelligence Efforts**: In the Pacific, Japanese espionage sometimes relied on local sympathizers or radio interception. But they failed to develop a robust codebreaking capability compared to the Allies. Their biggest intelligence victory was arguably Pearl Harbor's surprise, though even that success soon gave way to Allied codebreaking dominance.

Deception Campaigns: Masking Invasions and Tricking Foes

Alongside sabotage and spying, deception was a cornerstone of WWII espionage. The Allies orchestrated elaborate ruses to mislead enemy planners. The most famous example: **Operation Bodyguard**, encompassing multiple sub-operations designed to hide the true location and timing of the Normandy landings.

- **Operation Fortitude**: Within Bodyguard, the Allies created a fake "First US Army Group" under General Patton, complete with inflatable tanks, dummy landing craft, and false radio traffic, to convince the Germans that the main invasion would strike at the Pas de Calais. German commanders diverted significant forces there, weakening Normandy's defenses.
- **The "Man Who Never Was"**: Another British deception placed a corpse dressed as a Royal Marine officer carrying fake invasion plans off the coast of Spain. German intelligence took the bait, rerouting defenses away from the actual target.

Such deceptive maneuvers saved countless Allied lives. The Germans often fell for these illusions due to internal biases and the belief that the Allies would attack logical points. In the Mediterranean, Allied deception efforts helped the invasion of Sicily succeed with lower resistance than expected.

Propaganda Machines in Overdrive
Beyond cloak-and-dagger missions, propaganda shaped wartime psychology. Each belligerent power used radio broadcasts, newspapers, posters, and film to rally its own population and demoralize the enemy.

- **Nazi Propaganda**: Joseph Goebbels's Ministry of Public Enlightenment and Propaganda churned out materials glorifying Hitler and the Aryan race. They demonized Jews and Bolsheviks. When Allied bombers hit German cities, newsreels blamed "terror fliers," fueling hatred and calls for revenge.
- **Allied Response**: The BBC in Britain broadcast news into occupied Europe, encouraging resistance and sharing coded messages for agents. In the US, Hollywood produced war films praising American might. Famous animations like Disney's short propaganda pieces ridiculed Axis leaders, while War Bonds drives used patriotic themes to spur citizen contributions.
- **Soviet Propaganda**: Soviet authorities broadcasted calls for heroic defense of the Motherland, pushing the idea of a "Great Patriotic War." Posters showed fearless Red Army soldiers crushing Nazi hordes. Stalin's image was carefully managed to appear as a wise, paternal figure—despite his purges and brutal policies.

In Asia, Japanese propaganda promoted the "Greater East Asia Co-Prosperity Sphere" to justify occupation, though local populations quickly saw the gap between ideals and on-the-ground brutality.

Radio Propaganda Stars: Tokyo Rose, Lord Haw-Haw, Axis Sally
A unique aspect of WWII propaganda involved radio personalities broadcasting in the enemy's language to sow demoralization or confusion:

- **Tokyo Rose**: This was a name applied to several English-speaking female broadcasters in Japan. They aimed to undermine American morale by claiming US forces were losing, playing popular music, then inserting messages about the hopelessness of the Allied cause.
- **Lord Haw-Haw**: William Joyce, an Irish-American with fascist sympathies, broadcast from Germany. He mocked Britain's war effort, ridiculed Winston Churchill, and claimed the Axis had unstoppable weapons.
- **Axis Sally**: Mildred Gillars, an American living in Germany, produced shows telling US soldiers their girlfriends were being unfaithful at home, or that the war was pointless.

While these broadcasts annoyed some Allied troops, they rarely shattered morale. Many soldiers treated them as a curiosity, even making jokes about "listening to Tokyo Rose" for the latest big-band tunes, ignoring the propaganda. After the war, some of these broadcasters were tried for treason.

Resistance Radio and Underground Press
In occupied lands, clandestine radio stations and underground newspapers offered a lifeline of truth amidst enemy propaganda. Small groups built or smuggled radio transmitters, broadcasting short messages of encouragement or instructions for resistance. Newspapers were printed secretly in cellars, circulated at night by couriers. For example, in Nazi-occupied France, newspapers like *Combat* or *Libération* overcame relentless Gestapo crackdowns.

Such efforts were risky. If discovered, the SS or local collaborator police raided the hideouts, arrested everyone, and often executed them. Yet, these channels ensured locals knew about Allied victories, continuing the fight in small, relentless ways. The written word and the surreptitious broadcast became weapons just as potent as rifles in keeping the spirit of resistance alive.

Spy Gadgets and Ingenious Inventions
World War II saw an explosion of creative devices for espionage and sabotage, many developed by agencies like SOE's "Churchill's Toyshop" or the OSS labs. Some notable gadgets:

- **Explosive Rats**: The SOE filled dead rats with plastic explosives. The plan was to slip them into German factories so that when workers disposed of them by burning, the rats would explode. The Germans never encountered many but spent resources worrying about them.
- **Sten Gun**: A cheaply produced British submachine gun that resistance fighters could easily assemble.
- **Cyanide Pills**: Issued to Allied spies for suicide if captured, avoiding torture-induced betrayals.

- **Pen Guns and Sleeve Pistols**: Concealable firearms for quick kills in close quarters.
- **Miniature Cameras**: Hidden in cigarette cases or matchboxes, essential for photographing enemy documents or installations.

The creativity of these inventions highlighted the war's desperation. No idea was too bizarre if it might yield a strategic edge—even if only psychologically.

Double Agents and Misdirection

Throughout the war, MI5 in Britain ran one of the most successful double-agent programs in history. After capturing German spies who parachuted into the country, British officers gave them two choices: cooperate or face execution. Many chose to cooperate. Under careful supervision, these agents transmitted disinformation back to their German handlers.

- **Garbo (Juan Pujol García)**: Perhaps the most famous double agent. He invented an entire network of fictitious sub-agents, sending reams of fake reports. Germany awarded him the Iron Cross, never suspecting his loyalty lay with the Allies. His biggest success was feeding false data about D-Day's landing sites, reinforcing German belief that Calais was the real target.
- **Zigzag (Eddie Chapman)**: A British criminal turned spy, who "sabotaged" a British factory with the help of MI5. In reality, the explosion was staged. The Germans congratulated themselves on a successful infiltration.

These double agents contributed immeasurably to Allied strategic deception. The scale of their achievements only came to light decades after the war.

Soviet Partisan Networks and NKVD Control

On the Eastern Front, espionage and sabotage took on a huge dimension. Soviet partisans operated in forests behind German lines, ambushing convoys, blowing up rail tracks, and relaying troop movements to Red Army commanders. The NKVD coordinated many of these networks, distributing parachuted supplies and receiving intelligence via hidden transmitters.

Some partisans were patriotic villagers outraged by German atrocities. Others were communist loyalists. The movement wasn't always harmonious—disputes arose over resources, leadership, or even punishing local populations accused of collaboration. Still, the cumulative effect was enormous, tying down countless German units and ensuring that no territory was entirely safe. When winter snows isolated German armies, partisan attacks intensified, hitting supply depots and command posts, unraveling Axis control over vast areas.

Japanese Occupied Territories and Allied Spies

In Asia, the **OSS** and British **Force 136** (a branch of SOE) infiltrated Burma, Malaya, and parts of China. They helped local guerrillas coordinate strikes against Japanese outposts and gather intelligence on troop movements. However, jungles and mountainous terrain posed unique challenges for infiltration and exfiltration.

- **Burma Campaign**: Groups like the Kachin Rangers, composed of native Kachin tribesmen allied with the Allies, used knowledge of the terrain to ambush Japanese patrols. OSS advisors taught them demolitions and radio operation.
- **Malayan People's Anti-Japanese Army**: Primarily communist-led guerrillas, they received modest Allied support but faced brutal reprisals from the Japanese. Force 136 air-dropped supplies and liaison officers.
- **China**: The US built a relationship with Nationalist China under Chiang Kai-shek. The OSS attempted to unify Chinese resistance, but the internal friction with Communist forces under Mao Zedong complicated matters.

Neutral Countries as Spy Hubs

Nations like **Switzerland**, **Sweden**, **Portugal**, and **Turkey** maintained neutrality but became hotbeds of espionage. Rival intelligence services converged in these capitals, quietly trading information or courting informants. Luxury hotels doubled as clandestine meeting spots. Diplomats, businessmen, and refugees formed webs of rumor and intelligence.

- **Switzerland**: Close to Axis territory, with many banks and intact infrastructure, it served as a crossroads. German and Allied spies rubbed shoulders in Bern.
- **Sweden**: Exchanged goods with Germany under strict conditions but secretly aided Allied intelligence. Some Norwegian and Danish resistance cells had safe houses here.
- **Turkey**: At a key intersection between Europe and the Middle East, Turkey balanced relations with both sides. German and British intelligence vied for influence in Ankara, bribing or blackmailing officials for information.

Psychological Warfare: Leaflets and Rumors

Alongside secret agents, the Allies flooded Axis-occupied zones with leaflets dropped from planes. These pamphlets aimed to erode enemy morale, highlight Axis defeats, or promise lenient treatment for surrendering troops. In some cases, they contained carefully crafted "rumors" hoping to spark fear or confusion within German or Japanese ranks.

Rumor campaigns also targeted civilians in Axis countries, suggesting that the war was lost, that their leaders were lying about battlefield conditions, or that conspiracies existed within their government. While measuring the exact impact is difficult, the fear of infiltration and sabotage led Axis leadership to extreme suspicion. Paranoia at times hampered German and Japanese operational efficiency as they scoured for imaginary networks of Allied spies.

Underground Railroads and Escape Lines
Helping downed Allied airmen or escaped POWs reach safety was a vital aspect of clandestine work. In Europe, networks like the **Comet Line** or **Pat O'Leary Line** guided escapees from occupied France through Spain to British Gibraltar. These escape lines were mostly run by ordinary civilians—teachers, farmers, nuns—coordinated by a handful of resistance leaders. If caught, both helpers and escapees faced torture and execution.

- **Comet Line**: Founded by a Belgian woman, Andrée de Jongh ("Dédée"), it successfully escorted hundreds of Allied airmen across mountainous terrain.
- **Dangers**: German patrols, collaborator informants, treacherous weather. Many guides died or ended up in concentration camps if compromised.

The success of these routes underscored the synergy between espionage organizations and local patriotic networks, all risking their lives to help Allied personnel evade capture.

Assassinations and Targeted Hits
In the realm of secret operations, assassinations were not off-limits. The Allies and local resistance groups sometimes targeted high-ranking Gestapo officers, SS members, or collaborationist leaders. For example, **Operation Anthropoid** (1942) saw Czech and Slovak agents trained by the British parachute into Czechoslovakia to assassinate **Reinhard Heydrich**, the SS official overseeing the Protectorate of Bohemia and Moravia. Heydrich was mortally wounded in an ambush, provoking horrific Nazi reprisals, including the destruction of the villages Lidice and Ležáky.

Such missions had a dual edge. They removed dangerous figures but often incited brutal retaliation against civilians. Debates linger about their moral justification: were they worth the reprisals? In any case, they revealed how far clandestine efforts could go to strike at the heart of enemy power.

Extent of Success and Controversies
By 1945, espionage, sabotage, and propaganda had significantly shaped the war's outcome. Codebreaking at Bletchley Park and in the US gave the Allies a persistent advantage. SOE and OSS missions undermined Axis occupation. Resistance movements, guided by Allied agents, tied down enemy resources. Deception operations guarded the Allies' strategic secrets.

However, these successes came with controversies:

- Some blame British intelligence for not doing more to warn about the Holocaust, claiming they had intercepts indicating mass atrocities. Yet the full scale and details were never conclusively deciphered in time.
- Stalin's paranoia about Western spies complicated Allied coordination, particularly as Soviet troops advanced into Eastern Europe.

- Disinformation sometimes caused confusion or inflicted harm on civilians if Allied propaganda incited uprisings prematurely (e.g., the Warsaw Uprising in 1944).

In the immediate post-war period, revelations about espionage or propaganda rarely emerged. Many operations stayed classified, leaving the public with an incomplete picture of the "secret war."

Propaganda's Last Gasp and Home Front Morale
As the war in Europe reached its final stages, Goebbels tried frantic measures to sustain German morale, proclaiming "miracle weapons" (Wunderwaffen) like the V-1 and V-2 rockets would deliver victory. Faith in Hitler's leadership eroded, but fear of Soviet retribution and Allied bombing kept many Germans fighting. Propaganda remained potent, if only to stave off complete surrender. Meanwhile, the Allies also struggled with war-weariness among their populations, using victory parades and heroic narratives to maintain unity until total victory was secured.

In Japan, a similar phenomenon played out with talk of the "sacred homeland" and kamikaze tactics. The Emperor's broadcasts encouraged citizens to resist an Allied invasion with bamboo spears if necessary. Allied leaflet drops and radio messages urged Japan to surrender, highlighting the futility of continued resistance. Ultimately, the atomic bombings and Soviet entry into the war made further propaganda meaningless.

CHAPTER FOURTEEN

Starvation, Siege, and Suffering

Introduction: Warfare Without Mercy
In the brutal calculus of World War II, cutting off an enemy's supplies became a common strategy. Bombing factories, sinking merchant ships, and blockading ports aimed to starve the opposition into surrender. But these tactics, combined with harsh occupations, also meant civilians bore the worst consequences. Millions perished from hunger, disease, and exposure—often trapped in besieged cities or isolated regions. From the grand scale of Leningrad's siege to the smaller but equally tragic blockades elsewhere, starvation turned warfare into a slow, grinding horror.

This chapter surveys some of the most heart-wrenching episodes of siege and famine during WWII. We'll see how entire populations were reduced to eating rats, grass, or even turning to cannibalism. We'll examine the policies that led to such desperation—sometimes motivated by ideology, sometimes by raw military goals. This aspect of the war exposed the fragility of modern societies when faced with total encirclement and resource denial, leaving scars that lasted well beyond the final ceasefire.

The Siege of Leningrad: A City Starved
Perhaps no siege in history is more emblematic of sustained starvation than the **Siege of Leningrad** (1941-1944). After launching **Operation Barbarossa**, German armies encircled this Soviet metropolis (now St. Petersburg), hoping to force its surrender by cutting off food and supplies. Finnish forces collaborated from the north, effectively blocking land routes. Adolf Hitler intended to erase Leningrad from the map, ordering that no surrender be accepted—starvation, he believed, was cheaper than an assault.

- **900 Days of Isolation**: The siege dragged on for nearly two and a half years. Soviet authorities attempted to supply the city via Lake Ladoga—dubbed the "Road of Life"—but the quantity of food that arrived was never enough.
- **Rations**: Bread rations dwindled to a few hundred grams per day, often bulked with sawdust or cellulose. People fainted on the streets, fought over scraps in garbage bins.
- **Cannibalism**: In the harsh winter of 1941-42, with temperatures plunging below -30°C, thousands died each day. Some resorted to cannibalism out of sheer desperation, though Soviet secret police enforced strict laws against it.
- **Civilian Resolve**: Despite unimaginable suffering, Leningrad never surrendered. Workers continued to manufacture arms in bombed-out factories. Children attended makeshift schools. The city's defenders clung to the notion of eventual relief by Soviet armies.

By the siege's end, estimates suggest at least a million civilians perished, mostly from hunger. Survivors bore life-long trauma, and the city's historical treasures were heavily damaged by shelling. The siege remains a symbol of both the cruelty of total war and the endurance of human spirit under the direst conditions.

The Rape of Resources: The Hunger Plan

The siege of Leningrad was part of a broader Nazi strategy in the East. Hitler's **Generalplan Ost** envisioned starving millions of Slavs to free up farmland for German settlers. The so-called "Hunger Plan," developed by economists within the Nazi regime, aimed to divert Soviet food supplies to the German military and homeland, leaving the local population to starve. This policy was a deliberate act of genocide by economic means.

- **Ukraine's Grain**: Occupied Ukraine, known historically as a "breadbasket," was systematically stripped of harvests. The German occupiers seized grain, livestock, and farm equipment, leaving peasants with bare fields.
- **Prisoner of War Starvation**: Soviet POWs were often denied adequate food, locked in open-air camps (like the "Russenlager"), resulting in mass death.
- **Brutal Realities**: Civilians not sent to forced labor in Germany faced starvation in their villages. German authorities cared little for them, viewing Slavs as subhuman.

Though not all of the Hunger Plan's goals were fully realized, the partial implementation killed millions, especially during the harsh winters of 1941–42. Many who died were women, children, and the elderly, left with no recourse under a merciless occupying power.

China's Famine Under Occupation and War

China had endured famines for centuries, but Japan's invasion magnified food crises. As the Imperial Army advanced, farmland was ruined, irrigation systems collapsed, and large-scale conscription robbed villages of able-bodied men. Forced requisitions took whatever grain was left for Japanese troops.

- **Henan Famine (1942–1943)**: Triggered by drought and exacerbated by the Sino-Japanese War. Nationalist forces commandeered resources for military use, while the Japanese seized supplies to feed their soldiers. Starving peasants resorted to begging or selling children into servitude. Death toll estimates vary, but it likely claimed millions of lives.
- **Scorched Earth Policies**: Both Chinese Nationalists and Japanese armies sometimes burned fields to deny them to the enemy, further compounding hunger. Civilians found themselves with no farmland, no seeds, and no hope of relief.

China's plight went relatively unnoticed in Western media focused on Europe, yet the scale of starvation there was massive. Survivors' diaries detail families cooking tree bark or grass, risking execution if caught stealing from military storehouses. Disease outbreaks followed malnutrition, turning entire villages into ghost towns.

The Greek Famine Under Axis Occupation

When Axis forces (German, Italian, and Bulgarian) occupied Greece in 1941, they seized agricultural produce and disrupted trade routes. The British naval blockade further prevented imports, aiming to weaken Axis resources. The result was a humanitarian catastrophe within Greece, particularly in urban centers like Athens.

- **Winter of 1941–42**: Mortality rates soared as food vanished. People dropped dead on the streets. Desperate families ate stray cats, boiled weeds, or rummaged through garbage heaps.
- **International Red Cross**: Eventually, the Allies allowed some shipments of grain after seeing the scale of starvation. Swedish ships transported limited relief, but it was never enough.
- **Resistance**: The famine galvanized support for the Greek resistance (EAM-ELAS). Guerrillas attacked Axis supply lines and tried to distribute stolen food to starving villagers.

Estimates suggest at least 300,000 Greeks died from hunger or related diseases. The famine left deep scars on Greece's social fabric, fueling post-war political turmoil.

North Africa: Scarcity and Forced Migration

The war in North Africa saw battles between Axis and Allied forces from 1940 to 1943. Civilians in Libya, Egypt, and Tunisia found themselves in the crossfire, their farmland trampled by tank columns. Italian colonial rule in Libya already caused local suffering. The war worsened it: food supplies were requisitioned, and towns near the front lines were evacuated.

In Egypt, the Nile Delta remained somewhat fertile, but inflation and disruption of shipping pushed prices beyond the reach of many. Communities living in desert oases relied on trade routes that were cut or heavily monitored. Nomadic tribes faced forced sedentarization by occupying armies that suspected them of smuggling or espionage. While the African front did not see the same scale of famine as Eastern Europe or Asia, local populations still experienced severe hardships under the shadow of desert warfare.

Japanese Home Front: Famine's Glimpse
By 1944–45, the US submarine blockade and relentless bombing of Japan's merchant marine caused a collapse in food imports. Japan had always relied on overseas resources from Korea, Taiwan, Manchuria, and Southeast Asia. As those links were severed, rationing became severe. Rice, fish, and soy products dwindled. Urban populations turned to sweet potatoes, acorns, or thin millet gruel.

Children scavenged in fields for any edible plants. Malnutrition soared, weakening civilians as they endured bombing raids. While true famine was somewhat contained by rationing systems, if the war had continued into 1946 with a home island invasion, many more Japanese civilians would likely have starved. The atomic bombings and subsequent surrender came before a complete societal collapse, but hunger had already taken root in major cities.

U-Boat Campaigns and the Battle of the Atlantic
Germany's U-boat strategy aimed to starve Britain by sinking merchant convoys carrying food and raw materials from North America. During the early years, U-boat "wolf packs" inflicted heavy losses. Rationing in Britain tightened, with families receiving limited quantities of meat, sugar, butter, and other staples. Nevertheless, an extensive system of ration books and government oversight managed to prevent widespread famine.

- **Dig for Victory**: British citizens were encouraged to grow vegetables in home gardens and public parks. "Victory gardens" mitigated shortages, fostering a sense of communal effort.
- **Allied Countermeasures**: Improvements in sonar, radar, and escort tactics gradually reduced U-boat effectiveness. By 1943, Allied shipbuilding outpaced sinkings, ensuring Britain would not be starved into submission.

Though Britain avoided mass starvation, the sense of vulnerability was acute. Bomb shelters and barbed-wire beaches were constant reminders that isolation was a real threat if the Battle of the Atlantic turned against them.

Blockade of Germany and Occupied Europe
The Allies responded with their own blockade of Germany, cutting off imports of vital resources. Neutral countries like Sweden continued some trade, but the noose tightened as Allied air raids destroyed transport networks. By 1945, German civilians faced severe shortages of meat, dairy, and fuel. Urban dwellers scoured the countryside to barter for potatoes or beets. Malnourishment, especially among children and the elderly, became widespread.

For forced laborers and concentration camp inmates, these shortages were devastating. Rations in camps—already minimal—became even smaller. Many starved to death, especially toward the war's end when the collapsing Nazi state could not sustain its war machine, let alone feed prisoners. In this sense, the Allied blockade, combined with Nazi brutality, contributed to the death toll in the final months.

Starvation as a Weapon: Policy or Indifference?
Whether in the Soviet Union or Asia, occupying powers often claimed they lacked the means to feed local populations, even if they had the capacity to provide minimal relief. In truth, for ideologically driven regimes like Nazi Germany or Imperial Japan, feeding subjugated peoples was not a priority. The war machine and homeland consumption came first. Local civilians were expendable, especially if they belonged to "inferior" races.

In some Allied strategies, like the British blockade or the US submarine campaign against Japan, civilian suffering was an accepted byproduct of crippling the enemy. Allied leaders argued these measures would shorten the war, thus saving lives overall. The moral debate about starving an adversary into surrender remains contentious. War planners rarely weighed the immediate humanitarian cost beyond viewing it as a tool for victory.

Civilian Coping Mechanisms
Under blockade or siege, civilians resorted to various strategies:

- **Urban Gardens**: Leningraders grew vegetables in every available patch of land—parks, balconies, rooftops—despite harsh winter conditions.
- **Black Markets**: Even a crust of bread or handful of beans fetched high prices. Families sold heirlooms or furnishings for food. In Greece, the black market thrived as urbanites traded jewelry for flour from rural smugglers.
- **Foraging and Hunting**: Wild plants, mushrooms, or small game (like pigeons or rats) became essential survival foods.
- **Bartering and Community Kitchens**: Some neighborhoods formed collective soup kitchens, pooling resources for communal meals.

Such measures gave short-term relief but could not fully prevent starvation. Disease often struck malnourished populations, leading to tragic mortality spikes.

Case Study: The Warsaw Ghetto's Starvation
Although primarily a result of Nazi racial policies, the **Warsaw Ghetto** also epitomized siege-like conditions. Over 400,000 Jews were crammed into a walled-off district with scant rations. Smuggling became a lifeline:

- **Children Smugglers**: Young kids slipped through cracks or tunnels, sneaking bread and potatoes from the outside. SS guards often shot them if caught.
- **Starvation Deaths**: Corpses littered the streets, and daily death counts soared. The official German ration offered only a fraction of necessary calories.
- **Wealth Disparities**: Some individuals used hidden funds to access the black market, while the poor wasted away. Soup kitchens tried to help but lacked resources.

Conditions were so dire that some historians label it a deliberate slow extermination before mass deportations to death camps. Starvation acted as one more tool of genocide.

Hunger in the Netherlands: The "Hunger Winter"
In late 1944 and early 1945, the Netherlands suffered the **Hongerwinter** after a failed Allied attempt to liberate Arnhem (Operation Market Garden). German forces cut off food shipments to the western provinces, turning the region into a bleak landscape of hunger during a harsh winter.

- **Fuel Shortages**: People stripped trees from city parks, broke down furniture for firewood. Frozen canals offered limited transport routes.
- **Tulip Bulbs as Food**: Some resorted to boiling tulip bulbs to create a starchy meal. The taste was foul, but it was better than nothing.
- **Death Toll**: Estimates suggest over 20,000 Dutch civilians died of starvation or cold.

Even after Allied liberation, distributing relief supplies took time, as roads and bridges were destroyed. The Hunger Winter left an indelible mark on Dutch memory, influencing post-war politics and social policies.

Sieges on the Eastern Front Beyond Leningrad
While Leningrad stands out, other Soviet cities endured horrific mini-sieges:

- **Sevastopol** on the Crimean Peninsula faced repeated German and Romanian assaults. Civilians trapped in the city starved as supply lines were cut. Soviet defenders held out until mid-1942, with scarcities of ammunition and food.
- **Stalingrad** became a symbol of brutal house-to-house combat. Though the city wasn't encircled for as long, the intense fighting meant any supply line was perilous, and civilians caught in the ruins had little to eat. Those not evacuated in time starved or were killed in the crossfire.

In these urban hellscapes, the synergy of bombing, shelling, and food shortages created living nightmares. The Soviet state's willingness to sacrifice millions to hold symbolic cities demonstrated the war's ruthless nature.

Disease Outbreaks in Besieged Areas

When starvation strikes, disease follows quickly. Malnutrition weakens immune systems, making communities ripe for epidemics of typhus, tuberculosis, cholera, and dysentery. In besieged Warsaw, Leningrad, and beyond, hospital wards overflowed. Doctors lacked supplies, and public health measures collapsed under constant shelling.

Sewage systems often failed when bombs destroyed pumping stations. Clean water became scarce, especially in destroyed cities. People drank from puddles or contaminated rivers. With no functioning trash collection, garbage piled up, attracting rats and vermin. Infectious diseases spread unchecked, sometimes killing more civilians than bombs or bullets.

Psychological Toll and Acts of Desperation

Starvation undermines not only the body but also the mind. Civilians under siege reported psychological breakdowns: parents unable to feed children, neighbors turning against each other for a morsel of bread. Crime soared as hunger trumped morality. Some rummaged through cemeteries at night, exhuming corpses for clothing or valuables. In extreme cases, cannibalism emerged, although typically limited and met with social condemnation or harsh legal penalties if discovered.

Yet, glimmers of hope also appeared. Citizens formed mutual aid groups, teachers held clandestine classes to preserve a sense of normal life, and artists or writers documented the tragedy, believing that bearing witness could retain their humanity. After the war, diaries, letters, and sketches from besieged cities like Leningrad or Warsaw became haunting testaments to the power of resilience amid mass despair.

Allied Relief Efforts and Challenges

As the Allies advanced, they sometimes tried to air-drop supplies to besieged enclaves—like the US airdrops to the Philippine guerrillas or the Red Army's attempts to fly food into encircled Soviet cities. Logistics were precarious: planes could be shot down, weather could disrupt flights, and dropped supplies often fell into enemy hands.

Post-liberation relief was also fraught. Roads and rail lines lay in ruins, so delivering large quantities of food or medicine took time. Occupying armies had priorities—securing the area, disarming enemy forces, re-establishing order—while starving civilians could not wait. Relief agencies like the Red Cross or UNRRA (United Nations Relief and Rehabilitation Administration) stepped in eventually, but bureaucratic hurdles and continuing conflict often delayed assistance. Meanwhile, black market profiteers exploited the desperate, selling meager provisions at skyrocketing prices.

Comparisons to World War I Blockades

Some historians draw parallels between WWII blockades and those of World War I, during which Germany faced mass hunger due to Allied naval blockades. The difference in WWII was the total warfare ideology—ruthless occupation regimes, racist doctrines advocating the annihilation or subjugation of entire populations, and the added dimension of aerial bombing. The scale of famine and devastation soared beyond prior conflicts. Modern technology allowed for more efficient strangulation of supply lines and more lethal bombings of infrastructure.

Legacy of Starvation Warfare

The famines and sieges of WWII had lasting repercussions. Survivors carried emotional scars. Many developed obsessive behaviors around food—hoarding supplies or refusing to waste even a crumb—traits that lingered for decades. Governments learned that hunger could be weaponized effectively, but also discovered the difficulty of rebuilding shattered societies afterward. In the post-war period, global relief organizations expanded, partly in response to these catastrophic events.

Politically, post-war reconstruction efforts often overlooked the psychological toll. Soviet propaganda framed the siege of Leningrad as an example of heroic sacrifice, glossing over the government's early failures to evacuate or supply the city. In Japan, the near-starvation of 1945 shaped immediate post-war occupation policies by the US, which shipped in food to avert chaos.

CHAPTER FIFTEEN

Children of War – Lost Innocence

Introduction: A Shattered Youth
World War II disrupted countless childhoods across the globe. In peaceful times, children would go to school, play games, and grow up free from the chaos of adult conflicts. But from 1939 to 1945, the boundaries that protected their innocence dissolved in the face of bombings, occupations, genocides, and forced movements. In this chapter, we explore the lives of these children—what they experienced, how they were used by armies and governments, and the lasting scars they carried.

Many children became orphans, uprooted from homes, or forced to flee. Some were forced to take on adult responsibilities overnight, caring for siblings or working to help families survive. Others were victims of racial policies that designated them for extermination or "re-education." Still others became child soldiers or members of youth organizations twisted into war's purpose. No region was spared. Whether in Europe, Asia, Africa, or the Pacific, the war devoured childhood joys and replaced them with hunger, fear, and brutality.

Bombings and Evacuations
One of the earliest disruptions for many children was evacuation to the countryside to escape aerial bombardment. In Britain, the government organized massive relocations—"Operation Pied Piper"—moving thousands of children from major cities like London, Liverpool, and Birmingham to rural areas. Parents made agonizing decisions: send their children away for safety, or keep them close during the Blitz?

- **Separation Anxiety**: Children were often bewildered, clutching small suitcases and gas masks. Host families in the countryside might treat them well or, in some cases, exploit them for labor.
- **Return to Ruins**: After the worst of the bombings subsided, some children returned home to find neighborhoods flattened, friends killed, and daily life forever changed.
- **German Children**: In Germany, large-scale evacuations (the *Kinderlandverschickung*) sent youngsters to rural regions or even to the Austrian and Czech areas for "safety" from Allied bombers. However, toward the war's end, front lines shifted so quickly that many children became trapped or forcibly moved again.

For these evacuees, the war robbed them not only of their homes and normal schooling but also of the comforting presence of parents. Some spent years away, returning as near-strangers to families shattered by loss.

Occupation and Forced Displacement

Outside the bombed cities, many children faced displacement under occupation. In Eastern Europe, German policies uprooted entire populations, sending some families to forced labor in Germany while leaving children behind. In the Soviet Union, orphans multiplied as parents died on the front lines or in partisan warfare. Japanese conquests in Asia led to similar disruptions: children fled villages burnt by advancing armies, or were compelled to labor on farms or railways under the watchful eye of occupying troops.

- **Polish Children**: Targeted for "Germanization" if they had "Aryan" features. Some were taken from parents and placed in Nazi-run homes or adopted by German families. This practice aimed to "rescue" racially suitable children from "inferior" backgrounds. Many never saw their birth parents again.
- **Chinese Children**: Forced to migrate internally, sometimes trekking hundreds of miles as their families followed the shifting front lines to evade Japanese occupation. Epidemics of cholera and typhus ravaged refugee camps, killing children especially quickly.
- **Children in the Netherlands**: Endured the Hunger Winter of 1944–45, rummaging for scraps, while many were forcibly evacuated if they lived near battle zones such as Arnhem.

In these scenarios, children were rarely asked for their opinion; they were simply bundled along, often experiencing repeated traumas.

Child Soldiers and Youth Militias

Though child soldiers are more famously associated with later conflicts, World War II also saw underage combatants. Some children lied about their age to enlist, driven by patriotism or the loss of family members to enemy action. In partisans or resistance movements, young teenagers acted as couriers, spies, or even fighters, exploiting their perceived innocence to pass enemy checkpoints unnoticed.

- **Soviet Komsomol and Partisans**: Soviet youth organizations sometimes funneled willing teens into guerrilla units. The NKVD oversaw some "hero boy" stories, immortalizing young snipers or saboteurs who became propaganda symbols.
- **Hitler Youth**: In Germany, membership in the Hitlerjugend (HJ) became mandatory for most teenage boys and girls. Boys received paramilitary training, learning to march, handle small arms, and idolize the Führer. By 1945, as the Third Reich collapsed, some Hitler Youth members (barely in their teens) were thrown into desperate battles, manning flak guns or forming last-ditch militias in Berlin.
- **Japanese Military Training**: In Japan, school curriculums included military drills. By late 1944, high-school-age boys were organized into local defense militias. In the face of the Allied invasion threat, the government prepared them to fight with bamboo spears if necessary.

These children were robbed of normal adolescence, their minds shaped by propaganda, violence, and loyalty to regimes on the brink of destruction.

Education Turned Upside Down
Schools became instruments of propaganda. In Nazi-occupied Poland, Jewish and Polish children were barred from higher education, with only rudimentary classes allowed to prepare them for menial labor. In Germany itself, the curriculum focused on racial ideology, militarism, and worship of Hitler. Teachers who disagreed were removed or worse.

- **Nazi Germany**: Math problems involved counting bombs or calculating how much money could be saved by not supporting the disabled. Biology lessons promoted eugenics.
- **Japan's Emperor Worship**: Textbooks glorified the Emperor as divine, stressing loyalty and sacrifice. Children were taught bushido values, fueling a willingness to die for the Emperor.
- **Soviet Union**: Under Stalin, schools hammered home communist ideology, denouncing "fascist beasts." Patriotic lessons justified total devotion to the Motherland, and older students joined paramilitary or pioneer organizations for "home defense."

Wherever war spread, education was co-opted to raise a generation loyal to the wartime cause. Independent thinking and creativity often died under strict ideological control.

Holocaust and Genocide Victims
No account of children in WWII is complete without acknowledging the Holocaust's targeting of Jewish children (along with Roma, disabled, and other groups). Nazi policy singled them out as having "no productive value." They were among the first to be murdered upon arrival at death camps.

- **Ghettos**: Children in ghettos like Warsaw or Łódź starved or froze in cramped, diseased conditions. Smuggling food became a key survival activity for many. Some kids were known as "bread smugglers," risking immediate execution if caught.
- **Concentration Camps**: Children who couldn't work were often sent straight to gas chambers. Those who seemed older or stronger might perform forced labor until they collapsed. Infamous SS doctors, including Josef Mengele, performed experiments on twins or other children, subjecting them to torture disguised as "research."
- **Hidden Children**: Some Jewish families entrusted children to Christian neighbors, orphanages, or convents. These hidden children often posed as Christians, learning new names and prayers. After the war, reuniting them with biological families was difficult—many parents had perished, and the children had forgotten their real identities.

Tragically, countless children vanished into mass graves, their stories known only through the testimonies of a few survivors or the diaries they left behind.

Abuse and Sexual Violence
War also exacerbated sexual violence against minors. Occupying soldiers, whether Axis or Allied, sometimes exploited vulnerable children. In the chaos of bombed-out cities, separated families, or forced labor camps, pedophiles and sexual predators found opportunities. Surviving documentation is scarce, as societies often silenced these crimes.

- **Comfort Women**: While mostly older teenagers or young adults were forced into Japanese "comfort stations," some were underage. The trauma shattered their lives, leaving survivors with deep shame and health issues.
- **Liberated Zones**: Even after Allied forces liberated territories, some troops committed sexual violence. Children were not always spared. Military justice systems occasionally prosecuted offenders, but many cases remained hidden amid the larger swirl of chaos.

These dark truths rarely appear in official histories. For child victims, the war's end did not erase their suffering; it shaped their entire future with enduring psychological wounds.

Daily Survival and Adaptation
Children proved resilient in small but significant ways. Many adapted to routines of war—dodging bombs, scavenging for food, and supporting older relatives. Sometimes they found or created fleeting moments of play amid ruins or ration lines.

- **Makeshift Toys**: In Europe, children crafted dolls from scraps of cloth or carved toy cars from wood. In Asia, they improvised games with stones or empty cans.
- **Helping Family**: They ran errands, nursed younger siblings, and learned adult chores like cooking and firewood gathering. Some joined black market activities, bartering stolen goods for rations.
- **Friendships Despite Barriers**: Occasionally, children of different ethnic or national groups played together, ignoring adult hatreds. German children in occupied France sometimes befriended local kids, sharing sweets or language lessons—though such friendships could provoke anger or suspicion on both sides.

This resilience had limits. Many children suffered nightmares, bed-wetting, or became emotionally numb—symptoms we now associate with severe trauma.

Propaganda Targeting Children
Governments recognized the power of shaping young minds. From Hitler Youth rallies to Stalinist pioneer camps, from Japanese youth brigades to American War Bond ads featuring cartoon characters, propaganda aimed to instill loyalty from a young age. Disney cartoons depicted Axis leaders as buffoonish villains, while Nazi children's books demonized Jews. In Japan, textbooks and illustrated magazines glorified kamikaze pilots as heroic role models.

Children absorbed these messages, learning to chant slogans and see the enemy as less than human. Once the war ended, some found it hard to reconcile the propaganda with the harsh realities revealed. In Germany, for instance, devoted Hitler Youth members experienced a profound crisis of identity when confronted with Nazi atrocities.

Fleeing as Refugees
Many children traversed borders as refugees. Some ended up in neutral countries like Switzerland, Sweden, or Turkey. Others ventured across oceans—the Kindertransport rescued Jewish children to Britain from Nazi territories. In Asia, families from Chinese coastal cities fled inland to Chongqing or beyond.

- **Separation Trauma**: Children struggled with unfamiliar languages, climates, and customs. They missed extended family left behind in war zones.
- **Enduring Guilt**: Survivors safe in exile often felt guilt later, learning of relatives who perished. They wrestled with the question, "Why was I saved and not them?"

- **Adjustment**: Some refugee children integrated successfully, forging new identities in adoptive countries. Others faced discrimination or returned home post-war, finding no home or family left.

Their journeys highlight the global nature of WWII, displacing families to distant lands in search of any safe haven.

Street Children and Orphans
In ravaged cities—Warsaw, Berlin, Manila, Shanghai—thousands of war orphans roamed the streets, living hand-to-mouth. Orphanages overflowed or were bombed. Child gangs formed for mutual protection and petty theft. Allied soldiers sometimes encountered ragged kids picking through rubble, offering chocolate or cigarettes to gain their trust. Charitable organizations, if present, were overwhelmed.

For these children, future prospects were bleak. Even after liberation, post-war governments struggled to reunite them with surviving relatives. Some orphans ended up in state institutions or disappeared into the black market of illegal adoptions and forced labor. The war's end did not instantly solve the problem; in Eastern Europe, Soviet authorities forcibly re-located orphans in "people's homes," shaping them into model communist youths, often ignoring their personal trauma.

Health and Malnutrition
Malnutrition stunted growth and caused diseases like rickets, scurvy, or tuberculosis. Schools that remained open had meager lunches (if any). Medical clinics often lacked medicine. In besieged cities—like Leningrad—infants were born underweight, with mothers themselves malnourished. Infant mortality soared.

Long-term studies after the war showed that children who endured severe hunger often had lifelong health issues: weaker bones, compromised immune systems, and chronic conditions. Their mental health also suffered, with higher incidences of depression, anxiety, and post-traumatic stress. Yet these findings only emerged gradually; at the time, survival overshadowed all else.

Children in Resistance Movements
Beyond formal militias, some children played key roles in resistance networks:

- **Couriers**: Young girls and boys could slip past checkpoints more easily than adults. They smuggled messages, weapons, or ration coupons.
- **Informants**: They listened unnoticed to occupation soldiers' conversations in cafes or on the street, relaying gleaned intelligence to partisan leaders.
- **Sabotage**: In some rare instances, older kids planted small bombs or cut telephone wires.

These acts of bravery came with heavy risk. The Gestapo or Kempeitai showed no leniency for "child terrorists." Many kids paid with imprisonment, torture, or death if captured. Survivors often carried a sense of pride in contributing to the war effort, mingled with grief for lost comrades.

Allied and Axis Youth in Post-War Trials
After the war, legal proceedings sometimes involved children—both as witnesses and participants. Some youth militia members faced questions: were they perpetrators or victims? The Hitler Youth, for instance, had been indoctrinated. Did that absolve them from war crimes committed in the final battles? Allied tribunals generally focused on adult leaders, sparing minors from prosecution. Still, the moral complexities ran deep.

In Soviet-occupied territories, teenagers suspected of collaboration with Germans sometimes landed in harsh re-education camps. Meanwhile, Jewish child survivors testified in trials against camp guards. Their testimonies, though important, forced them to relive traumas, further complicating their psychological recovery.

Rebuilding Childhood after 1945
With the war's end, humanitarian groups tried to restore normalcy. The United Nations Relief and Rehabilitation Administration (UNRRA), the International Red Cross, and various charities opened schools, orphanages, and counseling centers. "Displaced children" camps dotted Germany and Austria, where kids of all nationalities resided, awaiting identification or adoption.

- **Identity Confusions**: Some children had no documents, barely remembered their real names, or only spoke the language of their occupiers.
- **Adoption and Emigration**: Some families in the US, Canada, or Australia adopted war orphans, offering them a fresh start. Others remained in Europe or Asia, living in transitional homes until local governments resettled them.
- **Mixed Results**: While many found loving homes, others languished in underfunded institutions or landed in refugee limbo. Governments struggling with reconstruction had limited capacity to handle a massive influx of orphaned or homeless kids.

Legacy of War Trauma
As these children grew into adults, the experiences shaped entire generations. Many rarely spoke of their past, burying painful memories to focus on rebuilding. Others wrote memoirs, turning personal trauma into collective history. Child survivors of the Holocaust, particularly, became outspoken witnesses, ensuring the world understood the atrocity of targeting children for extermination.

Studies in the decades following WWII revealed higher incidences of psychological disorders among those who were children during the conflict, including anxiety, depression, survivor's guilt, and recurring nightmares. Societies tried to address these needs unevenly. In places like the Soviet Union, PTSD was not officially recognized, and veterans or war survivors had little psychological support. In the West, child trauma research emerged slowly, culminating in better understanding of how war disrupts development.

Children on the Home Front: The United States and Beyond
In the United States, children did not experience the direct devastations of bombings or occupation. However, many felt the war's imprint: fathers or older siblings went off to fight, rationing limited their diets, and they participated in collecting scrap metal or buying war stamps. Propaganda taught them to hate the "Japs" or "Huns." Japanese-American children, meanwhile, were interned in camps due to racist fear, losing homes and normal childhood freedoms.

In Canada, Australia, and other Allied nations, kids also joined the war effort symbolically—knitting socks for soldiers or practicing air raid drills in schools. Though spared the worst horrors of war, they grew up in a global conflict's shadow, listening to news of battles and casualties. Some would eventually volunteer as soldiers near the war's end, lying about their age or forging papers.

Stories of Hope and Solidarity
Despite the darkness, stories exist of remarkable kindness toward children. In liberated areas, Allied soldiers often brought sweets, chocolate, or chewing gum—delighting starved or traumatized youngsters. Soviet troops occasionally adopted orphaned kids they found wandering in the rubble. Catholic convents, Protestant missions, and even Buddhist temples sheltered children of all backgrounds, ignoring differences for the sake of saving young lives.

Parents, too, displayed heroic resilience—mothers crossing battle lines to find medicine for a sick child, or fathers risking arrest to gather extra rations. Child evacuees sometimes formed lifelong bonds with foster families who treated them with genuine love. These glimpses of humanity stood out in a sea of violence, suggesting that even in the darkest times, compassion for children persisted.

Representation in Post-War Culture
In the years after 1945, the experiences of wartime children began appearing in literature, film, and art:

- **Diaries and Memoirs**: Anne Frank's Diary, though incomplete, became one of the most famous accounts of a Jewish child hiding from Nazis. It symbolized the stolen innocence of so many.

- **Films**: Post-war European cinema, especially in Italy (Neorealism), depicted street children in bombed-out cities, revealing the raw heartbreak of orphanhood.
- **Books**: Works like *When Hitler Stole Pink Rabbit* by Judith Kerr described a young girl's exile from Nazi Germany, capturing the confusion and resilience of a child refugee.

These cultural reflections helped society process the war's toll on children, though it would take decades to fully acknowledge the widespread trauma.

Conclusion: A Generation Scarred Yet Resilient

Children in World War II lost more than just their homes or families—they lost the sanctuary that childhood is supposed to provide. Many were forced to grow up overnight, facing hunger, violence, or indoctrination by regimes bent on total victory. Others found hope in small kindnesses, forging bonds that transcended the adult hatreds raging around them.

As we reflect on their plight, we see that the war was not fought solely on beaches or city streets—it was also fought in classrooms, orphanages, and hidden corners where children tried to make sense of a shattered world. Their resilience remains a testament to the human spirit, even as their trauma reminds us of war's terrible power to rob the innocent of what should be a time of safety and wonder.

CHAPTER SIXTEEN

Psychological Tactics and Fear

Introduction: Waging War on the Mind
In the vast theater of World War II, physical battles were only part of the conflict. Equally important were the psychological campaigns—efforts to demoralize enemy soldiers, manipulate civilian populations, and maintain morale among one's own side. Some tactics were blunt, like public executions or terror bombings; others were subtle, like rumors, propaganda, and the careful staging of misinformation. Fear became a weapon as lethal as bullets.

This chapter digs into the psychological dimension of WWII: how governments coerced cooperation, how fear was deliberately spread to break resistance, and how entire societies were molded by deception or intimidation. Some methods were carefully orchestrated at high levels; others emerged spontaneously in the chaos of occupation. By examining these tactics, we gain insight into the intangible but powerful aspect of how wars are fought not just on battlefields, but in minds and hearts.

Terror as State Policy
Both the Axis and Allied powers used fear deliberately, though the scale and brutality varied. In Nazi-occupied Europe, the SS and Gestapo systematically employed terror to keep populations in line. Random arrests, public shootings, and collective punishment for partisan actions sent a clear message: any defiance would be met with overwhelming cruelty.

- **Hostage Executions**: In France, Belgium, and Poland, the Germans would seize hostages—often civic leaders or random civilians—and announce they'd be killed if partisans attacked. This strategy aimed to isolate resistance fighters from local support.
- **Japanese Kempeitai**: Their reputation for torture and sudden nighttime raids cowed civilians in China, Malaya, and the Philippines. People feared even minor infractions, as the Kempeitai's brutality was both well-known and unpredictable.
- **Soviet NKVD**: Behind Red Army lines, the NKVD ruthlessly dealt with any suspected collaboration or defeatism. Fear of being labeled a traitor ensured compliance with Stalin's war directives.

Through these agencies, governments turned fear into a tool of control, often more effective than armies alone.

Propaganda: Shaping Perceptions
We've touched on propaganda in previous chapters, but from a psychological standpoint,

it went beyond mere information. Propaganda sought to mold entire worldviews, to maintain loyalty and demonize the enemy.

- **Racial Propaganda**: Nazis inundated Germans with pseudo-scientific theories of Aryan supremacy, portraying Slavs, Jews, and others as threats to be eliminated. In Japan, newspapers and radio insisted the Japanese were liberating Asia from Western imperialism, even as they committed atrocities.
- **British and American Propaganda**: Emphasized freedom versus tyranny, urging citizens to endure hardships like rationing and bombing. Posters used heroic imagery: "Keep Calm and Carry On" in Britain, "We Can Do It!" in the US.
- **Soviet Propaganda**: Stalin's regime glorified the Red Army's heroic stand, ridiculing Nazi ideology. Meanwhile, the terror of purges lingered in citizens' minds, preventing open criticism.

By consistently repeating certain messages, these propaganda machines shaped the emotional and intellectual climate, making entire populations more receptive to government directives—even those that required great sacrifice.

Rumors and Disinformation

Beyond official propaganda, clandestine agencies actively spread rumors within enemy territories to sow confusion or despair. The British Political Warfare Executive (PWE) created false narratives about Hitler's failing health or internal Nazi quarrels. German intelligence tried to incite panic in Allied nations by circulating stories of unstoppable secret weapons.

- **Operation Mincemeat**: The "Man Who Never Was" hoax (previously mentioned) used a corpse with faked invasion plans to mislead the Germans about Allied landings. This type of disinformation was aimed at German high command, playing on their existing fears and assumptions.
- **Local Rumor Networks**: In occupied areas, word-of-mouth rumors spread like wildfire, especially when official news was censored. These stories could erode morale quickly, leading civilians to overestimate enemy strength or believe rescue was impossible. Occupying forces often tried to counter such rumors by punishing those who discussed them.

Rumors thrived in conditions of scarcity—when real information was lacking. Fear and uncertainty made people cling to the wildest gossip, furthering the psychological toll of war.

Symbolic Acts of Fear: Parades, Flags, and Uniforms

Armies and regimes understood the visual power of ceremonies, uniforms, and symbols. A swastika-draped building, a row of goose-stepping SS soldiers, or an imposing banner in a city square—all served to project power and instill awe or dread.

- **Nazi Spectacles**: The Nuremberg Rallies before the war were prime examples, forging a sense of unstoppable unity. During occupation, Hitler's face on every poster, paired with the black-and-red swastika, reminded locals who was in control.
- **Soviet Counter-Imagery**: The Red Army's bold insignia and monumental statues of Stalin or Lenin symbolized communist might, intimidating locals in newly "liberated" areas. Some saw them not as liberators but as a new brand of overlord.
- **Japanese Surrender Ceremonies**: The flamboyant show of force by the Allies in Tokyo Bay or recaptured territories symbolized a complete psychological break for defeated Japanese troops, who had been told never to surrender.

Uniforms, parades, and iconography often replaced reason or debate. They hammered home a message of invincibility, compelling observers to capitulate mentally before any shot was fired.

Axis Fear Tactics on the Home Front
Controlling one's own population was equally crucial. In Germany, the Gestapo and SS enforced loyalty through networks of informants. Families feared a neighbor might report them for defeatist talk. Public morale had to remain high, or Hitler's regime might lose control.

- **Nazi Courts**: People accused of criticizing the Führer or the war effort were tried before special courts. Sentences included execution or confinement in concentration camps.
- **Homefront Bombing Propaganda**: As Allied raids increased, Goebbels hammered out messages of defiance, urging civilians to remain loyal. Still, the underlying fear that any sign of dissent might lead to arrest kept most Germans outwardly compliant.

In Japan, the Kempeitai policed civilian life. Voices questioning the war risked imprisonment or torture. Students were taught absolute obedience; mothers who lost sons at the front were expected to display stoic pride rather than grief. This emotional repression underscored how deeply fear penetrated daily life.

Allied Fear Tactics: Strategic Bombing and Leaflet Drops
While Nazi terror overshadowed many war crimes, the Allies also used fear. The strategic bombing of German and Japanese cities was partly intended to break civilian morale, forcing the population to pressure their governments into surrender.

- **Area Bombing**: RAF Bomber Command targeted urban centers like Hamburg or Dresden with incendiaries, knowing they'd cause firestorms. The shock and horror might push Germany toward collapse.

- **Leaflet Campaigns**: Before major bombing raids, Allied planes sometimes dropped leaflets warning civilians to evacuate. While seemingly humanitarian, these pamphlets also aimed to spread panic and chaos, burdening German authorities with fleeing refugees.
- **Japan's Civilian Psyche**: US B-29 firebombings inflicted mass terror, culminating in the atomic bombings. Fear of an endless American onslaught contributed to Japan's eventual decision to surrender.

Though Allies justified these tactics as necessary to shorten the war, the line between targeting military infrastructure and terrorizing civilians blurred significantly.

Occupation Fear and Collaboration

Under occupation, fear often birthed collaboration. Local officials or police joined the new regime to spare themselves or their families. Ordinary citizens avoided involvement in resistance, dreading savage reprisals. The occupiers leveraged this psychology:

- **Divide and Rule**: Encouraging ethnic tensions, they rewarded one group with privileges and used them to control others. In Eastern Europe, some local militias sided with the Nazis to eliminate rival groups, often out of fear that not collaborating spelled doom.
- **Public Trials and Executions**: Occupation authorities staged show trials of alleged partisans or spies, parading them before condemning them to death. This demonstration hammered home the lethal cost of resistance.
- **Civilian Hostages**: Taking hostages to guarantee local compliance was a classic method. The threat of these hostages being executed spread paralyzing fear, limiting sabotage or aid to partisans.

Collaboration did not always mean genuine sympathy for the occupier's cause. Often, it was a survival mechanism born from terror, suspicion, and the need to protect loved ones in a world with no mercy.

POW Camps: Breaking the Will to Resist

As described in previous chapters, prisoners of war were subjected to fear-based discipline. Japanese guards in the Pacific used beatings and executions to stifle any thought of escape. In Nazi camps, intimidation was equally ruthless. Starvation, forced labor, and random cruelty reinforced a sense that resistance was futile.

- **Torture Tactics**: For suspected escape organizers, the SS or Kempeitai inflicted brutal torture. Public beatings or hangings made examples of them, quelling rebellious spirits among POWs.
- **Propaganda in Camps**: Some POWs were shown films or given leaflets claiming their homeland was bombed into ruin. The goal was to demoralize them or coax them into collaboration (like working on propaganda broadcasts).

- **Psychological Warfare**: Even small acts—like playing sad music on camp loudspeakers—reminded prisoners of their helplessness. Guards might spread false rumors about incoming mass executions to keep inmates subservient.

Fear pervaded every corner of prison life, a constant, suffocating presence that few could escape mentally.

Racial Hatreds and Dehumanization

A significant pillar of WWII psychological tactics was dehumanizing the enemy. Germans called Slavs "Untermenschen," while Americans circulated caricatures of buck-toothed, bestial "Japs." Soviets railed against "Fascist beasts." This language eroded empathy, facilitating atrocities because soldiers and civilians felt their victims were subhuman.

- **Army Training Manuals**: Some US training materials depicted Japanese as cunning, treacherous. German manuals mocked Soviet backwardness, portraying them as hordes lacking culture.
- **Genocidal Ideologies**: Dehumanization underpinned the Holocaust. By labeling Jews or Roma as "vermin," the Nazi regime lowered moral barriers to mass murder.
- **"Kill or Be Killed" Mindset**: In the Pacific, after hearing stories of Japanese brutality, many Allied soldiers concluded that mercy was dangerous. This spiraled into mutual savagery, fueling cycles of revenge.

Such language and imagery hammered fear into the hearts of soldiers—fear that the enemy was less than human, unstoppable unless destroyed entirely.

Child Indoctrination and Fear-Based Education

As seen with the Hitler Youth, Soviet Pioneers, or Japanese school militarization, children were molded from an early age to fear the enemy and revere the state. Teaching methods included:

- **Nightmarish Depictions of the Foe**: Stories of monstrous Allied or Axis soldiers raping, torturing, or killing. Pupils were taught that surrender to such monsters meant death or worse.
- **Peer Pressure**: Children who showed reluctance faced bullying or official punishment. Fear of ostracism kept them aligned with the party line.
- **Patriotic Martyrs**: The glorification of child heroes who died for the cause instilled both admiration and fear—admiration for their bravery, fear that failing to emulate them meant being labeled a coward.

This next generation grew up in an environment where fear and hatred were normal emotions toward distant or local enemies.

Countering Fear: Morale Building

Despite widespread use of fear, each side also recognized morale's importance. Allies and Axis alike tried to bolster their populations with uplifting messages, communal events, or comedic relief.

- **Entertainment Propaganda**: Radio comedies, musicals, or variety shows kept spirits up during bombings. British dance halls stayed open, encouraging people to "keep dancing" as an act of defiance.
- **Victory Myth**: Both Hitler and Churchill spoke confidently of inevitable victory, even in dire times. Stalin insisted the Soviet Union would triumph. These reassurances offered hope amid the gloom.
- **Spiritual Support**: In many countries, religious leaders urged congregants not to lose faith. Services sometimes acted as emotional relief from the daily stress of war.

Morale and fear existed in tension. Rulers tried to strike a balance, keeping citizens frightened enough to obey but hopeful enough to keep working or fighting until victory.

Resistance to Psychological Control

For all these tactics, not everyone bowed to fear. Resistance movements thrived, even under the harshest occupations. People found ways to maintain dignity, from clandestine newspapers to secret religious gatherings. The knowledge that entire communities opposed the occupier offered psychological support.

- **Humor and Satire**: Underground jokes mocked Nazi pompousness or collaborator buffoonery. Laughter proved an act of rebellion, chipping away at fear's grip.
- **Civil Disobedience**: In places like Denmark, some citizens sheltered Jews despite threats of execution. They refused to let fear dictate moral choices.
- **Internal Dissidents**: Within Germany and Japan, a minority opposed the regimes from within, often at great personal risk. The White Rose movement of student activists in Munich, for example, distributed anti-Nazi leaflets. They were executed, but their courage inspired others.

Such acts remind us that the human spirit can resist even overwhelming psychological pressure, though it often came at a high cost.

Psychological Warfare on the Front Lines

On the battlefield, psychological operations (PsyOps) targeted opposing troops. Loudspeakers blared messages urging surrender; artillery bombardments were timed to disrupt enemy sleep. Some Allied units used "ghost armies" of fake tanks or playback of recorded engine noises to create illusions of larger forces.

- **Surrender Leaflets**: Dropped behind lines, these offered safe passage to POW camps if soldiers deserted. Some included explicit instructions on how to approach Allied lines, hoping to reduce enemy will to fight.
- **Fear of Encirclement**: Generals exploited the threat of encirclement to induce mass surrenders. When rumors spread that a unit was surrounded, morale could collapse.

On the Eastern Front, the Red Army sometimes broadcast messages at night, reminding Axis troops of harsh winter conditions and the impossibility of rescue. The psychological strain often led to entire units giving up, too exhausted and terrified to continue.

Occupier vs. Occupied: Day-to-Day Intimidation

For civilians, fear was not merely about large-scale atrocities but also daily interactions with occupiers. A wrong word in a market queue might invite a beating, a gesture of disrespect might spark rage from an armed soldier. The unpredictability of violence created a pervasive sense of vulnerability.

- **Curfews**: People dreaded nighttime. Anyone found outside could be shot on sight.
- **Knock on the Door**: Occupation police or Gestapo raids at dawn were nightmares come to life. Families huddled in corners, praying they wouldn't be taken.
- **Identity Papers**: Constant checks. If your papers were missing, forged, or suspicious, you risked arrest. This forced many to live under false identities, a source of constant tension.

Even mundane errands could be fraught with terror, as no one knew when a soldier might lash out or a bomb might fall.

War Crimes Trials and the Denial of Fear
After the war, some Nazi or Japanese defendants claimed ignorance or insisted they merely "followed orders." Fear was thus invoked as justification—they complied or risked punishment. Allied tribunals largely rejected this defense, emphasizing individual responsibility.

However, the environment of fear shaped entire societies. Many who participated in atrocities were not natural sadists but ordinary people pressured by propaganda, intimidation, or a desire to survive. This does not absolve them, but it illustrates how fear can erode moral compasses on a massive scale. In the post-war years, some nations confronted their complicity; others buried it. The fear-driven decisions of the war's darkest days left deep moral quandaries that endured for generations.

Psychiatric Insights Post-War
Research in subsequent decades delved into how terror-based systems manipulate behavior. WWII provided a grim laboratory. Psychologists examining Holocaust perpetrators (like SS officers) or Japanese guards discovered how social pressure, dehumanizing rhetoric, and fear for one's own safety could lead to compliance in horrific acts. The concept of "groupthink" and "obedience to authority" gained traction, famously studied by social psychologists like Stanley Milgram (though his experiments occurred later).

Returning soldiers suffered "battle fatigue," what we now recognize as PTSD. Civilians also displayed psychological trauma—insomnia, anxiety, and hypervigilance triggered by memories of sirens or gunfire. Fear lingered well after the conflict ended.

Legacy of WWII Psychological Tactics
The war's psychological dimension set precedents for the future. Propaganda, mass indoctrination, and terror as policy continued into the Cold War, where both sides used fear (of nuclear annihilation, of communist infiltration, of capitalist subversion) to maintain control. Many WWII survivors carried on the lessons, either adopting a "never again" stance or, in some cases, employing similar methods in post-war conflicts.

Intelligence agencies refined disinformation and clandestine manipulation. The moral line between legitimate propaganda and unethical psychological warfare remained blurry. As a result, the use of fear as a political tool did not end with WWII, a sobering testament to how deeply war-time innovations in control and manipulation can embed themselves in society.

Hope as a Counterweight

Despite oppressive fear, hope remained a powerful counterforce. Resistance movements, Allied support, and small acts of humanity kept alive the belief that tyranny would not last forever. Even in concentration camps, secret gatherings, music, or religious ceremonies gave inmates psychological sustenance.

- **Spiritual Strength**: Many turned to faith or moral convictions, refusing to internalize the occupier's message of hopelessness.
- **Allied Victories**: As news (often from underground radios) spread of the Axis losing key battles—Stalingrad, El Alamein, Midway—occupied peoples found renewed courage to resist.
- **War's End**: The moment Allied or Soviet troops rolled into towns often triggered euphoric release—tears, shouts of joy, a physical and emotional relief from years of pent-up fear.

That surge of hope overshadowed fear in the final months, though the war's psychological scars would not vanish overnight.

CHAPTER SEVENTEEN

The Tide Turns – Brutal Retaliations

Introduction: The Shift in Momentum
By late 1942 and early 1943, the seemingly unstoppable Axis war machine began to show cracks. Germany's "lightning" successes in Europe and North Africa stalled. Japan's rapid conquests in the Pacific slowed under the combined pressure of Allied air, land, and sea power. The Allies—bolstered by American industrial might, Soviet manpower, and British resilience—started to push back. Victory was far from certain, but the tide was turning.

However, shifting tides did not mean a smooth or merciful resolution. As Axis forces retreated, they often resorted to scorched-earth tactics, destroying everything behind them. In response, partisans and Allied troops unleashed their own forms of vengeance. Civilians bore the brunt of it all, caught in the crossfire or singled out for collective punishment. In this chapter, we see how the war's momentum reversed, leading to a wave of brutal retaliations across multiple fronts. The human cost soared as both armies and resistance groups sought payback for years of oppression and atrocities.

Stalingrad: The Great Turning Point
Among the pivotal events marking the Axis's decline, the **Battle of Stalingrad** (August 1942–February 1943) stands out. The German Sixth Army, under General Friedrich Paulus, pushed deep into the Soviet city on the Volga River, expecting a swift victory. Hitler saw Stalingrad as symbolically important—named after Stalin—and also strategically vital for controlling Soviet oil routes and the Caucasus.

- **Urban Hell**: Street-by-street fighting raged in rubble-strewn districts, with snipers, flamethrowers, and countless ambushes. Civilians hid in basements. Each building changed hands multiple times, leaving corpses everywhere.
- **Soviet Counteroffensive**: In November 1942, Marshal Zhukov's forces launched Operation Uranus, encircling the German Sixth Army. Caught in a freezing cauldron, lacking supplies, the Germans starved and froze as Soviet artillery pounded them.
- **Surrender and Horror**: Despite Hitler's orders to fight to the last man, Paulus surrendered in February 1943. Of some 250,000 Axis troops trapped, only a fraction survived captivity. The Soviets paraded thousands of emaciated POWs through Moscow as living proof of Nazi failure.

Stalingrad shattered the myth of German invincibility. The psychological blow to the Wehrmacht was enormous, emboldening Soviet forces to press westward. It also triggered brutal reprisals: as the Red Army reclaimed villages, they discovered mass graves and scorched-earth devastation, fueling a desire for vengeance that would shape the war's later stages.

Turning Points Elsewhere: El Alamein and Midway
While Stalingrad raged, other fronts saw similar Axis setbacks:

- **North Africa**: At the **Second Battle of El Alamein** (October–November 1942), British General Montgomery halted Erwin Rommel's Afrika Korps and began driving it back across Libya. Deprived of supplies and hammered by Allied air power, the once-feared "Desert Fox" had no choice but to retreat. By May 1943, Axis forces in North Africa capitulated, opening the door for an Allied invasion of southern Europe.
- **Pacific Theater**: The **Battle of Midway** (June 1942) crippled Japanese naval aviation, and the **Guadalcanal Campaign** (August 1942–February 1943) ended in a costly Japanese withdrawal. The Allies seized the initiative, shifting to offensive "island hopping." Japan's hopes for a swift knockout blow against the US fizzled, replaced by a desperate defensive stance.

These turning points were not mere military maneuvers; they signaled a global shift. The Axis, though still dangerous, was on the defensive. Allied morale soared. But as Axis troops pulled back, they often exacted brutal tolls on civilians, determined to leave nothing for the advancing enemy.

Brutality on the Eastern Front: Scorched Earth Revisited
Nowhere was retaliation more vicious than on the Eastern Front. After Stalingrad, the Red Army advanced, recapturing territories that had endured Nazi occupation for over a year. The Soviets discovered entire towns razed, with survivors recounting executions, forced labor, and mass graves.

- **German Retreat**: The Wehrmacht torched farms, blew up bridges, and destroyed factories to slow the Soviet tide. Villages were burned to deny shelter. Thousands of slave laborers, including Soviet POWs, were herded toward Germany or executed if they couldn't march fast enough.
- **Partisan Vengeance**: Soviet partisans emerged from forests to strike retreating Axis columns. In some areas, partisans executed local collaborators—sometimes after hasty "trials." This could include families accused of betraying neighbors to the Germans.
- **Soviet Reprisal Killings**: The Red Army itself sometimes shot or hung captured SS officers or known pro-German officials. Stalin's orders allowed little mercy, especially for units that had committed atrocities against Soviet citizens.

As Soviet forces pushed the front beyond their own borders and into Eastern Europe, the cycle of brutality continued, with retribution fueling each new wave of violence. Civilians in regions like Ukraine and Belarus often found themselves hammered first by German scorched earth, then by Soviet revenge tactics.

Occupation Collapses in the Balkans

In the Balkans, Axis forces struggled with rampant partisan movements. Yugoslavia was especially divided: Communist partisans under Josip Broz Tito clashed with Chetnik forces, both opposing German and Italian occupation. By 1943, with Italy's capitulation, the region descended into chaos:

- **Italian Collapse**: After Mussolini was deposed in July 1943, the new Italian government sought an armistice with the Allies. German troops swiftly occupied former Italian zones, disarming or executing confused Italian units. Yugoslav partisans exploited this power vacuum to seize territory.
- **German Retaliation**: Retreating Germans carried out mass reprisals, burning villages that harbored partisans. Civilians caught with partisan propaganda were shot. Meanwhile, local ethnic feuds flared—Croats, Serbs, and Bosnians took the chance to settle old scores, sometimes with the backing of Axis or Allied arms.
- **Tito's Offensive**: By 1944, Tito's partisans had effectively liberated swaths of Yugoslavia. When they overran towns that had supported the Axis puppet regimes, they executed collaborators. Some entire families were labeled "traitors," culminating in summary killings.

The Balkans became a tapestry of revenge, fueled by years of harsh occupation and deep-rooted ethnic hatreds. As the Axis retreated north, each side unleashed brutal vendettas, turning the region into one of Europe's bloodiest theaters of local civil conflict wrapped within the broader war.

Italy's Long Surrender and Civil War

After Mussolini's fall and Italy's armistice (September 1943), German forces occupied much of the country, freeing Mussolini to lead a puppet Fascist regime in the north (the Italian Social Republic). This led to a civil war between Italian partisans (backed by the Allies) and the remaining fascists alongside German troops.

- **German Tactics**: The Wehrmacht treated Italy as a betrayal. Units like the SS Panzer Division Leibstandarte Adolf Hitler repressed local populations with ruthless force. Towns suspected of aiding partisans were subjected to mass shootings and burnings.
- **Partisan Warfare**: Italian partisans sabotaged rail lines, staged ambushes, and helped Allied landings. Retaliations from German and fascist forces were swift: entire communities were shot or deported. The **Ardeatine Caves Massacre** in Rome (March 1944) saw 335 Italians executed in reprisal for a partisan attack.
- **Allied Advance**: The Allies slogged up the Italian peninsula through Monte Cassino and the Gothic Line. Civilians, caught between German fortifications and Allied bombing, suffered. Meanwhile, partisans who captured fascists often conducted summary executions, driven by anger at years of oppression.

By 1945, northern Italy was a patchwork of liberated towns and fascist holdouts. When final collapse came in April, Mussolini was captured by partisans and executed. His body was hung in a Milan square, a macabre display of triumphant revenge.

The Western Front: Normandy and Beyond
In June 1944, the Allies launched **Operation Overlord**, storming Normandy's beaches. Though the Germans resisted fiercely, Allied forces broke out and liberated Paris by late August. As they swept through France, local resistance groups emerged from hiding, seizing the moment to settle scores with collaborators.

- **Purge of Collaborators**: Known as the "Épuration," France witnessed mob justice. Women accused of sleeping with German soldiers (sometimes out of coercion or for survival) were publicly humiliated, their heads shaved. Officials who served the Vichy regime were arrested or executed, occasionally without fair trials.
- **Fighting in Belgium and the Netherlands**: Retreating Germans unleashed punishments on civilians suspected of aiding Allied paratroopers. In the Netherlands, the failed Operation Market Garden (September 1944) led to German retaliation and the Hunger Winter. Some Dutch collaborators were executed post-liberation, while others faced imprisonment.
- **Destruction of German Towns**: As the Allies pressed into Germany itself, the US and British air forces continued massive bombing. German towns and cities turned into rubble, with civilians caught in the crossfire. Some Allied units, angered by the Battle of the Bulge's brutality, took fewer prisoners, especially SS troops known for atrocities.

The Western Front's final months saw waves of euphoria in liberated areas, but also unleashed vigilante actions. Years of pent-up rage exploded against real or alleged collaborators, sometimes in savage, disorganized retribution.

Operation Bagration: Soviet Steamroller in the East

While D-Day garnered headlines in the West, the **Red Army's Operation Bagration** (June–August 1944) was arguably the war's most devastating offensive. Attacking the German Army Group Center in Belarus, Soviet forces encircled and destroyed entire divisions. The scale of German losses dwarfed those in Normandy.

- **Liberation and Retaliation**: As Soviet troops reclaimed Belarusian towns, they discovered ruins—villages turned to ash, with only blackened chimneys standing. Locals told of Nazi massacres. Soviet soldiers responded harshly. Captured Germans or local collaborators were often shot on the spot.
- **Poland's Ordeal**: Crossing into eastern Poland, Soviet armies encountered remnants of the Jewish ghettos, forced labor camps, and sites of mass executions. Again, the desire for vengeance was immense. At the same time, the Polish Home Army tried to assert independence, leading to tensions with Soviet command—who sometimes arrested or disarmed Polish partisans opposed to communist influence.

Operation Bagration hammered the German Eastern Front so thoroughly that the path to Berlin was laid open. But in each liberated zone, bloodshed continued, with civilians suffering from both Nazi retreats and Soviet reprisals.

Warsaw Uprising and Betrayal

A tragic highlight in the push west was the **Warsaw Uprising** (August–October 1944). Polish resistance forces, hoping to liberate their capital before Soviet arrival, fought fiercely against well-armed German garrisons. Initially successful in seizing parts of the city, the insurgents pleaded for Soviet assistance. But Stalin, wary of supporting a non-communist Polish underground, halted his armies on the Vistula River's far bank.

- **German Retaliation**: Under SS General Erich von dem Bach-Zelewski, German troops, including Dirlewanger's notorious penal brigade, unleashed savage counterattacks. Entire districts, such as Wola, saw mass executions. Tens of thousands of civilians were shot, hospitals burned with patients inside.
- **Abandoned by Allies**: Airdrops from the British and Americans fell short of sustaining the uprising. The Soviets refused to grant Allied planes landing rights, crippling supply efforts. After 63 days, the Home Army capitulated.
- **Aftermath**: Hitler ordered Warsaw systematically destroyed. Almost 85% of the city's buildings were leveled. Survivors were deported. The uprising's failure remains a symbol of Allied-Soviet mistrust and a prime example of the brutal retaliations that accompanied the war's final chapter.

Bombing of German Cities: A Desperate Defense

As the Allies advanced from the west and Soviets from the east, the Third Reich reeled under relentless bombing. Cities like Hamburg, Berlin, and Dresden faced repeated raids. Dresden, a cultural center with limited military value, was firebombed in February 1945, leaving tens of thousands dead in a firestorm. This raid spurred controversy among Allied leaders themselves, questioning if such terror bombing was necessary so late in the war.

- **Nazi Propaganda**: Goebbels used bombed-out cities to stoke hatred, insisting the Allies aimed to exterminate Germans. He pressed for total war, urging civilians to fight on.
- **Volkssturm**: Hitler mobilized teenagers and old men into a last-ditch militia, handing them Panzerfausts and outdated rifles. Fear of Allied occupation spurred many to keep fighting, especially on the Eastern Front, where tales of Soviet vengeance spread.
- **Disintegration of Morale**: Despite propaganda, many Germans realized the war was lost. Desperate attempts to hold Berlin at all costs led to a climate of mass paranoia: desertion was punishable by death, and roving SS squads hanged suspected defeatists from lampposts.

This final descent into madness underlined how total war could devour a society. As bombs fell, the regime clung to illusions, dragging civilians into deeper ruin.

Allied Advances in the Pacific: The Philippines and Beyond

While Europe convulsed in 1944–45, the Pacific war also saw momentum shift decisively to the Allies. American forces recaptured the Philippines (October 1944–August 1945). Japanese troops, low on supplies, vented frustration on civilians.

- **Manila Massacre**: In February–March 1945, cornered Japanese marines committed mass killings of Filipino civilians. Hospitals, schools, churches—none were spared. Over 100,000 died. The city was left in ruins.
- **Kampeitai Brutality**: As the Allies liberated Southeast Asia, they uncovered POW camps and comfort stations. Local populations, forced into labor or starved, turned on Japanese collaborators with lethal vengeance.
- **Iwo Jima and Okinawa**: US Marines faced fanatical Japanese resistance on these islands (February–March 1945 for Iwo Jima, April–June 1945 for Okinawa). Japanese propaganda told civilians the Americans were monsters, leading some to commit suicide en masse. The fierce Japanese stand inflicted enormous casualties, foreshadowing how an invasion of the home islands might cost millions more lives.

Japan's leadership, though aware of their dire position, refused to surrender, prompting more destructive battles. The stage was set for the war's final, terrifying acts.

Civilian Revenge in Occupied Asia
As Allied forces ousted the Japanese from places like Burma, Malaya, and parts of China, local partisans or militias took revenge. Villages that had collaborated were attacked; families of pro-Japanese policemen were slaughtered. This pattern echoed the European experience:

- **Chinese Reprisals**: In recaptured regions of China, those who served in Japanese puppet governments were publicly denounced. Some faced "people's trials" leading to executions. The Chinese Nationalist and Communist factions each tried to assert authority, occasionally using the excuse of collaboration to eliminate political rivals.
- **Singapore and Hong Kong**: Locals targeted individuals who had worked with the Japanese administration. British authorities, upon returning, had to restrain mobs from lynching suspected collaborators.
- **Korea**: Under Japan's rule since 1910, Korea endured forced assimilation and labor conscription. As Japanese control collapsed in 1945, anti-Japanese sentiment exploded. Some Koreans attacked Japanese settlers or police, forcing a chaotic exodus.

In each region, the flames of vengeance burned hot. Years of oppression had built up a reservoir of anger that was released violently once the occupying power lost its grip.

Collapse of Fascist Hungary and Romania
In Eastern Europe, Germany's Axis allies, like Hungary and Romania, faced internal and external pressures as Soviet armies loomed. Romania switched sides in August 1944 after a coup deposed pro-German leader Antonescu. Hungary resisted but was occupied by Germany in March 1944, then ravaged by the Soviet advance.

- **Budapest Siege**: From December 1944 to February 1945, the Red Army encircled Budapest. Hungarian and German troops fought desperately, inflicting horrors on civilians. Jews were rounded up by the Hungarian Arrow Cross fascists, shot along the Danube. After the city fell, Soviet soldiers unleashed their own wave of rapes and lootings.
- **Romanian Retaliations**: After Romania joined the Allies, newly emboldened forces clamped down on pro-fascist elements. Political purges erupted, with some Arrow Cross or Iron Guard members executed without trial.

The interplay of shifting alliances and Soviet occupation created a chaotic environment, where old loyalties meant death sentences, and revenge overshadowed any attempt at orderly justice.

Retreating SS Units and Last Stand Brutality
As the Red Army neared Germany's borders, SS units tried to wipe out evidence of

concentration camps, forcing death marches. Prisoners too weak to walk were shot. Scenes of horror unfolded across Poland, Silesia, and eventually the heartland of the Reich.

- **Death Marches**: Camp guards evacuated inmates westward, hoping to keep them from liberation. Thousands died of exposure, hunger, or execution en route.
- **Abandoned Camps**: Allied soldiers found camps half-empty or hurriedly abandoned. The SS burned records and tried to blow up gas chambers. Still, the piles of corpses and skeletal survivors testified to the scale of genocide.
- **Civilian Vigilantes**: Some local populations attacked fleeing SS men. In a few cases, Polish or Czech villagers lynched captured guards. The thirst for retribution after witnessing mass murder was enormous, leading to unrestrained acts of violence.

This final phase of Nazi brutality, combined with local revenge, produced a swirl of horror that epitomized the war's last months on the Eastern Front.

Mounting Atrocities in Germany Itself
By early 1945, Soviet forces crossed the Oder River, just 60 miles from Berlin. Reports of Soviet mass rapes and pillaging in East Prussia, Pomerania, and Silesia fueled a huge refugee crisis. Millions of German civilians fled west, often strafed by Allied planes or attacked by partisans. Scenes of columns of refugees clogging frozen roads became common.

- **Hitler's Orders**: He declared "no retreat," demanding total defense of every German town. Nazi officials who advocated evacuation risked execution for defeatism.
- **Werewolf Plan**: A last-ditch Nazi idea to leave clandestine operatives behind Allied lines. Though mostly ineffective, rumors about "Werewolves" stoked Allied fears.
- **Civilian Suffering**: Many Germans were now on the receiving end of war's devastation—bombs, artillery, hunger, and the terrifying approach of Soviet tanks. The war's "chickens came home to roost," as once-occupied nations took revenge on German soil.

Allied Moral Quandaries
As evidence of Nazi and Japanese atrocities mounted, some Allied soldiers and commanders believed harsh retaliation was justified. Others argued for adhering to the Geneva Conventions, worried that succumbing to vengeance would tarnish Allied ideals. Still, in the heat of battles or after liberating death camps, some Allied troops lost restraint.

- **American and British Troops**: Instances occurred where Allied soldiers killed surrendering SS or Gestapo men. Observers reported that GIs, upon finding murdered POWs or camp inmates, sometimes shot captured Germans out of rage. Such incidents were not official policy, but anger and exhaustion made them more frequent.
- **Soviet High Command**: Stalin's regime largely condoned pillaging and rapes in Germany as a form of retribution for the USSR's suffering. Though some Soviet officers tried to discipline looters, large-scale atrocities still happened, particularly in the first weeks of occupation.

This moral gray zone underscored the difficulty of maintaining discipline and justice in a war so deeply stained with hatred and revenge.

Civil Wars Hidden in the Wider Conflict
World War II also served as a cover for local civil wars. The Greek Civil War flared after the German withdrawal, pitting communist partisans against monarchist forces. In Yugoslavia, Tito's communists vied with royalist Chetniks, culminating in brutal retributions. In Italy, after the fascist regime collapsed, ideological battles erupted between leftist partisans and conservative groups.

- **Executions and Purges**: These conflicts went beyond fighting foreign occupiers, as Italians killed Italians, Greeks killed Greeks, etc., with each side punishing collaborators or ideological opponents.
- **Foreign Influence**: The Allies or Soviets supported factions aligned with their post-war visions, intensifying local disputes. Many of these "internal wars" spilled over into the post-war era, fueling further violence.
- **Civilians Again Caught**: Villages torn by loyalty to different factions faced repeated occupations or forced conscriptions. Betrayals led to cycles of vendettas, overshadowed by the major Allied vs. Axis narrative but just as brutal for those on the ground.

Japan's Desperate Measures: Kamikazes and More
On the Pacific side, 1944–45 saw Japan throw everything into last-stand tactics, including **kamikaze** missions. Thousands of Japanese pilots deliberately crashed planes into Allied ships, a suicidal strategy that both terrified and baffled the Americans.

- **Impact on Morale**: Allied sailors dreaded kamikaze attacks, which could come swiftly and with no regard for pilot survival. But the toll on Japanese youth was devastating—green pilots sacrificed en masse.
- **Civilian Militias**: Japanese propaganda told civilians to fight invading Americans with bamboo spears. Schoolchildren practiced bayonet drills on straw dummies. Fear of savage Allied retribution, fueled by stories of Japanese brutalities, drove many to prefer suicide over capture.

- **Retaliations by Allied Troops**: After bitter fights on Iwo Jima and Okinawa, some US troops saw Japanese soldiers as fanatics unworthy of mercy. Incidents of battlefield executions or the refusal to accept surrenders multiplied.

The Pacific war thus intensified into a clash of unwavering wills, with brutalities on both sides. Japan's refusal to concede ensured the eventual endgame would be catastrophic.

Mounting Civilian Death Tolls
All these retaliations, scorched-earth withdrawals, and final stands contributed to a staggering civilian death toll. Historians estimate tens of millions of non-combatants died in WWII. This included genocide victims, forced laborers, bombing casualties, famine victims, and those caught in vengeful retributions.

Even as the war neared its conclusion, no end to the suffering was in sight. In newly liberated cities, basic services were destroyed. Disease spread among displaced populations. Refugee camps teemed with traumatized survivors. The Allies struggled to feed these masses while continuing the fight. Meanwhile, hatred brewed in the hearts of those who had lived under brutal occupation, fueling cycles of payback that often went unchecked.

CHAPTER EIGHTEEN

The Final Thunder – Endgame Horrors

Introduction: The Gathering Storm of 1945
By the dawn of 1945, the Axis powers stood on the brink of defeat, yet they still fought with desperation that made the last months of World War II among its most violent. Hitler hunkered in his Berlin bunker, prophesying that new miracle weapons would save the Reich. In Japan, Emperor Hirohito's government told civilians to defend the home islands to the death. Meanwhile, Allied forces closed in—determined to finish the job.

This chapter charts the war's culminating events: the Battle of the Bulge in Western Europe, the Soviet onslaught toward Berlin, the final stand of Japanese forces in the Pacific, and ultimately the nuclear strikes that forced Japan's surrender. The tension and dread mounted, and with them came atrocities, mass displacements, and the horrifying unveiling of humanity's capacity for destruction. The war's end was near, but it arrived with thunderous brutality, leaving behind ruins and ghosts that would haunt the post-war world.

The Battle of the Bulge: Germany's Last Gamble
In December 1944, the Germans launched a surprise counteroffensive in the Ardennes region of Belgium and Luxembourg, hoping to split the Allied lines and capture Antwerp. This became the **Battle of the Bulge**—Hitler's final major offensive in the West.

- **Initial German Success**: Poor weather grounded Allied aircraft, allowing German panzer divisions to punch through thinly spread American lines. Panicked Allied troops retreated, creating a large "bulge" in the front.
- **Bastogne and Siege**: The 101st Airborne Division found itself surrounded in Bastogne, refusing German surrender demands. General McAuliffe's famous reply—"Nuts!"—became a morale-boosting symbol.
- **Allied Counterattack**: Once the weather cleared, Allied airpower decimated German supply lines. Patton's Third Army relieved Bastogne. Germany's fuel shortages and exhausted manpower spelled doom for the offensive.

The Allies recovered in January 1945, pushing the Germans back. American forces discovered massacres of POWs, such as at Malmedy, where SS troops shot surrendering US soldiers. Such incidents fueled Allied rage, leading some GIs to retaliate by shooting captured SS men. Though the Bulge delayed the Allied advance, it also drained the last reserves of German strength in the west.

Crossing the Rhine and Entering Germany
With the Bulge repulsed, Allied armies surged toward the Rhine River. By March 1945,

they seized key crossings, including the Ludendorff Bridge at Remagen, unexpectedly intact. German attempts to blow it failed, giving the Allies a crucial bridgehead.

- **Resistance Crumbles**: German defenders, including Volkssturm and Hitler Youth, fought with fanaticism but lacked heavy equipment. Allied armor and overwhelming air superiority shattered any organized resistance.
- **Discovery of Camps**: As Americans and British units advanced, they stumbled upon concentration camps like Buchenwald, Bergen-Belsen, and Dachau. The sight of skeletal inmates and piles of corpses shocked even battle-hardened soldiers. Anger skyrocketed, and some soldiers executed captured camp guards on the spot.
- **Bombing Continues**: Despite Germany's imminent collapse, Allied bombers hammered cities like Würzburg and Pforzheim, unleashing devastating firestorms. The logic was to hasten surrender, though critics questioned the necessity of such total destruction.

Civilian misery in western Germany was profound—bombed-out towns, refugees fleeing the eastern front, and collapsing infrastructure spelled chaos. Nonetheless, Nazi propaganda insisted the Allies would enslave or slaughter Germans, pushing many to cling to Hitler's orders for total resistance.

Soviet Juggernaut: Vistula-Oder to Berlin
On the Eastern Front, the Soviets launched the **Vistula-Oder Offensive** in January 1945, smashing German defenses in Poland and driving swiftly west. By mid-February, Soviet forces stood at the Oder River, less than an hour's drive from Berlin.

- **Liberation of Auschwitz**: The Red Army liberated Auschwitz on January 27, 1945, exposing the world to the full horror of extermination camps. The few survivors told of gas chambers, forced labor, and mass executions. Evidence of the Holocaust was undeniable, fueling Soviet anger even more.
- **Prague, Budapest, and Vienna**: Major cities fell under Soviet control, often after fierce battles in the streets. Budapest's siege inflicted catastrophic damage. Vienna, declared a "city of culture," saw brutal fighting as well. The Soviets targeted symbolic hearts of German influence, determined to avenge years of Nazi terror.
- **Rape and Pillage**: As the Red Army advanced, numerous reports emerged of mass rapes and looting in East Prussia, Pomerania, Silesia, and eventually Berlin. Though Soviet command discouraged such actions officially, discipline broke down in many units. German civilians, especially women, lived in terror of the approaching Soviet columns.

The unstoppable Soviet juggernaut left only Berlin as the final prize. For Hitler, the capital was the last stand of National Socialism.

The Fall of Mussolini and Italian Horror

Meanwhile, in Italy, Allied forces fought a grinding campaign through the Apennines. By April 1945, they broke the Gothic Line, forcing a German-Fascist withdrawal. As previously noted, Mussolini fled north but was captured by partisans near Lake Como on April 27.

- **Mussolini's Execution**: The following day, partisans shot him along with his mistress, Clara Petacci. Their bodies were hung upside down in Milan's Piazzale Loreto, a public display of revenge for years of fascist oppression. Crowds jeered, spat, and mutilated the corpses.
- **End of Fighting**: German forces in Italy capitulated in early May. Partisan squads scoured remaining fascist hideouts, often executing suspects on sight. Though some Allied officers tried to curb vigilantism, the thirst for vengeance could not be fully contained.

Italy's war ended in a swirl of violence that symbolized the downfall of fascism and the deep bitterness left by two decades of Mussolini's rule.

Battle of Berlin: A Capital in Flames

The Red Army finally struck at Berlin in April 1945. The city's defenders included remnants of the Wehrmacht, the SS, and an assortment of Volkssturm militias, many armed with only old rifles or Panzerfausts.

- **Encirclement**: Soviet Marshals Zhukov and Konev raced to encircle Berlin. Artillery and rockets pounded the city without respite. Streets became barricaded mazes, and each district was a battlefield.
- **Civilians Trapped**: Over two million civilians remained. Food and water ran out. Bomb shelters overflowed. Some Berliners ventured outside only to be killed by crossfire. The city's famed architecture crumbled under Soviet shells.
- **Bunker of Despair**: Deep underground, Hitler ranted about imaginary armies that would save Berlin. He refused to flee, eventually marrying Eva Braun before committing suicide on April 30. Propaganda Minister Goebbels followed suit after poisoning his children. The regime's top figures either fled or died by their own hands.

By early May, Soviet troops raised the Red Flag over the Reichstag. Berlin fell in a storm of destruction—thousands of civilians died in the final assault, and the Soviets indulged in looting and widespread sexual violence. Germany's capital had become a graveyard of Hitler's ambitions.

Germany's Capitulation and Occupation
With Berlin lost and Hitler dead, Grand Admiral Dönitz briefly assumed leadership, trying to negotiate a partial surrender to the Western Allies. But Stalin demanded total capitulation. On May 7, 1945, at Reims, and again on May 8 in Berlin, Germany unconditionally surrendered. **VE Day** (Victory in Europe Day) was declared.

- **Chaos of the End**: German troops across Europe laid down arms. Some units tried to flee west to avoid Soviet capture. Millions of displaced persons—forced laborers, camp survivors, POWs—roamed the roads.
- **Allied Occupation Zones**: Germany was carved into zones controlled by the US, UK, France, and the USSR. Austrian territory was similarly divided. Berlin, in ruins, was jointly occupied. Tensions already emerged between the Western Allies and the Soviets, hinting at future conflicts.
- **Retribution**: Local populations sometimes attacked fleeing or surrendered Germans. Eastern Europeans demanded payback for atrocities. Western civilians purged collaborators. The war in Europe officially ended, but emotional battles for justice or revenge continued.

Germany now lay prostrate—a ruined landscape of bombed cities and shattered industries. Meanwhile, the Pacific war raged on, overshadowed by the cataclysm in Asia yet to come.

The Pacific's Final Battles: Iwo Jima and Okinawa
While Europe celebrated VE Day, the US confronted some of the toughest fights in the Pacific. The capture of **Iwo Jima** (February–March 1945) cost nearly 7,000 American lives

and over 20,000 Japanese, many perishing in caves rather than surrender. Next came **Okinawa** (April–June 1945), a bloody 82-day battle:

- **Ferocious Defense**: Japanese General Ushijima turned the island into a fortress of tunnels and ridges. Kamikaze attacks plagued the US fleet offshore, sinking or damaging scores of ships.
- **Civilian Casualties**: Okinawan civilians, taught to fear Americans, hid in caves or were forced at gunpoint to become human shields. Some jumped off cliffs to avoid capture.
- **Casualty Figures**: The Allies suffered over 49,000 casualties (including thousands dead). Japanese losses topped 100,000 soldiers plus tens of thousands of civilian deaths—estimates vary widely.

Okinawa's carnage convinced many US planners that invading the Japanese home islands would be even worse, potentially costing millions of lives on both sides. The savage fighting fueled a search for alternatives, setting the stage for a new, terrifying weapon.

Bombing Japan: Firestorms and Civilian Devastation
Even before Okinawa ended, the US Army Air Forces targeted Japanese cities with incendiary raids. General Curtis LeMay orchestrated low-level night bombings to maximize fire damage in Japan's wooden urban districts.

- **Tokyo Firebombing**: On March 9–10, 1945, B-29s dropped napalm and other incendiaries over Tokyo, igniting a colossal firestorm. Over 80,000 died that single night, rivaling the toll of atomic strikes to come.
- **Industrial vs. Civilian Targets**: The US argued that Japan's cottage industries were interwoven with civilian neighborhoods, making entire areas fair game. Critics questioned the morality of burning entire cities to the ground.
- **Effects on Japanese Morale**: Many civilians grew desperate, losing faith in the government's claims of victory. Yet the militarist clique refused to capitulate, insisting on honorable death over surrender.

These raids killed hundreds of thousands and left millions homeless. Still, Japan's leadership vowed to keep fighting, ignoring calls for unconditional surrender.

Soviet Entry into the Pacific War
At the **Yalta Conference** (February 1945), Stalin promised to join the war against Japan after Germany's defeat. True to his word, on August 8, 1945—just after the first atomic bomb fell on Hiroshima—the USSR declared war on Japan and invaded Manchuria. The **Manchurian Offensive** (sometimes called Operation August Storm) overwhelmed the Japanese Kwantung Army.

- **Soviet Blitz**: T-34 tanks and mechanized divisions swiftly crushed Japanese defenses. Many Japanese units, already stripped of equipment for the Pacific front, collapsed.
- **Civilians Flee**: Japanese settlers in Manchuria panicked, fearing both Soviet vengeance and Chinese retribution for years of occupation. Manchurian roads clogged with refugees.
- **Accelerated Collapse**: Stalin's move sealed Japan's fate. Surrounded by Allies on all sides, the Japanese government could no longer hope for negotiations to preserve the empire.

This Soviet intervention, combined with the devastation from atomic bombs, forced Japan's leadership into a dire choice.

The Atomic Bombings: Hiroshima and Nagasaki
On August 6, 1945, a B-29 named **Enola Gay** dropped the first atomic bomb on **Hiroshima**. The blast obliterated much of the city, killing an estimated 70,000–80,000 instantly, with tens of thousands more succumbing to burns and radiation sickness. Three days later, a second bomb hit **Nagasaki**, causing similarly catastrophic losses.

- **US Rationale**: Officials argued the bombings would save lives by avoiding a costly invasion of Japan. They also aimed to demonstrate power (especially to the Soviet Union) and force a swift surrender.
- **Unimaginable Horror**: Survivors recounted a blinding flash, searing heat, and shock waves that turned people into shadows on walls. Burns, radiation poisoning, and cancers haunted them for decades.
- **Global Shock**: The world learned of a new destructive capacity—one that overshadowed even the conventional brutality seen so far. In Hiroshima and Nagasaki, the war ended in a nightmare of charred ruins and silent, invisible death.

The bombs did indeed accelerate Japan's collapse, but the moral debate over their use would rage indefinitely. For the immediate war, however, they represented the final thunder—unmatched destruction that broke Japan's resolve.

Japan's Surrender
On August 14, Emperor Hirohito announced Japan's acceptance of the Allies' terms. In his radio broadcast, he cited the "new and most cruel bomb" and the Soviet entry as reasons to end the war. Official surrender documents were signed aboard the USS Missouri on September 2, 1945.

- **Armed Forces Reaction**: Hardline militarists attempted coups to prevent surrender, but they failed. Soldiers wept, some committing suicide rather than endure the shame of defeat.

- **Occupation of Japan**: General Douglas MacArthur oversaw the occupation. Japan's society, battered by bombings and near-starvation, submitted to Allied directives. War crime trials loomed for key leaders, while the Emperor remained but with curtailed authority.
- **Asian Reaction**: Occupied territories from Korea to Southeast Asia erupted in celebration or vendetta. Japanese troops, once lords of the local population, now faced hostility. Many were killed by partisans before official Allied repatriation could occur.

With Japan's surrender, World War II ended. Yet, the sudden cessation of global conflict did not erase the scars or halt the waves of retribution and communal violence that followed.

Immediate Aftermath in Europe

While the Pacific war ended in September, Europe had been under uneasy calm since May. The Allies turned their attention to stabilizing conquered Germany, assisting displaced persons, and preparing for trials of Nazi leaders.

- **Denazification**: US and British authorities removed former Nazi officials from power, but the process was inconsistent. Ordinary Germans scrambled to distance themselves from the regime, destroying uniforms or membership records.
- **Displaced Persons Camps**: Millions of Poles, French, Russians, Jews, and others found themselves far from home, some freed from camps, others forced laborers. Their return or emigration took years.
- **Hunger and Ruins**: Cities lay in rubble; Europe's transportation and agriculture were in shambles. Famine threatened many regions. Allied relief agencies raced to distribute food and rebuild infrastructure, but progress was slow.

In Eastern Europe, Soviet control replaced Nazi rule. Countries like Poland or Hungary found themselves under communist regimes. The seeds of the Cold War were already planted in the war's final months.

Repatriation and Revenge in Asia

In Asia, the end of Japanese occupation triggered its own chaos. Chinese Nationalists and Communists eyed each other warily. In Southeast Asia, colonial powers like Britain and France attempted to reassert control, leading to new conflicts.

- **Korean Independence**: After 35 years of Japanese rule, Korea was split along the 38th parallel by Soviet and American forces, setting the stage for future conflict.
- **Revenge Killings**: Former collaborators with Japan were lynched or imprisoned. In places like Indonesia and Vietnam, nationalist movements quickly turned on returning colonial armies.

- **POW Liberation**: Allied forces rushed to free POWs scattered across Asia. Some were found in dire conditions, days from death. Their stories of forced labor and torture fueled anger, leading to demands for Japanese war crime trials.

Thus, Asia, like Europe, faced a post-war period marked by retribution, political realignments, and lingering animosity.

Discovery of Full-Scale Atrocities

As Allied soldiers entered camps in Germany and Eastern Europe, the Holocaust's scale emerged. In the Pacific, the liberation of places like Singapore or Hong Kong laid bare the Kempeitai's cruelty. Unit 731's experiments in Manchuria came to light, though much data was hidden or destroyed.

- **Holocaust Shock**: Film footage of emaciated survivors and bulldozed mass graves horrified the world. The Allies organized Nuremberg Trials to prosecute top Nazi leaders for war crimes and crimes against humanity.
- **Japanese War Crimes**: Trials in Tokyo (the International Military Tribunal for the Far East) scrutinized leaders for aggression and atrocities like the Rape of Nanjing, forced labor, and torture. Some officers faced execution, but others escaped justice due to political deals.
- **Public Outrage**: Civilians worldwide, especially in Allied countries, demanded severe punishment for those responsible. This sense of moral fury helped shape the post-war order, but it also sometimes overshadowed Allied excesses or crimes that rarely faced equivalent scrutiny.

Understanding these atrocities shaped international law, leading to conventions on genocide and human rights. But the war's immediate aftermath was too chaotic for full accountability.

Psychological Burden of Survivors

Those who survived the final weeks or years of the war emerged traumatized. Soldiers returned home with nightmares of charred cities and dead comrades. Civilians, especially in bombed-out Germany or atomic-ravaged Japan, faced shattered lives. Holocaust survivors grappled with unimaginable loss.

- **PTSD and Shell Shock**: Terms like "battle fatigue" barely captured the scale of mental scars. Some veterans turned to alcohol or isolated themselves. Many civilians also exhibited long-term anxiety, depression, or distrust.
- **Families Torn Apart**: Orphans abounded; entire families had disappeared into camps or mass graves. Reunions were joyous but overshadowed by missing loved ones.
- **Rebuilding a Future**: Governments struggled with reconstruction. In Western Europe, the US-led Marshall Plan eventually aided recovery. Eastern Europe fell

under Soviet influence, with forced political and economic transformations. Asia faced a mosaic of civil wars, decolonization struggles, and US occupation in Japan.

Thus, the endgame horrors continued into the peacetime transition, forging a generation scarred by memories of devastation.

Allied Occupations and New Conflicts

With Germany and Japan defeated, Allied forces occupied both nations. While the US, UK, USSR, and France split Germany, the US alone oversaw Japan's transformation. In both places, a delicate balance existed between punishing war criminals, reforming governments, and rebuilding economies.

- **Deindustrialization vs. Reconstruction**: In Germany, some early Allied plans favored dismantling factories to prevent future war-making potential. Yet the Cold War's onset shifted policies toward rebuilding West Germany as a bulwark against communism.
- **Japan's Emperor**: Despite calls to try Hirohito for war crimes, MacArthur's administration decided to keep him as a figurehead to maintain stability. This move angered many who viewed the Emperor as complicit in militarist expansion.
- **Local Grievances**: Civilians faced housing shortages, food rationing, and unfamiliar foreign troops occupying their cities. Distrust lingered. In East Germany and Eastern Europe, Soviet influence introduced repressive systems.

While major combat ended, political and social upheavals seeded future tensions, culminating in the early stages of the Cold War.

Continued Violence: Post-War Insurgencies

Even after official surrenders, violence continued in pockets. Some diehard Nazis or Japanese soldiers refused to surrender. In Eastern Europe, anti-communist partisans fought Soviet-backed regimes for years. Asia saw a surge of independence movements, leading to conflicts in Indonesia, Vietnam, and elsewhere.

- **Werewolf Resistance**: A small group of fanatic German youth attempted guerrilla resistance in occupied zones, assassinating local officials. The Allies reacted forcefully, but the threat was minimal.
- **Japanese Holdouts**: In the Pacific, scattered Japanese soldiers in remote islands did not believe the war ended. Some survived in jungles for years, occasionally clashing with locals before being found or surrendering decades later.
- **Colonial Wars**: France tried to reassert control in Indochina, sparking war with the Viet Minh. The British faced unrest in Malaya. Old imperial systems crumbled as nationalism and communism expanded globally.

Thus, the "final thunder" of WWII set off aftershocks that reverberated for decades, shaping geopolitics and fueling new wars.

Human Cost and Reflection
By war's end, estimates suggest over 60 million people died—soldiers and civilians combined. The war's last year alone accounted for a significant portion of the death toll, reflecting the ferocity of endgame battles and mass killings. Entire cities vanished from maps, and entire families from memory.

- **Mourning and Memorials**: Across continents, people built memorials to the fallen. War cemeteries dotted Europe, Africa, Asia, and the Pacific. Families visited mass graves or never found them at all.
- **Lessons and War Crimes Legacies**: The Nuremberg and Tokyo Trials established precedents for prosecuting aggression and genocide. Yet partial justice in some cases (e.g., immunity deals with Unit 731 scientists or minimal sentences for certain Nazi officials) left lingering resentments.
- **UN Formation**: In the war's aftermath, the United Nations took shape, aspiring to prevent another global catastrophe. Its Charter reflected the desire for collective security, though the Cold War soon paralyzed much of its function.

For survivors and the next generation, WWII's final thunder was a grim reminder that human civilization could nearly self-destruct. The atomic bombs, especially, hinted at an even darker future if global tensions continued unchecked.

CHAPTER NINETEEN

Aftermath Shadows – Trials and Torments

Introduction: A World Left in Ruins
When the guns finally fell silent in 1945, the relief that swept across much of the globe was overshadowed by the colossal devastation left behind. The physical destruction was staggering: entire cities flattened by bombings, roads and rails mangled, farms scorched, and factories reduced to twisted metal. Even more profound was the human toll—tens of millions dead, countless maimed or displaced, and survivors grappling with unimaginable trauma. Such was the backdrop against which the victors, and even some defeated nations, tried to forge a measure of justice.

This chapter explores the immediate aftermath of World War II. It delves into the war crimes trials that sought to bring major perpetrators to account, the collapse of regimes and ideologies, the resettlement nightmares for refugees and prisoners, and the emotional burden borne by survivors. Though the war was officially over, suffering persisted, shaped by vengeance, political opportunism, and the sheer scale of rebuilding required. The lines between justice and revenge sometimes blurred, leaving controversies that persist to this day.

Immediate Chaos and Displacement
Even before the final surrenders, vast populations were already on the move. Liberated concentration camps and forced labor sites revealed multitudes of emaciated survivors who had no homes to return to. Millions of Soviet prisoners, Polish civilians, and French forced laborers found themselves scattered deep within Germany or Eastern Europe.

Meanwhile, ethnic Germans in countries like Czechoslovakia, Hungary, or Yugoslavia faced expulsion from lands where many had lived for generations.

- **Refugee Columns**: In Europe, roads teemed with wagons, carts, or simply families walking with bundles of clothes. Some tried to go home, only to find their towns in ruins or under new political rule.
- **Displaced Persons Camps**: The Allies established camps to shelter and feed these uprooted masses, now known as "DPs." Organizations like UNRRA (United Nations Relief and Rehabilitation Administration) coordinated basic relief—distributing rations, blankets, and medical care. Conditions were rough, with shortages of everything.
- **New Borders, New Problems**: As Soviet forces occupied much of Eastern Europe, millions of Polish citizens discovered their homes were now in territory annexed by the USSR. Some chose relocation to the new Polish borders, further adding to the chaotic flow of humanity.

Emotions ran high in these camps—anger, depression, hope to find lost relatives. Many saw the aftermath as a second ordeal, a test of endurance after surviving the war's brutality.

The Fate of Collaborators and Revenge Killings

In every liberated country, local populations faced the question of how to handle collaborators who had aided the Nazi or Japanese occupiers. Some had joined out of genuine ideological sympathy, others for survival or personal gain. Either way, the end of hostilities triggered a wave of "score-settling."

- **Extrajudicial Retribution**: Mobs targeted individuals known or suspected of collaborating. In France, women accused of "horizontal collaboration" (relationships with German soldiers) were publicly humiliated—hair shaved, paraded through streets. Some collaborationist officials were lynched or shot without trial.
- **Official Purges**: Governments in exile returning to power also conducted formal purges. In Norway, Vidkun Quisling faced trial and execution. Belgium, the Netherlands, and Denmark similarly prosecuted thousands for treason.
- **Moral Dilemmas**: These purges sometimes swept up individuals who had little choice—like civil servants forced to sign documents under threat—or teenage girls who had sought food for their families from occupying troops. The line between necessity and betrayal was not always clear.

The fervor of vengeance slowly subsided as new administrations realized the need for stable societies. But the scars remained, and for many, the label "collaborator" could never be shaken off.

Nuremberg Trials: Confronting Nazi War Crimes

In the European theater, the most prominent legal reckoning unfolded in **Nuremberg**, Germany. Between November 1945 and October 1946, major Nazi figures faced the International Military Tribunal (IMT) on charges including "crimes against peace," "war crimes," and "crimes against humanity." The Allies hoped these trials would lay down a precedent that aggression and genocide would not go unpunished.

- **High-Profile Defendants**: Hermann Göring, Rudolf Hess, Joachim von Ribbentrop, and others. Heinrich Himmler and Joseph Goebbels had committed suicide, as had Adolf Hitler. Field Marshal Wilhelm Keitel and others were indicted for executing orders leading to mass civilian deaths.
- **Evidence and Revelations**: Allied prosecutors presented detailed records of extermination camps, forced labor, and medical experiments. Survivor testimonies and captured documents left no doubt about the regime's atrocities. Filmed footage from liberated camps shocked even the judges.
- **Verdicts**: Twelve defendants received death sentences (including Göring, who took poison hours before his hanging). Others got prison terms or were acquitted. This caused controversy—some felt sentences were too lenient, while others argued the trials were "victor's justice."
- **Subsequent Trials**: The IMT was followed by additional proceedings targeting lesser-known Nazi officials, SS doctors, and industrialists. While many were convicted, others escaped or served minimal sentences, fueling debates about inconsistency in Allied justice.

Still, Nuremberg established legal concepts like "crimes against humanity," shaping future international law. It also put on record the Holocaust's scale, ensuring denial could not flourish without confronting overwhelming evidence.

Tokyo Trials and the Asian Parallel

Across the globe, Allied authorities in the Pacific set up the **International Military Tribunal for the Far East (IMTFE)** in Tokyo to try major Japanese war criminals. This paralleled Nuremberg but faced different complexities.

- **Defendants**: Former Prime Ministers Hideki Tojo and Kuniaki Koiso, plus generals, admirals, and cabinet officials. Emperor Hirohito, however, was not indicted—General Douglas MacArthur decided to keep him as a constitutional figurehead to stabilize Japan. This angered many Asian victims who believed the Emperor bore ultimate responsibility.
- **Charges and Evidence**: The tribunal addressed aggression (the invasion of China and other territories), mistreatment of POWs, forced labor, the "Rape of Nanjing," and other atrocities. However, evidence from Unit 731 (biological experimentation) was partly suppressed, as US intelligence reportedly struck deals to obtain data in exchange for immunity.

- **Verdicts and Criticisms**: Several top leaders were sentenced to death (including Tojo), while others received life imprisonment. Critics said the trials overlooked Allied misconduct and gave a free pass to Emperor Hirohito. Japanese nationalists denounced the proceedings as another form of victor's justice.

Though the Tokyo Trials confirmed Japan's wartime atrocities, incomplete prosecutions and political compromises cast a long shadow, affecting how Japan's wartime history would be remembered or misremembered.

War Crimes in Soviet Domains
The Soviet Union ran its own war crime trials. High-profile cases included captured German generals and SS officers tried in cities like Kharkov or Leningrad, with the public invited to witness. Some trials were fairer than expected, but the NKVD's methods raised doubts about coerced confessions. The convictions often ended in execution or long sentences in Gulag labor camps.

- **Mass Trials**: Soviet authorities tried thousands of German POWs for crimes committed in occupied Soviet territory. Some truly guilty SS men or policemen faced swift retribution. But many regular Wehrmacht soldiers also suffered harsh punishments.
- **Deportations of Ethnic Minorities**: In parallel, Stalin deemed entire ethnic groups—like Chechens, Crimean Tatars, or Volga Germans—collectively guilty of collaboration. He deported them eastward in brutal conditions. This was a form of collective punishment, reminiscent of Nazi practices.
- **Limited International Oversight**: The Allies had little influence over Soviet trials. They sometimes accepted that Stalin's brand of "justice" was part of the cost of maintaining the anti-Nazi alliance. Many convictions occurred behind closed doors, with minimal due process.

Hence, in the vast Soviet-occupied zone, "justice" was often overshadowed by political motives and the desire to neutralize any potential opposition to Stalin's grip.

Industrialists, Financiers, and the Gray Lines of Guilt
A critical question in the aftermath was how to treat business leaders and bankers who profited from wartime economies or exploited forced labor. In Germany, companies like Krupp, I.G. Farben, and Siemens had used slave labor from concentration camps. In Japan, zaibatsu conglomerates benefited from expansions in Manchuria.

- **Allied Dilemma**: Some Allied planners wanted to dismantle these industrial giants to prevent future militarism. Others believed they needed them to rebuild economies and avoid chaos.
- **Nuremberg Follow-up Trials**: Certain top industrialists faced trial (e.g., Alfried Krupp), receiving prison terms only to be released early in the 1950s. Some

corporate structures changed names but kept many of the same executives, fueling resentment among survivors.
- **Japan's Corporations**: Mitsubishi, Mitsui, and others underwent partial reforms under US occupation, but many war-time profits were not confiscated. A few executives faced censure, but the swift pivot to Cold War alliances meant the US wanted a strong Japan as a bulwark against communism.

This realpolitik approach left many survivors feeling that justice was incomplete and that economic elites who had fueled the war machine got off lightly.

Dealing with Holocaust Perpetrators

Beyond the Nuremberg main trial, subsequent proceedings tackled the intricate network of Holocaust facilitators: SS camp guards, Einsatzgruppen leaders, concentration camp doctors, and bureaucrats who organized deportations. However, the sheer number of perpetrators overwhelmed Allied courts. Many disappeared into post-war chaos, forging new identities.

- **Eichmann and Others**: Adolf Eichmann, responsible for coordinating mass deportations of Jews, escaped to Argentina. He was captured by Israeli agents in 1960, tried in Jerusalem, and executed. Other Nazis like Josef Mengele evaded capture, living under assumed names in South America.
- **Limited Resources**: As the Cold War loomed, Allies reallocated intelligence resources. Nazi-hunting took a back seat to anti-communist efforts. Some ex-SS men were even employed by Western intelligence to gather info on the Soviets, complicating moral lines.
- **Survivors' Testimonies**: Jewish and Roma communities pressed for thorough prosecutions, but often faced bureaucratic indifference. Over time, a few high-profile trials resumed in West Germany decades later, but the majority of lower-level perpetrators never stood trial.

Though the Holocaust had been extensively documented, achieving full justice for its countless victims proved elusive in the political climate that followed.

Reparations and Economic Rebuilding

Another key dimension of the post-war scenario involved reparations and reconstruction. The Treaty of Versailles after World War I had famously contributed to resentment in Germany. This time, the Allies approached the issue more carefully, though initially, Stalin insisted on large-scale German reparations.

- **Soviet Plunder**: In Eastern Germany and other liberated zones, Soviet soldiers dismantled factories and shipped machinery east. This was considered war booty to compensate for Soviet losses. The scale of removal significantly hindered East Germany's recovery.

- **Western Approach**: The US, Britain, and France soon shifted focus to rebuilding western Germany's economy. Under the Marshall Plan (1948), the United States poured resources into Europe, including West Germany, to foster stability and counter Soviet influence.
- **Japan's Economic Reforms**: Under MacArthur, the Allied occupation restructured Japan's economy, breaking up large zaibatsu monopolies, promoting land reform, and laying foundations for eventual rapid growth. War damages for Asian nations occupied by Japan were handled unevenly, leading to long-standing disputes over compensation.

Hence, the post-war economic order was a patchwork—some areas gutted for reparations, others receiving generous aid. The disparity set the stage for future East-West tensions.

Prisoners of War Return and Forced Labor Survivors

Allied POWs in German and Japanese camps returned home with stories of cruelty. Many needed extensive medical treatment. The Japanese had withheld Red Cross aid from many Western POWs, resulting in catastrophic death rates. Survivors struggled with bitterness but found some relief in the war crimes trials.

- **Soviet POWs**: Among the war's most tragic figures were Soviet soldiers who survived Nazi captivity only to be treated as potential traitors upon returning to the USSR. Stalin suspected any soldier captured by the enemy of collaboration. Many ended up in Gulag camps.
- **Forced Laborers**: Millions of Europeans, including Poles, French, and Soviet citizens, had been dragged to Germany for slave labor. Liberation gave them freedom but not an easy path to normal life. Some found their hometowns under

new borders or destroyed. Others had to wait months or years before traveling home, sometimes receiving minimal assistance from Allied authorities.
- **Emotional Scars**: POWs and forced labor survivors often faced mental health struggles, nightmares, and difficulties reintegrating. Their experiences were overshadowed by the broader narrative of victory, leading many to suffer in silence.

Resettling these former prisoners took years. Governments offered limited compensation; charities did what they could. Yet the scale was overwhelming, and resources stretched thin.

Civilian Trauma and Medical Crises
Aside from POWs, civilian populations across Europe and Asia were in poor health. Malnutrition and disease were rampant. Tuberculosis, typhus, and dysentery flared in bombed-out cities lacking clean water or intact sewage systems. Orphaned children lived in the streets, forming gangs for survival.

- **Shortage of Medical Staff**: Many doctors had died or been conscripted. Hospitals were bombed, supplies scarce. Allied medics and relief agencies attempted to stem epidemics, but progress was slow.
- **Psychological Toll**: Wartime atrocities—bombings, sieges, massacres—left countless survivors with trauma symptoms. Yet formal mental health support was nearly nonexistent. Many tried to bury memories and rebuild, while unprocessed psychological wounds lingered.
- **Genetic Impacts**: In Hiroshima and Nagasaki, atomic bomb survivors faced radiation sickness, burns, and higher cancer rates. Children born years later suffered birth defects. Doctors scrambled to understand radiation's effects, but knowledge was limited, and many victims found care too little, too late.

Thus, large swaths of the world faced a humanitarian crisis unprecedented in history. The relief efforts, while substantial, could never fully remedy the immediate suffering.

Political Shifts and the Seeds of the Cold War
Amid the rubble, political realignments took shape. Soviet influence expanded into Eastern Europe, establishing communist regimes. Western Allies, alarmed by Stalin's methods, began fostering "friendly" governments in Western Germany, Italy, and elsewhere. The ideological rift that emerged would soon freeze into the **Cold War**.

- **Division of Germany**: The Western zones merged into the Federal Republic of Germany (West Germany), while the Soviet zone became the German Democratic Republic (East Germany). Berlin itself split.
- **Iron Curtain**: Winston Churchill's 1946 speech about an "iron curtain" descending across Europe symbolized the dividing line between Western democracies and Soviet-controlled states.

- **Asian Aftermath**: In China, the civil war between Nationalists and Communists reignited by 1946. Korea, divided by the 38th parallel, set the stage for future conflict. Meanwhile, nationalist uprisings in French Indochina and Dutch Indonesia sparked new wars of decolonization.

The war's end thus did not guarantee peace—rather, it laid the groundwork for decades of geopolitical tension.

Occupation of Japan: A New Order

Under General MacArthur's supreme command, the US occupation of Japan introduced sweeping changes. The Allies disbanded Japan's military, released political prisoners, and started democratizing reforms. Women gained the vote, and the constitution was rewritten to renounce war. Yet the Emperor remained as a symbol, albeit stripped of political power.

- **Trials and Scandals**: As in Germany, top Japanese war criminals faced the Tokyo Trials. Lower-level officers faced local prosecutions. However, controversies over immunity deals for certain scientists or officials dogged the process.
- **Economic Rehabilitation**: Land reform broke the power of large landlords, while zaibatsu conglomerates were partially dismantled. US advisers hoped to build a strong capitalist ally.
- **Cultural Shifts**: Press censorship dissolved, new textbooks replaced militarist propaganda, and American influences swept across popular culture. Still, many older Japanese harbored resentment, mourning the war dead and the lost empire.

By 1952, Japan regained sovereignty but remained under American influence. Its rapid post-war recovery would surprise the world, yet the memory of Hiroshima, Nagasaki, and other devastations shaped its future pacifist policies.

Rebuilding Lives and Searching for the Missing

Families torn apart by bombings or deportations sought to reunite. Newspapers published lists of missing persons. Aid organizations set up offices to trace relatives across shattered countries. Some found joyous reunions; others discovered entire bloodlines erased.

- **Holocaust Survivors**: Jewish agencies like the Jewish Agency or the Joint Distribution Committee compiled records to help survivors locate relatives. Many discovered they were the lone survivors of entire extended families. Disbelief and grief mingled with the challenge of forging new lives.
- **Child Displacement**: Tens of thousands of children lost track of their parents—or had never known them. Orphanages struggled to cope, and adoption systems faced confusion over identities. In some cases, political authorities blocked efforts to return children forcibly "Germanized" by the Nazis to their real families, citing bureaucratic obstacles.
- **Postal Services and Red Cross Messages**: Rebuilding mail routes was crucial for connecting the displaced. Red Cross messages served as a lifeline for families across borders. Over time, many discovered tragic truths or, in rarer cases, that loved ones were alive in distant DP camps.

This vast search for missing persons highlighted the war's toll on personal identities. Some never found closure, uncertain if relatives died or vanished in the chaos.

New National Boundaries and Forced Relocations

As post-war treaties and the Potsdam Conference redrew maps, entire populations were uprooted. In Central and Eastern Europe, the Allies sanctioned massive shifts in national borders. Poland moved west, gaining territory from Germany but losing lands to the Soviet Union. Ethnic Germans in Silesia, Pomerania, and the Sudetenland were expelled to a shrunken Germany.

- **Expulsions**: Historians estimate 12 to 14 million Germans were driven from Eastern Europe, often violently. Thousands died in transit from starvation or disease.
- **Ethnic Cleansing**: These forced relocations, though sanctioned by the Allies, resembled the Nazi-era displacements in their brutality. Czechs, Poles, and others justified it as "just retribution," but the scale of suffering was enormous.
- **Long-Term Consequences**: The region's ethnic mosaic was replaced by more homogenized states. This shaped the political and cultural face of post-war Europe, leaving behind deep resentments and a sense of permanent estrangement among displaced families.

Such policies indicated how the war's logic of collective guilt lingered, reinforcing that entire populations could be punished for the crimes of regimes or militaries.

Healing Wounds or Stirring Anger?
While official trials attempted to address major crimes, many survivors felt no sense of closure. Their individual tormentors remained unpunished, or they saw ex-Nazi or ex-collaborator figures reintegrate into society. The Allies themselves, especially in the West, prioritized rebuilding a stable, anti-communist Germany over exhaustive prosecutions.

- **Jewish Communities**: Survivors sought restitution for stolen property or businesses "Aryanized" under Nazi rule. Some received token payments; many got nothing. Israel's founding in 1948 offered a new homeland for some, but also triggered further geopolitical tensions.
- **Roma and Sinti**: Often overlooked, these groups also suffered genocide. Post-war European governments largely ignored their claims, offering minimal reparations. Many Roma families remained marginalized, a legacy of centuries of discrimination exacerbated by the war.
- **Asia's Partial Atonement**: Countries like China or the Philippines demanded compensation for destruction by the Japanese. Japan signed various reparations treaties but did not comprehensively address atrocities such as the comfort women system. Survivors struggled for recognition even decades later.

Thus, while some symbolic efforts at "justice" occurred, the overwhelming scale of atrocities and the messy politics of the post-war world left countless wounds unhealed.

Rise of the United Nations and International Law
Amid the ruins, the desire to prevent another global catastrophe found expression in the **United Nations (UN)**, formed in 1945. Nations signed the UN Charter in San Francisco, pledging to resolve disputes peacefully and protect future generations from the "scourge of war."

- **Security Council**: The major victors (US, USSR, Britain, France, and China) became permanent members with veto power. This structure aimed to maintain peace but often paralyzed action when superpowers clashed.
- **Universal Declaration of Human Rights (1948)**: Driven by horror at the Holocaust and other atrocities, the UN developed new frameworks for individual rights. Though non-binding at first, it set moral standards recognized globally.
- **Geneva Conventions**: Revised in 1949, the Conventions strengthened protections for POWs and civilians. The shadow of WWII's brutalities drove signatories to promise more humane conduct in future conflicts—though reality would sometimes fall short.

International law thus advanced significantly, yet cynicism abounded. Observers questioned whether lofty principles could truly stop aggression when major powers had nuclear arsenals.

War's End as the Dawn of Nuclear Fear

The US atomic bombings of Hiroshima and Nagasaki ushered in the nuclear age. While they forced Japan's surrender, they also alerted the world to a new existential threat. The Soviet Union accelerated its own atomic research, successfully testing a bomb by 1949. Britain, France, and others followed suit.

- **Cold War Context**: The arms race overshadowed the spirit of anti-war sentiment that had briefly blossomed post-1945. Instead of disarming, superpowers stockpiled weapons capable of far greater devastation than anything seen during WWII.
- **Public Anxiety**: Survivors of Hiroshima or Nagasaki testified before global audiences, warning of nuclear horrors. Yet governments pressed on, each seeing nuclear deterrence as essential to preventing future total war.
- **Legacy of Terror**: Thus, World War II's final months—the "final thunder" of atomic blasts—became an immediate prologue to a new era where entire civilizations lived under the specter of nuclear annihilation. The horrors of WWII ironically planted seeds for an even more frightening standoff.

For many who had endured the bombs or witness testimonies, the notion of "never again" was overshadowed by the unstoppable momentum of superpower rivalry.

Memorials, Memories, and Cultural Impact

As time passed, societies erected memorials—Auschwitz turned into a museum, Hiroshima built a Peace Memorial Park, and national cemeteries welcomed the fallen. War stories appeared in films, literature, and personal memoirs. Children learned about WWII in schools, sometimes shaped by national narratives that highlighted certain heroics while downplaying inconvenient truths.

- **Holocaust Remembrance**: Jewish communities worldwide worked to preserve testimonies, diaries, and historical records. New synagogues displayed memorial plaques with thousands of names. Each year, commemorations recognized the Shoah's victims, seeking to ensure the world would not forget.
- **Varied National Perspectives**: In Germany, a long process of Vergangenheitsbewältigung ("coming to terms with the past") began, culminating decades later in official acknowledgments of guilt. Japan's remembrance was more contentious, with some textbooks minimizing wartime aggression. The Soviet Union glorified the "Great Patriotic War," often ignoring Stalin's purges.
- **Art and Expression**: Countless novels, paintings, and later films captured personal anguish. Survivors attempted to convey experiences so extreme that

language sometimes failed. Post-war culture was forever shaped by the memory of concentration camps, the firebombing of cities, and the stark atomic shadows imprinted on buildings.

In these memorials and arts, the war continued to reverberate, weaving itself into the identities of nations and the conscience of future generations.

Conclusion: Shadows That Stretch Beyond War
World War II ended with official signings of surrender and the exultation that a nightmarish conflict was finally over. Yet for millions, the torment persisted in hunger, displacement, psychological scars, and the silent absence of those who never came home. Governments attempted war crimes trials, distributed relief, and redrew maps. Some of these measures offered partial justice or relief, but the scale of wrongdoing was so vast that many perpetrators evaded genuine accountability.

The world that emerged in 1945–46 was not the same as the one that had existed before 1939. Empires crumbled, superpowers arose, entire populations had been uprooted, and the seeds of new conflicts were planted. In this complex aftermath, survivors struggled to piece together shattered lives, states navigated precarious political shifts, and the evolving concept of human rights tried to address the atrocities that had rocked civilization's foundations.

In **Chapter Twenty**, we turn to the bigger lessons and haunting reminders left by WWII—how the ghosts of that conflict still linger in our collective memory and why the war's example of unleashed cruelty and apocalyptic potential demands vigilance from every subsequent generation.

CHAPTER TWENTY

Lingering Ghosts and Haunting Lessons

Introduction: Beyond the Smoke and Rubble
Chapter Twenty completes our journey through the dark corridors of World War II by focusing on the enduring legacy, the moral inquiries left unanswered, and the lessons gleaned—or sometimes forgotten—by subsequent generations. Despite the official end in 1945, the war's ghosts never ceased to roam. Survivors, their children, and even societies untouched by actual fighting carried the war's memory in cultural, political, and ethical debates.

We will reflect on how WWII reshaped international relations, fueled anti-colonial movements, advanced technology, and introduced new moral frameworks. We will examine how the Holocaust became a defining symbol of absolute evil, forcing humanity to confront its capacity for genocide. We'll also see how WWII's terror underscored the importance of preventing future global conflicts—yet ironically laid the groundwork for Cold War standoffs. In short, the war's conclusion was less a finale than a pivot to new challenges and a reminder that vigilance is needed to keep such horrors at bay.

Redrawing the Global Map
One of the most obvious legacies of WWII was a radically altered political map. European colonial empires, already weakened, began to crumble amid rising nationalism in Asia and Africa. The US and USSR emerged as superpowers, overshadowing traditional powers like Britain or France.

- **End of Empires**: In the decade after 1945, nations such as India, Indonesia, and Vietnam fought or negotiated for independence. Some struggles turned violent, with colonial powers reasserting control before eventually withdrawing. WWII had undermined the myth of colonial invincibility.
- **Divided Europe**: Germany's partition into East and West symbolized the continent's new fault line. Eastern Europe fell under Soviet-aligned regimes, while Western nations formed alliances like NATO.
- **Rise of the Third World**: Former colonies in Latin America, Africa, and Asia aligned with or against the superpowers based on ideological or economic interests. The concept of a "Third World" bloc signaled new global politics, shaped indirectly by WWII's outcome.

Thus, WWII sparked a wave of decolonization, shifting power away from old imperial centers toward new states, many of which faced internal struggles rooted in the war's legacies.

Cold War Anxiety and Militarization
The dawn of nuclear weapons and the rivalry between the US and USSR replaced WWII's alliances with suspicion. Each superpower invested heavily in arms, aiming to deter or outmatch the other. The memory of how quickly Hitler had turned on treaties fueled paranoia.

- **Arms Race**: The US tested the first hydrogen bomb in 1952; the Soviets soon followed. The potential for annihilation overshadowed all other war memories. Civilians, especially in Europe, found themselves trapped between two nuclear-armed blocs.
- **Proxy Conflicts**: The moral clarity of WWII—fighting fascism—gave way to murkier conflicts where superpowers backed opposing sides in Korea, Vietnam, or Africa. WWII veterans recognized echoes of old horrors but lacked a unifying sense of righteous cause.
- **Allied War Crimes Overshadowed**: As both sides recruited ex-Nazi scientists or intelligence officers for their own aims, interest in further Nazi prosecutions dwindled. Political convenience trumped moral imperatives.

Ironically, the war to end tyranny led to a new era of vast military preparations and the perpetual fear of a catastrophic new conflict, one that could surpass WWII's devastation in mere hours.

Technological Leap and Ethical Questions
WWII accelerated scientific and industrial developments: rockets, jet engines, radar, advanced medicine, and above all, nuclear energy. While these innovations spurred post-war economies and research, they also introduced profound ethical dilemmas.

- **Rocketry and Space Race**: German V-2 missile technology formed the basis for US and Soviet space programs. Former Nazi engineers like Wernher von Braun played major roles at NASA. Ethical critics asked whether "progress" was built on forced labor and complicity in war crimes.
- **Medical Advances**: The drive to treat mass battlefield injuries led to improved antibiotics, surgical techniques, and the use of blood transfusions. But the shadow of Nazi and Japanese human experiments tarnished these gains.
- **Atomic Age**: The atomic bombs ended WWII but opened a Pandora's box of potential global destruction. Nuclear power offered cheap energy yet posed catastrophic risks if misused. The moral question of whether unleashing nuclear war was ever justifiable loomed large.

Hence, WWII's technology shaped the modern world. But behind each breakthrough lay a reminder that necessity—and sometimes brutality—had spurred its creation.

Holocaust Memory and the Fight Against Genocide

The Holocaust, once discovered, seared itself into global conscience as the epitome of industrial-scale genocide. Over time, it became a key reference point for activism against racism, anti-Semitism, and mass atrocities. But this evolution in public awareness took decades.

- **Early Silence**: Immediately after the war, many Holocaust survivors found it hard to speak. The enormity of their experiences was often met with incomprehension or a desire to forget. Many countries—West Germany included—struggled to face the full scope of Nazi crimes.
- **Gradual Recognition**: By the 1960s, with trials like Adolf Eichmann's, the Holocaust emerged into broader discourse. Education programs, museums, and memorial days were established. "Never again" became a moral rallying cry, even if the world's actions didn't always uphold it.
- **Genocide Conventions**: The UN's 1948 Convention on the Prevention and Punishment of the Crime of Genocide was a direct response to Nazi atrocities. It defined genocide legally, though enforcement remained inconsistent, as future genocides in places like Cambodia or Rwanda demonstrated.

Still, the memory of the Holocaust set a moral benchmark. It forced societies to confront how ordinary people can be swept into systematic murder when hatred and propaganda gain power.

National Myths and Historical Debates

Each country shaped its own narrative of WWII. Victorious nations glorified sacrifices and underplayed inconvenient truths. Defeated nations navigated guilt, denial, or selective remembrance.

- **Germany's Vergangenheitsbewältigung**: Over decades, West Germany moved from denial and silence to a deep reckoning with the Nazi past. East Germany, under communism, framed all crimes as "fascist" while claiming the GDR had inherited an antifascist legacy—ignoring complicities within its own population.
- **Japan's Divided Memory**: Some politicians and textbooks minimized Japanese aggression, fueling regional anger (especially in China and Korea). Others sought honest reflection, forming peace movements that championed pacifism.
- **Soviet and Post-Soviet Interpretations**: The USSR commemorated the "Great Patriotic War" as a heroic struggle, glossing over Stalin's pre-war purges and forced deportations. After communism's collapse, new Russian narratives emerged, sometimes reviving nationalist pride while downplaying Soviet abuses.
- **Western "Good War" Myth**: Allied nations often portrayed WWII as a righteous crusade against evil, ignoring episodes like colonial exploitation, firebombing, or forced relocations. Over time, more critical scholarship revealed darker Allied actions.

These competing narratives shaped how future generations understood WWII, sometimes fueling tensions between neighbors or within domestic politics.

Artistic Expressions of Trauma

Artists, writers, and filmmakers grappled with WWII's horrors. From immediate post-war documentary footage to fictionalized accounts, culture reflected an enduring attempt to process trauma.

- **Literature**: Authors like Primo Levi (an Auschwitz survivor) or Gunther Grass (revealing Germany's war complicity) forced readers to confront moral ambiguities. Holocaust memoirs gave voice to the voiceless, ensuring the dead were not erased.
- **Cinema**: War films emerged from all sides—Soviet epics about the Eastern Front, Hollywood's celebratory portrayals of D-Day or the Pacific, and later more introspective works dissecting moral dilemmas.
- **Poetry and Theater**: In Europe, existentialist and absurdist movements flourished, reflecting disillusionment. Japanese literature wrestled with the bombings, guilt for aggression, and the Emperor's role in the war.

Art became a space for questioning the logic that led entire nations into barbarism. It also preserved emotional truths that official histories sometimes sanitized.

Survivors' Lives: Continual Struggle

For individuals who survived concentration camps, forced labor, or frontline battles, the war did not simply end in 1945. Many dealt with chronic health problems, psychological trauma, and lost livelihoods. Societies—overwhelmed with reconstruction—often failed to provide comprehensive support.

- **Veterans' Issues**: Soldiers returned to a changed world. Some found families had moved on or died; others faced stigma if they had been POWs (like Soviet returnees). Economic booms in certain countries eventually brought jobs, but the transition was not always smooth.
- **Holocaust Survivors**: Many relocated to the US, Israel, or scattered across Europe. They formed communities, sharing experiences with fellow survivors. Public empathy was sometimes limited, especially in immediate post-war years.
- **Children's Long Shadows**: War orphans grew up in new countries or adoptive homes, shaping adult identities around fragmented memories. Child survivors of bombings or genocide carried nightmares well into old age, even as they built successful careers or families in safer lands.

Thus, the personal costs endured quietly in millions of households, shaping behaviors and attitudes that, in subtle ways, influenced future social policies or activism.

War's Role in Civil Rights and Social Change

WWII also catalyzed major social shifts, especially in the United States and other Allied nations, where the rhetoric of fighting for freedom abroad sparked questions about freedom at home.

- **Racial Inequalities**: Black American soldiers who fought against fascism returned unwilling to accept Jim Crow segregation. This helped propel the post-war Civil Rights Movement.
- **Women's Roles**: With so many men conscripted, women entered factories, offices, and military auxiliary units. Post-war, some societies tried to push women back into traditional roles, but the genie was out of the bottle—women had tasted economic independence, fueling future feminist movements.
- **Debates on Internment**: The US internment of Japanese Americans was later condemned as unconstitutional. Though reparations eventually passed decades afterward, the event exposed contradictions between Allied ideals and domestic practices of discrimination.

Hence, the war's ideological veneer—defending democracy against tyranny—spurred introspection about injustices within Allied societies themselves.

The Question of "Just War" and Morality

World War II is often invoked as the archetype of a "just war," particularly against Nazi Germany's genocidal regime. Yet debates persist around the moral cost of civilian bombings, the atomic bombs, and the Allied alliances with dictatorial regimes (like Stalin's USSR).

- **Realpolitik vs. Principles**: Allies allied with Stalin despite his own terror state. Many argue the exigencies of defeating Hitler justified such compromises, but this also cast a shadow over claims of moral high ground.
- **Aerial Bombardment**: Targeting civilian populations in Germany and Japan ignited ethical debates: Did these bombings truly accelerate surrender, or did they primarily terrorize innocents? Some veterans believed it was necessary revenge for Axis aggression. Others saw it as crossing a moral line.
- **Enduring Lesson?**: The popularity of the phrase "the ends justify the means" soared, but historians caution that adopting such logic can lead to atrocities on all sides, as exemplified by the war's spiral of violence.

Hence, WWII remains a reference point for statesmen, ethicists, and peace advocates wrestling with whether war can ever be waged cleanly or justly.

Influence on Future Generations: Education and Commemoration

Each post-war generation inherited some version of WWII's story, shaped by schools, media, or family stories. Monuments and museums dotted the landscapes of Europe, Asia, and the Pacific, serving as cautionary reminders.

- **School Curricula**: Nations adjusted textbooks over time, reflecting political shifts. In West Germany, a strong emphasis on Holocaust education eventually emerged, while in Japan, controversies rose over textbooks glossing over Nanjing or comfort women.
- **Pilgrimages to Battle Sites**: Veterans and descendants visited Normandy beaches, Auschwitz, Hiroshima's Peace Memorial. These journeys aimed to connect with personal or collective histories, often renewing commitments to peace.

- **Annual Observances**: Many countries honor a "Victory Day" or "Memorial Day," focusing on sacrifices and patriotic themes. Holocaust Remembrance Days highlight the moral imperative to remember genocide. Over time, these rituals can lose meaning if not accompanied by deeper reflection.

Still, the existence of such commemorations underscores the continuing impact of WWII on national identities and moral consciousness.

The Evolving Holocaust Scholarship

As decades passed, new documents, survivor testimonies, and academic inquiries refined understanding of the Holocaust and other atrocities. Researchers debated how "ordinary men" could commit mass murder, or how bureaucratic systems enabled genocide. These debates extended beyond Germany:

- **Comparative Genocide Studies**: Examining Rwanda, Bosnia, and other modern examples, scholars traced parallels with the Holocaust. WWII became the baseline for analyzing totalitarian regimes, groupthink, and scapegoating.
- **Denial Movements**: Some fringe groups continued to deny or minimize the Holocaust, or other wartime genocides. Survivors and historians countered with archival evidence, fueling legal battles in countries where Holocaust denial was criminalized.
- **Moral and Philosophical Lessons**: Philosophers like Hannah Arendt probed the "banality of evil," suggesting that ordinary people, not just fanatics, can commit atrocities under certain conditions. The Holocaust thus became a universal cautionary tale about human psychology.

This continual scholarship ensures WWII's darkest chapters remain not just past events, but living warnings.

Shifts in Military Doctrine
World War II profoundly influenced how modern armies planned. Blitzkrieg tactics, airborne assaults, amphibious operations, and combined arms approaches shaped post-war doctrines. The nuclear revolution overshadowed conventional strategies, but the fundamental lessons of logistics, intelligence, and industrial mobilization remained:

- **Total War Concept**: WWII exemplified how entire societies could be mobilized or targeted—economies, agriculture, and civilian morale were battlefronts. Nations developed civil defense measures, anticipating future total conflicts.
- **Air Power Doctrine**: Strategic bombing promised "quick victory" by destroying enemy industry and morale. Post-war air forces and navies expanded, though Vietnam and later conflicts challenged assumptions about bombing's effectiveness.
- **Amphibious Warfare**: The lessons of D-Day and Pacific landings shaped future operations, from the Korean War's Inchon landing to more modern amphibious doctrines.

Yet the advent of nuclear weapons cast doubt on whether another total war could be survived at all, pushing large-scale conventional strategies into a realm of uneasy irrelevance if nuclear escalation was on the table.

Veterans: War Heroes or Lost Generation?
Throughout Allied countries, returning soldiers were often welcomed as heroes. Nations erected memorials to the fallen, awarded medals, and introduced educational or housing benefits (like the US GI Bill). But not all veterans reintegrated smoothly:

- **Physical and Mental Health**: Many bore permanent injuries or PTSD, called "battle fatigue" then. Societies offered some support, but mental health remained poorly understood.
- **Demobilization Challenges**: Millions needed jobs, homes, or new skills. In the US, the GI Bill helped create a new middle class. Elsewhere, job shortages and destroyed infrastructure complicated their return.
- **Respect and Commemoration**: Ceremonies on anniversaries recognized their sacrifice, forging strong veterans' associations that lobbied for pensions or memorial services. Over time, these groups also influenced how WWII was remembered.

Veterans, thus, contributed to shaping post-war politics and culture, sometimes pressing for peace, other times fueling patriotism that justified future military expansions.

Women's Wartime Gains and Post-War Reversals
The war had ushered women into factories, farms, and offices. They operated heavy machinery, built munitions, served in auxiliary military roles, and ran entire households

alone. Post-war demobilization often forced them to relinquish jobs when male soldiers returned, but many resisted or found new roles.

- **Employment Shifts**: In the US and UK, "Rosie the Riveter" was thanked, but women were steered back into domestic life. Some acquiesced, seeking normality, while others demanded equal opportunity.
- **Women's Movements**: The seeds of modern feminism were partly sown in WWII experiences, as women realized their capabilities. By the 1960s and 1970s, these memories galvanized calls for civil and labor rights.
- **Soviet Women Veterans**: Red Army female snipers, pilots (the "Night Witches"), and tank crews returned to patriarchal communities that did not fully acknowledge their contributions. Some faced stigma, others became revered war heroes.

Though the war disrupted traditional gender norms, post-war societies were often uneasy about sustaining women's newfound independence, laying groundwork for future social struggles.

Global Aid and the Bretton Woods System

Allied conferences also laid the foundation for a new economic order. The 1944 Bretton Woods Conference established the International Monetary Fund (IMF) and World Bank to stabilize currencies and finance reconstruction. This system aimed to avoid the chaotic financial crises that fueled extremism in the 1930s.

- **Marshall Plan**: In 1948, the US launched a massive aid program for Western Europe, spurring recovery and growth. The Soviet bloc refused such aid, deepening the divide.

- **Japan's Reconstruction**: US occupation authorities pumped resources into rebuilding Japanese infrastructure, leading to an economic surge in the 1950s and 1960s.
- **Critiques**: Some argued this post-war economic framework favored capitalist powers, locking smaller nations into dependency. Nonetheless, it helped Western Europe and Japan achieve remarkable recoveries, contrasting with the slower reconstruction under communist regimes.

Hence, WWII's end spurred an international economic structure that defined global finance for decades, forging a measure of stability but also sowing inequalities.

Human Rights Movements and the UN Charter

Amid the rubble, voices demanded a new moral order. The Holocaust and other atrocities revealed how fragile human rights were under totalitarian or militaristic regimes. This realization fueled the push for universal human rights protections.

- **Universal Declaration of Human Rights (1948)**: Led by figures like Eleanor Roosevelt, it enshrined basic rights to life, liberty, and personal security. While not legally binding initially, it influenced constitutions and inspired global rights campaigns.
- **Refugee Conventions**: The experiences of WWII's displaced persons eventually led to the 1951 Refugee Convention, defining refugees and states' obligations.
- **Limitations**: The outbreak of the Cold War meant some human rights ideals took a back seat to superpower politics. Yet these documents remained moral yardsticks that activists worldwide invoked, referencing WWII's lessons of unchecked state power.

Thus, the moral shock of WWII atrocities shaped emerging frameworks for protecting individuals from state violence, though actual implementation varied drastically.

Redefining Warfare: The Geneva Conventions

Widespread violations in WWII—especially targeting civilians—prompted major updates to the Geneva Conventions in 1949. They expanded protections for POWs and civilians, codifying that indiscriminate destruction and maltreatment were unacceptable.

- **Civilians as a Focus**: WWII made clear that entire populations could be devastated, so the new conventions aimed to limit the horrors of occupation and protect non-combatants.
- **Enforcement Challenges**: States that signed these conventions sometimes ignored them in future conflicts. The principle that "military necessity" could override moral constraints persisted.
- **Legacy of Accountability**: Still, these documents allowed war criminals to be held responsible. Over time, they contributed to the formation of international courts,

eventually leading to institutions like the International Criminal Court (ICC), albeit much later.

While not eradicating war crimes, the updated Geneva Conventions at least set a baseline of agreed-upon norms that nations publicly claimed to respect.

The Perennial "Never Again"

From 1945 onward, leaders and citizens repeated the mantra "Never again"—never again genocide, total war, or global conflagration. Yet the subsequent decades saw genocides in Cambodia, Rwanda, and conflicts in Korea, Vietnam, the Middle East, and more. Each crisis tested humanity's resolve to avoid repeating WWII's mistakes.

- **Educational Programs**: Many nations embedded WWII lessons in their curricula, emphasizing tolerance, the perils of dictatorship, and the cost of letting aggression go unchecked.
- **Peace Movements**: The nuclear threat spurred activism for disarmament. Groups invoked Hiroshima as a symbol of what could happen if deterrence failed.
- **Reality of Political Interests**: Despite "Never again" sentiments, realpolitik often overshadowed moral imperatives. The memory of WWII's carnage served as a cautionary tale, but it did not prevent states from acting aggressively when national interests seemed threatened.

Still, the moral framework shaped by WWII—recognizing genocide as evil, calling for collective security—remains influential. It highlights how the war stands as a stark warning against complacency.

Conclusion: The War That Never Quite Ended
World War II officially ended in 1945, but its echoes refused to fade. Lives shattered by concentration camps, atomic bombs, scorched-earth campaigns, and forced deportations struggled for decades to regain stability. Nations rose from ruins to shape a new global order—one riddled with tension between ideals of peace and the harsh realities of power politics.

In the years that followed, the war's horror served as a constant reference point: a measure of absolute evil, a caution about the fragility of civilized norms, and a rallying cry for unity against future tyrannies. Yet the war also gave birth to massive arms races, the entrenchment of ideological blocs, and fresh conflicts that tested the sincerity of "Never again."

For all the terrifying facts we have recounted—blitzkrieg devastation, Holocaust atrocities, firebombed cities, human experiments, starvations, and atomic annihilation—World War II remains an epochal lesson. It is both a testament to human cruelty, orchestrated on an industrial scale, and to extraordinary perseverance, courage, and solidarity in the face of apocalypse.

Hence, if there is any final truth in these dark, scary stories, it may be that each generation must remember the horrors unleashed by hatred, propaganda, and unchecked militarism. The ghosts of WWII linger not to paralyze us with fear, but to remind us that vigilance, empathy, and respect for human dignity can stand against the worst impulses of humanity. Only in acknowledging how the war happened, and why, can we truly strive to ensure such cataclysm never recurs in any corner of our precarious world.

Help Us Share Your Thoughts!

Dear reader,

Thank you for spending your time with this book. We hope it brought you enjoyment and a few new ideas to think about. If there was anything that didn't work for you, or if you have suggestions on how we can improve, please let us know at **kontakt@skriuwer.com**. Your feedback means a lot to us and helps us make our books even better.

If you enjoyed this book, we would be very grateful if you left a review on the site where you purchased it. Your review not only helps other readers find our books, but also encourages us to keep creating more stories and materials that you'll love.

By choosing Skriuwer, you're also supporting **Frisian**—a minority language mainly spoken in the northern Netherlands. Although **Frisian** has a rich history, the number of speakers is shrinking, and it's at risk of dying out. Your purchase helps fund resources to preserve and promote this language, such as educational programs and learning tools. If you'd like to learn more about Frisian or even start learning it yourself, please visit **www.learnfrisian.com**.

Thank you for being part of our community. We look forward to sharing more books with you in the future.

Warm regards,
The Skriuwer Team

www.ingramcontent.com/pod-product-compliance
Lightning Source LLC
LaVergne TN
LVHW012105070526
838202LV00056B/5635